D0233038

Nature's Second Chance

Restoring the Ecology of Stone Prairie Farm

Steven I. Apfelbaum

BEACON PRESS

BOSTON

Beacon Press
25 Beacon Street
Boston, Massachusetts 02108-2892
www.beacon.org

Beacon Press books
are published under the auspices of
the Unitarian Universalist Association of Congregations.

12 11 10 09   8 7 6 5 4 3 2 1

This book is printed on acid-free paper that meets the uncoated paper
ANSI/NISO specifications for permanence as revised in 1992.

Text design by Yvonne Tsang at
Wilsted & Taylor Publishing Services

Library of Congress Cataloging-in-Publication Data

Apfelbaum, Steven I.
Nature's second chance : restoring the ecology of Stone Prairie Farm /
by Steven I. Apfelbaum.
p. cm.
ISBN-13: 978-0-8070-8582-0 (hardcover : alk. paper)
1. Restoration ecology—Wisconsin—Anecdotes.
2. Prairie restoration—Wisconsin—Anecdotes.
3. Stone Prairie Farm (Wis.) 4. Apfelbaum, Steven I. I. Title.

QH105.W6A74 2008
639.909775—dc22
[B]   2008013071

Contents

FOREWORD
by Nina Leopold Bradley   *v*

INTRODUCTION
A Place for Land   *ix*

Part I: Focus and Intentions

CHAPTER 1
A Place to Settle   3

CHAPTER 2
Ancient Landforms and Modern Inhabitants   13

CHAPTER 3
Jump-Starting Land Restoration   28

CHAPTER 4
Formative Ideas and Understandings   42

Part II: What Really Matters

CHAPTER 5
The Past Revisits and the Future Begins   61

CHAPTER 6
Taming the Old House   82

CHAPTER 7
Planting the Seeds of Restoration   96

CHAPTER 8
The Doctor Is In—
Symptoms of Ecological Health   108

CHAPTER 9
Playing with Fire   120

CHAPTER 10
Getting to Know Your Neighbors   135

CHAPTER 11
Globally Connected   147

Part III: Preparing for the Future

CHAPTER 12
Gone   157

CHAPTER 13
Exotic and Invasive Species   169

CHAPTER 14
The Invading Humans   184

CHAPTER 15
Ecological Reserves   197

CHAPTER 16
A Healthy Earth Ethic   211

CONCLUSION
Land Community Membership   219

AFTERWORD
Lively Seasons on the Restored Stone Prairie Farm   222

Foreword

Of all the memberships we identify ourselves by (racial, ethnic, secular, national, class, age, religious, occupational) the one that is most forgotten, and that has the greatest potential for healing, is place. We must learn to know, love, and join our place even more than we love our own ideas. People who can agree that they share a commitment to the landscape/cityscape— even if they are otherwise locked in struggle with each other— have one deep thing to share. *Gary Snyder*

In the spirit of place, Steve Apfelbaum and his partner, Susan Lehnhardt, have found a unique spiritual connection through their love of the land. To be "rooted in the land" involves actively participating in a known landscape. Steve and Susan have worked directly on the land, connecting both with it and with each other as members of a community of interdependent parts —soils, waters, plants, and animals. Or, collectively, the land.

My father, Aldo Leopold, through his own participation in the land community, came to a deeper personal understanding and appreciation of the land. On his Wisconsin sand farm he struggled to rebuild a diverse, healthy, aesthetically satisfying biota where there had been abuse and degradation. He developed a profound humility as he became more acutely aware of the complex factors involved in life and death, growth and decay. Ethical and aesthetic values became entwined with his scientific understanding. By recording and integrating all strands of his own firsthand experience, blending ecological science with philosophy, history, literature, and even poetry, he came to his final statement of the "land ethic": that land is a community is the basic concept of ecology, but that it is to be loved and respected is an extension of ethics.

Today, the concept of "restoration"—putting back into land what has been taken out of it—is evolving. In the 1930s, when my father worked in central Wisconsin restoring his abused acres, there were no detailed plans, experimental designs, or systematic treatments. The science of land health was yet to be born. What Aldo Leopold accomplished at his shack—a chicken coop turned simple cabin—in the sand counties of central Wisconsin rested upon simple knowledge and personal insight and commitment. He wrote in *Sand County Almanac*, "On this sand farm in Wisconsin, first worn out and then abandoned by our bigger-and-better society, we try to rebuild, with shovel and axe, what we are losing elsewhere."

With shovel and ax, Steven Apfelbaum has worked to bring the science of land health to fruition, acre by acre, landscape by landscape. Today, the rewards of his labor on Stone Prairie Farm are more than a healthy landscape—they exist as values deep within him. These values continue to direct his life. His emotional commitment is always evident as he works to bring back the elegance and the beauty that were indigenous to this land.

I rejoice in reading these chapters because I find myself entwined in Steve's excitement as he connects with the land physically and mentally. I rejoice because I, too, have found myself connected to the land, participating in this very process on my own acres.

The idea that humans themselves must actively participate in nature has origins that date back many generations. In our present consumerist society, we have reason for a renewed interest in the importance of viewing human communities as rooted in biological communities.

In the history of natural resource conservation, seldom has there been a more urgent need than now for people to connect with each other and with the land, and what better way to do so than through ecological restoration, a process of nurturing wild plant and animal communities back to health. In his 1992 book *The Diversity of Life*, E. O. Wilson wrote, "There can be no purpose more enspiriting than to begin the age of restoration, reweaving the wondrous diversity of life that still surrounds us."

My father, Aldo Leopold, wrote of a "land ethic," a moral theory of harmony between people and the land—a new thing under the sun. If morality is the glue that binds human communities, then, as we monitor some of the world's crises, are we watching that glue disintegrate?

These chapters vividly express the convergence of people and a place as they discover a new relationship between themselves and nature. Rediscovering our place in nature requires new ways of thinking about the relationship between humans and the natural world.

As the author worked to reclaim his own acres from generations of agricultural overuse, he employed practical measures to bring back their ecological health. Grubbing in the dirt, collecting seeds from native vegetation, planting, observing changes, and gaining understanding—all these were part of the process of giving nature a second chance.

Steve Apfelbaum weaves a story that would not have been nearly as rich without his soul mate, Susan. Both here at "the shack," on my family's land, and at Stone Prairie Farm, restoration has been a family affair. Susan, a botanist, artist, and hardworking advocate of nature, and Steve, an ecologist and educator, are highly motivated, creative, and productive people. Initially Steve and Susan restored their own 2.7 acres, learning as they worked. As their financial situation improved, they purchased an adjacent 80 acres. Be prepared, however, to be swept into this project of prairie planting on a more massive scale. They proceed, after measurable success on their farm, to help their neighbors, then the people in their local watershed, and finally the community in which they live. Perhaps Steve's success makes me rejoice for my father, who wrote, "A land ethic changes the role of *Homo sapiens* from conqueror of the land-community to plain member and citizen of it."

In his 2002 essay collection *The Art of the Commonplace*, Wendell Berry wrote, "one of the primary results . . . of industrialism is the separation of people and places and products from their histories." We do not know the histories of our families or our habitats or our food. In this book, the very process of restoring ecological health to the land helped the author and his partner participate in its history and ecological functions, while finding meaning in their own lives and a way of thinking based on land.

Weekends at our shack and the surrounding lands have transformed my family. Through our restoration we discovered our sense of place and acquired our relationship with nature. In the very process of planting, of seeing birds and other animals responding to changes, of learning from our successes and failures, we grew increasingly to appreciate and admire the interconnectedness of living systems. As we transformed the run-down sand farm, it transformed us.

In the flow of these chapters the reader is caught up in a similar spirit of transformation—in the excitement and in the developing sense of place.

Nina Leopold Bradley
Aldo Leopold Foundation, Baraboo, Wisconsin
January 2008

⌒

A Place for Land

We must understand and improve our relationship with the land.

Land provides the ideal vacation spot and wildlife habitat, and the beauty that inspires dreams. Each of us depends on plants that root into the soils, particularly where prairies and wetlands historically occurred, areas that now produce the deep black soils and lush crops of the midwestern breadbasket states. Dark green to the east of the Missouri River, the grayish green color of sage, bunch grasses, and cacti in the western grasslands and deserts, land gives us colors and vistas and adds untold richness to life. With no connection to soil and land, people have no heritage and become rootless wanderers in search of a place to call home. When we travel, we meet others and discuss the hometowns, regions, and districts that help make up our identity. Some cultures spend generations trying to reclaim their ancestral lands. Land is synonymous with life.

This book is about the midwestern land I know and love—what it is now, what it was like before corn and grazing cattle came to dominate it—and the human community that settled it. I worked the land because I needed to know and understand my lineage, to recognize, cultivate, and rekindle a historic connection to the earth.

Dirty hands and sweat welded my relationship with Stone Prairie Farm, an 80-acre expanse in Wisconsin where I have worked to give nature a second chance. My years of planting, of nurturing the resurgence of prairie, wetland, and forest cover where eroded farm fields once lay exposed, have created a deep, direct connection to nature. Because of the years of work that I, my partner, Susan, and countless friends and volunteers have put into the land, native plants, birds and butterflies, and other wildlife have all returned in abundance, and a diversity of life now exists far beyond what is commonly found in the region. The immediate delight of this is wonderful. Over time I began to understand that rare birds were returning, flying miles to find our farm. This realization turned my dreams into a broader vision for restoration and stewardship over a much larger landscape, local, regional, and national, that encompassed many ecosystems —deserts, mountain forests, eastern forests, and others.

I began wondering how I could inspire others to think about restoring their farms, or parts of them. I envisioned a network of restored lands that would reconnect dispersed and isolated habitats. This may be viewed as an ecological systems approach to re-thinking the landscape or a community land ethic where the health of the land—not just of individually owned parcels—is a measure of land community vitality. I also began contemplating expansion of the restored prairies beyond my fence lines. These visions have taken hold with some neighbors, resulting in a series of reasoned changes on their land. Some have planted prairie on parts of their farms, contributing to the ecological fabric of the community with a great increase in the number of bluebirds and wildflowers.

Documenting personal experiences in my restoration of Stone Prairie Farm sparked the notion of this book. A similar experience could have resulted anywhere, in any ecosystem. Corn, wheat, soybeans, and milk were produced here for over a hundred years, as they still are on neighboring farms. The difference on my land today is that a sweet corn patch is the only corn growing, and many dozens of species of wild birds and other wildlife have supplanted milk cows. This book is about the conversion—what's been required, the process, and the rewards. This book is not about homesteading, though many of our hobbies, like wine and furniture making, are activities commonly done by homesteaders, and they connected us to the land-change process during restoration. While we relish the home-made wild grape wine but more so, we've stayed focused on the changes that have attracted the birds and the seeds they distribute, including wild grape.

Beyond this farm, my livelihood is based upon restoring the land, using the same conversion process celebrated in this book. My ecological consulting firm, Applied Ecological Services, Inc. (AES), implements ecological restoration projects throughout North America and in many other parts of the world. Over the course of almost three decades, my design and implementation of these projects for many hundreds of clients has transformed and healed nature. I started AES in 1975 and, shortly thereafter, launched Taylor Creek Restoration Nurseries (TCRN), which grows seeds and plants of more than six hundred native prairie, wetland, and forest plant species used in AES's restorations. Today the firm—which is based in Brodhead, Wisconsin, but also has five remote offices around the United States—employs 140 growers, ecologists, restorationists, engineers, and designers. Multiple satellite nursery operations support regional plant production that meets the needs for those areas.

Through AES, I've worked on some of the most exciting and intriguing ecological restorations of recent years, affecting many millions of acres of land. These lands were monitored and visited frequently during, and sometimes decades after, the restoration work. They included reclaimed mined lands, where thousands of acres at a time were planted to prairie, forest, or wetland vegetation; landfills converted to parks through native plantings; and many tens of thousands of acres of converted agricultural lands, mostly with marginal crop-producing soils. The land was purchased by agencies, by nonprofit groups such as the Nature Conservancy, and by many private and corporate parties who saw value in restoration. AES was also instrumental in the restoration of Stone Prairie Farm, which began in 1980, shortly after I moved to southern Wisconsin. However, the relationship was informal and serendipitous. Sometimes I borrowed a tractor or seed drill on weekends and holidays at times when they were not in use. I also made arrangements for several years to have the waste seed and chaff from Taylor Creek Restoration Nurseries' seed-cleaning facility spread on sections of Stone Prairie Farm.

Over the course of the last twenty-eight years, my partner, Susan Marie Lehnhardt, her son, Noah Klinge, and our dog, Max, have all been involved in the restoration process on Stone Prairie Farm. It is with trepidation that I have used the word "I," when "we" would have been more appropriate to describe our shared experiences. My choice to write in the first person is not meant to belittle the importance of our shared experiences.

Susan and I have tried to understand this land we call home, a wonderful historic dairy farm of 80 acres, and its place on the broader landscape. My twenty-eight years and Susan's nineteen years working and watching this land, thinking and dreaming about it, have been life giving. Life has returned to previously degraded, badly eroded farm fields that produced only periodic crops of corn. Today, lively prairies, wetlands, forests, orchards, and gardens flourish. The 150-year-old farmhouse historically housed farmers, and kept the outside out. Now, nature resides inside and out. If the condition of the land is any reflection of dreams, ours are surely different from those of the prior tenants. We've celebrated the return of the corn snake and ambush bug, and the reintroduction and resurgence of hundreds of wild prairie plant species. The restoration and stabilization of the spring brook brought the return of native fishes. We found its revitalization to be symbolic of the larger restoration experience. It could not be stabilized, and the water did not begin to run clean and cold, until bordering uplands grew wild again. Then the furred, feathered, finned, and scaled inhabitants reinvaded.

Growing up five hundred miles apart—she in Walnut, Iowa, and I in Chicago—Susan and I began our parallel journeys in childhood, each groping for life in whatever wildness was available. We scratched the dirt, plucked seeds, and braided wild grasses, all the while looking out over the land like a raccoon feeling the submerged brook pebble while mindlessly looking elsewhere. Our dreamy stares focused on the land's myriad mysteries.

Since childhood, a passion for nature has impressed on me the importance of land, opening my eyes and heart. At this farm, Susan and I have been led beyond the fence lines, farther than the boundless rolling green surrounding us, to a better understanding of land, water, and wind, of politics, community, neighbors, and economics. The connections are unbreakable, ever growing and durable. We've found that sharing our experiences gives them a broader value. Every piece of land can provide a fellow human being with a rich, meaningful experience.

This book grew out of journaling keyed to cycles—daily, seasonal, and annual reactions, feelings, and awakening awareness. Wind, light, wild plants, and animal life captivated my primordial instincts. Observations gave pause for contemplation and reflection. Hard physical labor during restoration provided an enduring connection, augmented by blisters and words, photographs and questions. As a result of these connections, I've begun to learn and understand this place—and myself.

Somewhere in the early days of working on AES projects it became clear that working on someone else's project was not giving me a personal connection to the land. During the course of a normal AES project, I'd work on one piece of land for a few years, and then move on to the next project. I needed to work in an ongoing relationship with the land, not just that delimited, relatively short timeline. I yearned to cultivate a garden and prune an orchard. Since early 1981, my farm has been my home, my love, my passion, my peace.

This book is about the living land and my experiences at Stone Prairie Farm. It is organized around my getting to know the land, restoring it, and connecting with the community through the process, and will perhaps inspire others to do the same. I also contemplate what will become of this vigorous land, rich with life, that Susan and I have helped re-create.

The first section is a story of discovery that offers specifics about this patch of earth, its location and context. The second part describes the changes we wrought in order to restore the land and farm and to live more comfortably. Part III begins my contemplation of connections with the larger ecosystem and my community, setting the stage for a time when Susan, Noah, Max, and I are no longer here. The final section explores the future and speculates on ways to maintain the restoration Susan and I have cherished, and to expand this ethos using larger-scale land features and engaging others in developing a concern for the health of ecosystems. The Afterword provides a seasonal perspective on the dynamics of this place, from the cacophony of frogs in spring to the new wildlife and wildflowers that appear in summer to the bird migrations in fall and the vats of maple syrup in winter.

Steven I. Apfelbaum
Stone Prairie Farm
April 2008

PART I

Focus and Intentions

CHAPTER I

A Place to Settle

What I remember most is falling in love with the place. Instantly. I recall the minute details as well—the scent of moist hay, the hiss of the radiator as the engine of my mother's 1974 Toyota Celica cooled, the warm July sun against my skin, the feel of rich, fertile dirt under my feet, the rustle of wind through the rows of corn planted nearby. But mostly these particulars blended together into an exhilarating, unexpected sense of being deeply at home on this land I'd never before seen.

Stepping away from the car, I looked around, taking in the gentle roll of the land from north to south. The earth was lush and green in the early summer, cleared of large trees in most areas, with scatterings of gangly oaks and box elders, and a stand of what looked like young pines in the distance. An immense weeping willow arched over a large wooden farmhouse in front of me. Beyond it was a weathered wooden barn and, farther off, several dilapidated outbuildings teetered on the hillside. Beside them were a couple of old, cobweb-covered tractors. The distance in between was carpeted with plush foliage dotted by unruly patches of prairie wildflowers in their last stages of bloom, many already gone to seed. Next to me I could almost sense my mother thinking, "We'll get this place cleaned up and orderly in no time." Inside I reveled in its anarchic disarray.

The buildings were separated from the rest of the 80-acre farm with a fence of posts and barbed wire. A two-track dirt driveway ran between the house and the outbuildings and led to a gated pasture where I could see, hear, and smell a herd of black-and-white Holstein dairy cows, their tails in constant motion, swishing at flies. They had grazed the vegetation to ankle height. On this side of the fence the mix of weeds and unkempt former lawn grasses past the height of the house foundation, largely obscuring the front door.

My mom began walking through this high growth toward the farmhouse. She is a short woman, barely five feet tall on a good day, and the sight of her tromping through the greenery waving her arms was like a gentle parody of a machete-wielding jungle explorer blazing a trail through dense underbrush. I made to follow her, but my eye was drawn in another direction, toward a cluster of weeping willows, and particularly the dark, mossy recess on the ground between the trees. Perhaps it was just the opportunity to find shade from the warm sun that steered me that way, or perhaps it was my recent training as an ecologist. Maybe it was some innate connection with the land. Whatever the cause, I headed off toward the trees and, parting the tall vegetation with my arms, stumbled onto a treasure.

In the cool shade I found a torrent of clear water, a crystal-clear spring bubbling up from the earth. Looking closer, I saw a flurry of movement. The gushing stream was full of fairy shrimp—grayish-white, nearly translucent creatures, about a quarter inch in length, that darted about in undulating, wavelike patterns, powered by several rows of sweeping legs and spinnerets. The shrimp danced about against the background of a dark green algae-like aquatic plant, which itself waved back and forth in the current discharging from the spring. This was not the green slimy algae commonly found in the polluted water-ways and streams of Chicago, where I'd started out that morning. I reached into the water to touch this plant and found it attached firmly to a limestone rock. Around the rock was more life: a flurry of small aquatic insects, including mayflies and caddis fly larvae, which I knew from my training are typical of only high-quality water resources. They held tightly to the bottom and sides of the rock as though a strong displacing current was tearing at them.

There was also something here I had learned about in plant ecology classes but had never seen: a red algae species adhering to the underside of several rocks. Unlike some green and blue-green algae species, red algae, like the aquatic insects, indicates very high-quality water. I became so entranced by the spring, with its vegetation and shrimp and insects, that I stumbled backwards, hit my head on something behind me, and fell to the ground.

It was 1981 and I was twenty-six years old, a young research ecologist full of energy and idealism, and I was looking for a home, but not in the way many people look for an apartment—as a refuge from their work lives or a haven of comfort and convenience. Rather, I was searching feverishly for a place that would become the central focus of my living and my work. Somewhere I could walk the talk of environmentalism. I dreamt of a home that would allow me, two decades after the start of the back-to-the-land movement, to become deeply involved with the land, where I could live simply and build a relationship with nature and my work that was exciting and rejuvenating. This imagined farm I sought would be a root source of lifelong learning, an entrée to greater understanding of nature and of our relationship with the earth. It was a grand vision, but also a very tall order to fill given the meager amount of money I had at my disposal. No one in his right mind would consider research ecology—the science of applying ecological knowledge to solve environmental problems and manage natural resources—a smart money-making career choice. But I had chosen it nonetheless, and having land of my own was critical to my education and, perhaps, my sanity.

I'd spent long months looking for a place, often with my mother at my side. Each time my hopes would rise as we left suburban Chicago and drove into landscapes with farms and open sky. As we neared each potential location my heart would race with anticipation. I fell in love easily with half a dozen of the properties, for any number of reasons. I made an offer on one because of its view of a large bur oak tree on an adjacent property. At another I fell for the seclusion: it was a quiet place on a dead-end farm road, with no neighbors or through traffic for miles. But each time we'd return disappointed, as some feature spoiled each place—the absence of any even remotely livable farmhouse, a price tag that was far beyond my very limited means, or totally inappropriate neighboring farmers. In one case I was so taken with a nearly perfect farm that I almost failed to notice a large pork producer nearby, whose hogs created an unbearable stink.

I'd never pursued any purchase for so long, and my patience was in tatters. Each failure—be it the site, the funding, or the timing—seemed a disaster, a sure omen that I'd never find an appropriate farm, or be able to afford it if I did. After a dozen unsuccessful attempts I was truly discouraged. My dream seemed doomed to failure.

It was my mother who came to the rescue. She had faithfully driven down long country roads week after week and comforted me through the repeated letdowns, despite being unable to fully accept my career choice. She had continued to tell her friends that "little Stevie" was going to be a veterinarian years after I had begun my ecology studies. I don't think it was a question of pride or of being able to boast to her friends, although veterinarian was the closest shot any of her children gave her to "my son the doctor." Somehow my work just didn't compute for her. Nonetheless she had taken up the standard just as my spirits sagged, and she jumped into the hunt for a farm with tenacious vigor.

She worked for a police union in Barrington, a suburb of Chicago, and when the police chief mentioned that his family owned three farms, she pressed him for details. It turned out that one of the farms, located in southern Wisconsin, had long been a vacation spot for him, his brothers, and their extended families. It had been largely vacant for some time, with portions of the lands rented out to actual working farmers. We were forewarned that the old farmhouse was in great disarray, and that every room, including the kitchen, was wall to wall with beds: roll-aways, doubles, a bank of bunks for the gangs of children and friends that sometimes visited in the summers and winters.

The chief wasn't actually looking to sell the farm, but my mother can be very convincing and rarely takes no for an answer. I felt a little sorry for him, thinking back to my childhood, to how relentless she could be when she wanted something. I have a clear memory of her haggling for what seemed like hours with the local shoe store owner over the "outrageous" price of the annual installment of gym shoes for me and my brothers. And it's easy to recall other occasions when she spoke sternly with teachers and students alike, making sure the Apfelbaum clan was treated well at school. So it wasn't a stretch to imagine her pestering the police chief daily for updates on this piece of land, until he finally caved in. Soon we were on our way to view the place—given the keys and sent off on our own for what should have been a two-hour drive.

We didn't barrel down the road at high speeds, hell-bent on getting to the farm as fast as possible, as I would have had I been alone, driving my beat-up 1950 Willys. Instead we took the Celica and made endless gas station stops. And paused at deserted intersections for stoplights that seemed to last for hours. And Mom needed to go to the bathroom. And then go again. How many times can one person have to go during a hundred-mile drive? I didn't have to, so why did she? Then there was confusion over the directions, and long moments of scrutinizing maps that weren't detailed enough to include many of the narrow country roads. My frustration mounted. I was so anxious to get there and she seemed to be doing everything she could to slow us down.

"It's a long way," she said at one point, several miles down a poorly marked gravel road.

And again, a bit later, "I wouldn't want to drive this in the winter. All that ice and snow."

"I've got snow tires—it'll be great" was all I could answer.

Even though I was focused on our destination, and irritated by her seeming reluctance, I heard the worry in her voice: worry about my leading a rugged lifestyle she couldn't fathom away from the niceties and conveniences of modern urban America, worry for my safety, and, mostly, worry about my being so far from the family.

This was nothing to the long list of concerns she would develop as we discovered the rundown condition of the farm and it became increasingly possible that I might actually live there.

⌒

I hit the moist ground by the spring with a thud, more surprised than hurt. Something fell beside me, pinging off a small rock. A blue enameled tin cup. Clearly it had been hung on the tree branch for use in the spring. I dipped it in immediately, and took a deep sip of the mouth-numbingly cold, clear water.

"Mom! You've got to try this!" I yelled.

When she made it over to the spring from her cursory walk around the house, she looked skeptical.

"It's fantastic." I filled the cup for her.

"It might not be clean," she said. "Or safe."

"Not from the faucet. Right." I took another long sip and replaced the cup on the branch. "You're going to have to learn to trust me on some of this."

From the spring and the shade of the surrounding trees, my eyes were drawn across the road to a hill that glowed with the midsummer color and texture I had learned could only be that of a prairie. While Mom headed to the barn, I walked toward the hill. I paused at the wire fence beside the road. There was no sign posted, but thoughts of territorial farmers with shotguns or angry dogs flickered through my mind. The lure of the prairie, golden and wild, flecked with spots of color, drew me on. I continued up the hill, side-stepping beautiful flowers and oval-shaped badger burrows. At the top of the hill, amidst pale purple coneflowers that swayed in the warm midday breeze, I turned to look behind me.

The farmhouse and other buildings sat cradled by golden prairie, a rich contrast with the tarpaper and asphalt roofs and the weathered timber sidings. The belt of prairie was narrow, essentially patches of land in the middle of an intensely agricultural region that had been left fallow and reverted to a semi-wild state. From the hill I saw endless farms stretching into the distance, each connected to the next by dark cornfields. Other features accented the landscape—the occasional rich green of a waterway, slight gaps for property lines, and straight fencerows of intertwined trees. A euphoric feeling came over me, the same feeling I had when paddling my canoe through glassy waters, or hiking through untrammeled wilderness—the magical experiences that had steered my life in this direction to begin with, prompting me to study ecology and dedicate myself to communing with nature; the very experiences that had brought me to the farm that day, seeking a new place to put down roots.

Down below, Mom had gone into the farmhouse to inspect. The building had been sealed for quite some time, and as she opened windows and doors the musty smell of mildew spilled out. Inside it was a true mess. Stained mattresses were strewn everywhere, corners nibbled by mice that had left piles of droppings everywhere. She was mortified at first, but soon began strategizing how to fix the place up, where my bedroom would be, what could possibly be done with the decaying kitchen. None of this mattered to me at all. I quickly looked over the space, saw the chimney with its cracking mortar, and figured I could vent my wood-burning stove into it—the bare minimum needed to deal with the harsh Wisconsin winter. That, a water source, and a bathroom (inside or out, didn't matter) were enough for me. Mentally I was still back outside, looking over the farm, seeing the golden prairie and deep green cornfields blanketing the earth, the trees reaching into the blue sky, and the vibrant, flowing spring with its cold water feeding the land, supporting its own perfect microcosm of undulating insect and algae life.

The purchase negotiations were rocky. The property encompassed 80 acres, but the owners only wanted to part with the five around the buildings. This was a tiny scratch at my fantasy. Still, given my financial situation, it would be a decent start. However, the survey found that this 5-acre parcel violated the boundary of the cornfield behind the house, for which a tenant farmer had a multiyear contract. Ultimately I was able to purchase only 2.7 acres, bounded by fences and surrounded by corn, which was a mere toehold in this sea of greenery. But it was a toehold nonetheless.

The drawn-out negotiation process made me desperately impatient, so I moved onto the land in late summer, long before the sale was complete. I had permission to be there, but not to take up residence in the farmhouse. Instead I moved into the hayloft, a squatter with the gentle blessing of the landlords. I cooked by camp stove, drank and bathed at the spring, and slept in my worn blue down sleeping bag.

The first night I pushed together a thick pile of hay on the haymow platform, some twenty feet off the ground, laid my bag out on top, and crawled in, utterly exhausted by the effort of moving. In moments I'd drifted off to sleep. Hours later I awoke, disoriented, to a chorus of sounds—the erratic bellowing of cows in the nearby pasture. Why now? I thought. What has happened in the middle of the night to set them off? Bad dreams, perhaps? A cricket chirping too loudly? The distant howling of forlorn coyotes? I lay awake for some time listening to bellowing, not yet able to distinguish between the cows and the bulls, not yet aware how many nights during the following years I'd find myself listening to the persistent calls.

After drifting back to sleep despite the noise, I woke at dawn to rays of sunrise streaming in from the open haymow doors more than eight feet above me, bathing rough-hewn beams and wooden walls in a fiery red light. Nearby there was a chattering of birds. I searched about for a way to climb up, but no ladder or built-in steps were visible. Eventually I found myself balancing gingerly as I crept out onto the timbers that supported the loft. The wood under my feet was mostly smooth with age, but here and there a stray rough edge bit into my foot. Suspended too far off the floor for comfort, I looked down to see my shoes, innocently strewn beside my sleeping bag, mocking me. And as I looked down, I lost my footing for a moment, and found myself clutching at the beam, my heart racing. Finally calming myself, I continued my way out to the center timber. There I grabbed hold of the thick, dusty rope that ran to the door and carefully pulled myself along the beam.

I finally made it onto the platform and knelt, happy to be on a somewhat steady surface, just as a swarm of small shapes came flying toward my head, shrieking, and sent me sprawling. The birds, a handful of house sparrows and starlings, had been roosting in the rafters. Apparently my clambering about had startled them, and they came screeching out in a panicked burst, desperate to get out the doors before I blocked their exit. I lay face down on the platform, catching my breath from the fright. Directly below was my sleeping bag, its rich navy blue now peppered soundly with white splotches the birds had released as they took off. I'd been up for less than half an hour. I'd nearly fallen from the ceiling, and my bed was covered with feces. It was the first of many lessons on what to expect from living in and with nature.

As time passed, the haymow became my regular perch. The panoramic view that spread out for miles was glorious, and I would perch there for hours at a time, drinking in the beauty of the land around me, scanning the view, catching the movement of wildlife, and watching and listening to the human activity on the nearby farms. Eventually this lofty perspective would start the gears turning in my head.

CHAPTER 2

Ancient Landforms and Modern Inhabitants

After gazing out over the neighboring farms from my promontory those first days, my initial sense of a generalized vista refocused to a more precise mental mapping of the surrounding terrain. As a scientist I began to break down what was laid out before me. Most elements were pretty clear, and repeated in different versions on each rectangular property. There were tractors and other farming implements scattered over large corn and grain fields, and cattle grazing smaller fenced-in areas. Farmhouses and their outbuildings appeared in the midst of the few remaining older-growth trees. I could trace the line of the creek fed by my spring through four or five farms before I lost its trail beyond the hills. It turned out to be a tributary of Spring Creek, which was located downstream of my property, about one mile away to the north. My land was less manicured, not having been actively farmed for two years, but the same essential landscaping remained.

Five or six generations of farm families had carved out their livelihoods on these plots. Each had its own goals, but there would have been certain overlapping concerns. Farmer A wouldn't have wanted Farmer B leaching fertilizers into the creek upstream of his land if that supplied drinking water for him or his livestock. There would certainly have been questions regarding accuracy of fence lines, as well as questions of responsibility for large overhanging or fallen trees. For years boundary issues would have been worked out between neighbors, using fallen trees and other guides for simple solutions that kept the geometry and plot layout clear. I guessed that this community of farmers hadn't been engaged in dialogue about the interconnectedness of their lands within the larger landscape. They were neighbors, but they weren't exactly allies. They worked in rhythm with one another as they farmed their individual properties, but as with small children engaging in parallel play, their efforts had no significant linkage, no relation to the larger perspective in which I saw the land as a whole. There was clearly a code of mutual respect, since they were all in the same boat, and often a tool was borrowed or a tractor was lent. But there wasn't a concern with how their actions generally affected the ecosystem.

That realization made me nervous about being an outsider with a differing agenda. I hadn't decided exactly what to do with my land, but I had no intention of doing what they did. Still, I wanted amiable relationships with the surrounding families. I worried about how they would react to my plans once it was apparent that I wasn't running a commercial farming enterprise. Would they accept me if my land use deviated from what they expected? And if not, would it be simply awkward, or truly untenable?

They farmed to subsist. Cornfields engulfed their farmhouses. Cows butted against the fences encircling their yards. Everything was neat, clearly arranged, efficient in human terms. In contrast I wanted an Eden of flowers, birds, and wildlife.

Maybe a row or two of sweet corn in a small garden, sure. But my land would be unruly to the farmer's eye, and efficient only in natural terms.

The farmers worked their fields with skill, following generations of tradition. I was most interested in the remaining natural areas on their lands, slivers of wildness left behind like the remnants of fabric that have been made into a suit. On each farm I could see the same tired drama being played out between traces of free-reigning nature and encroaching cultivation. The natural elements that lingered on these lands—remnants of woodlands, meadows, and bubbling brooks—were always secondary to the pressing business of running a farm, which required maximal space for animals and crop yields. I fantasized about these vestigial parcels expanding if they were encouraged to develop naturally. Meanwhile my neighbors were calculating their bottom lines, turning land use into a purely mathematical formula, viewing these spaces as inefficiencies to be rectified.

My discomfort intensified within my first few weeks there, when the neighbor to the northeast razed a swath of remnant woodland that I had been scouting from afar. I had been considering how I might go about sneaking onto the property to witness it up close, since it looked to be a pretty mature grove of maples. Judging by the size of the trees and the settlement history of the area, the woodland would have predated nineteenth-century settlement, and therefore provided invaluable ecological records and clues to the history of the neighborhood. I had hoped to analyze soil samples, core some trees to determine their age, and experience the lively diversity of birds and wildflowers.

With binoculars glued to my eyes, I watched as the trees were razed and the area was transformed into an indistinct patch of farmland in a single afternoon. The huge maples were bulldozed into a barn-sized pile of sticks. The varied wildflowers that had dotted the woodland edge with color were heaped together and burned. The speed with which the high-tech scythe decimated the land and its magnificent heritage shocked me. I watched the entire day with the burning smell in my nose, and fell asleep where I sat with a canteen of water as the fire died down. Within days the frame for a large modern home emerged from the ashes of those beautiful trees.

That event unsettled me, and I couldn't bear to climb up to my perch and see the progress of the new structure. Instead I spent the next few days roaming the perimeter of my land and looking at the geometry of my neighbors' overtaxed fields. As I stared down perfect rows of young corn and let my vision blur in blowing wheat fields, I felt an awkward respect for the tenacity of the farmers and began worrying that my youthful idealism was a collection of fragile hopes that would shatter against the realities facing me. How did I expect to reveal Eden in this farm-belt grid?

I had questions that it would take some time to answer. Some anxieties would only ease with perspective born of experience. So I settled in and began to set up systems and routines that would allow me to develop a relationship with the soil and the trees and the creek. Naming the land helped, made it somehow more concrete for me. The name, Stone Prairie Farm, came to me while I was walking the rented cornfield, where swathes of stones were scattered across the ridge. I bent over and picked up one of the stones to find a fossilized imprint of some long-gone ocean creature. I marveled over it for a moment, then looked up to see another miraculous sight—a single remaining native prairie grass plant standing stalwart against the tug of the eroding topsoils, in the heavy gravelly clay soils.

As I settled in I could ground myself, and begin to call the land home, confident that the optimistic student that I was then would eventually integrate into the local community, and the intrepid scientist I was becoming would surely have the opportunity in the future to engage the neighbors in an ecological dialogue, and perhaps help design cooperative systems that would benefit each others' lands.

But I knew that kind of integration could take years to establish. I told myself to slow down. First I had to accept that the neighbors would do what they needed to do regardless of how I felt about it. I was the outsider, and I was young enough to allow things to play out. So what better thing to do than climb back up to that platform and continue my meditative daydreaming? The visioning process relaxed me and flowed into my peaceful nightly slumbers in the hayloft bed.

One muggy night I dreamed that I was flying along the creek line. From my bird's-eye view as I glided northward, I could see the riparian trees begin to thicken and the creek water become noticeably clearer. I was flying toward an unknown destination amidst a dense flock of passenger pigeons, the now extinct species that used to thrive in this neighborhood, darkening the skies with their numbers. Suddenly I was caught in an updraft and quickly ascended into thick clouds, which obscured my view of the land. No matter in which direction I steered myself, I couldn't find my way out of the clouds. A buzzing noise invaded, and I woke to find a large mosquito circling my head.

As I sat over hot tea later, absentmindedly sketching the neighboring farmhouse, I contemplated the meaning of that dream. It seemed that my subconscious was trying to go back in time to the source of the landforms. I flipped the page and started to sketch an aerial view of my property in its current state, but instead of replicating what existed, I exaggerated the creek, widening it and filling out the riparian strip. I added savanna oaks and replaced cornfields with swathes of prairie and wetlands in the lowest ground. This gave me the idea that I should do a bit of research, try to find survey records and actual aerial photos.

I didn't know exactly what I was looking for, but envisioning the stages of geographic development in the region seemed like a good exercise. The farms obstructed the interconnected pristine landscape, with its prairies and wetlands and woodlands. But the topography was still largely intact, and certain non-farmable features that still existed in the area might elucidate what had been plowed under, bulldozed down, or eroded away. I did a mental exercise, letting my mind slip backward in time to the creation of the landforms and the brook. The topography had been crafted by glaciers that stripped the earth, leaving behind flattened lands that became wetlands, then eventually forests and prairies, and finally the farm fields I had been contemplating.

A glacier is a super bulldozer two miles thick and hundreds of miles wide. It advances methodically on a slippery sheet of oozing, melting waters, propelled by its own weight like a snail. In the midwestern plains this relentless mass would grind down the underlying limestone, polishing its features while filling in eroded crevasses and canyons with millions of tons of crushed rock. And this towering, translucent, bluish wall, a behemoth that dwarfed the Grand Canyon in scale, reshaped the undulating terrain and its bedrock ridges and valleys not only once —about 10,000 years ago—but twice more in the preceding 200,000 years.

I visualized this watery slurry with its tinted, mineral-enriched rivers and streaming waterfalls, and imagined the incessant drone as it advanced and receded over my diminutive plot of land. What a calculation to consider the force of such an assault! Consider that a column of air one inch wide by one inch thick stretching several miles in height results in about fifteen pounds per square inch of pressure on the ground and on every being. This is the atmospheric pressure of the earth at sea level. Now imagine the weight of a stack of ice cubes two miles high, assuming one pound of weight for every foot in the stack. Even without calculating the encapsulated rock and other materials, the glacier would exert more than ten thousand pounds of pressure per square inch, a feat unduplicated by humankind, I am sure. By expanding that square-inch pressure over miles and millennia, I began to understand that my land had been sculpted in enormous elemental strokes: freezing and thawing, erosion and sedimentation, and upheavals of the soil that created the landforms discovered by the first settlers.

Current theory in the climate sciences suggests that the glaciers caused climate change even before completely receding, positing that the air plunging over the glaciers compressed and heated as it fell. So the air speeding away from the base created warmer conditions than one might assume next to a two-mile-high wall of ice. Warm air plus newly released nutrients and ground rock deposited by the receding glacier created the ideal growing conditions to support arctic wetlands and spruce forests as far north as the Arctic Circle. As the glacier moved even farther northward, conditions across temperate latitudes favored oak and pine forests, and grasslands took hold when seasonally warm and dry conditions eventually prevailed.

After that glacial clearing, and for several thousand years leading up the time of settlement, oak savanna and prairie vegetation spread virtually unimpeded in this part of the North American continent, interspersed with occasional wetlands. Animal habitats evolved in the balance of that perfect interconnected wilderness and existed in equilibrium for millennia. Then settlers, mostly European Americans pushing west, set into motion a tide of agriculture and development that would eventually fill in countless wetlands, plow under millions of acres of prairie vegetation, and clear-cut enough swaths of oak savanna to degrade ecosystems to their current alarming levels.

And what of those early settlers? Arriving in their new lands, they would have discovered a majestic, nearly self-regulating environment with four interdependent communities of flora: various types of prairies; oak savannas; rare and scattered wetlands; and isolated maple woodlands containing key plant species typically found only in locations resistant to wildfires. The Sugar, Pecatonia, and Wisconsin Rivers surrounding the region, as well as the steep coulees to the north and west, served as firebreaks that protected several thousand square miles within the surrounding prairie landscapes of Wisconsin and northern Illinois from intense burns.

According to the original land surveys, my home would have rested within the region once shielded by those former fire-protected forests. I would have been able to see, half a mile north, the oak-scattered savanna whose fire-tolerant prairie grasses and other assorted plant species would have safeguarded the larger northern forests from burns stoked by seasonal southerly and westerly winds. On a misty morning it is easy to envision stalwart gnarled bur oaks still growing on the sand-and-gravel knob ridge tops rolling along the sloping northern horizon.

Prior to the European settlers, Native Americans learned and developed what was necessary to live lightly on this land for perhaps several thousand years. Arrowheads and a hide scraper found behind our home tell of their presence even on Stone Prairie Farm. Then European settlers arrived with minimal resources beyond know-how and the urgent will to survive. Instead of taking the Native American approach, these settlers would have seen in this landscape an unending resource, awaiting the application of labor. And so trees were transformed into houses and firewood; prairies became pastures for livestock and endless fields of crops; creeks and springs became sources for irrigation and potable water. For some time these systems were sustainable. But as these farmlands became vital to markets farther and farther away, the business of farming slowly whittled away at the harmonious balance of between farmer and land. I am sure this shift seemed perfectly natural to the pioneers, just as it does to modern consumers and corporations, who value uniformity and productivity over variety and sustainability, and have come to accept the segregation of nature in the form of state parks and preserves as the best solution. Cities and suburbs aren't the only denuded areas; farmlands contain mere fractions of their original richness.

When I moved onto my land only scant traces of the natural

flora remained—a dozen fencerow trees, and several others scattered near the farmhouse. The box elder, black cherry, mulberry, and hackberry along the fencerows had an unnatural, flattened shape from years of tractors and corn harvesters swiping at their branches while working the fields on either side of the fence. Any limbs that ventured too far into the neighbor's lots were twisted back into the fencerow, most likely with the front-end loader on a farm tractor.

On the south side of the house, providing shade from the summer sun, were a sizable white ash and a large cultivated mulberry. There were also a couple of weedy box elders and, wedged in so close to the cement foundation that it had survived the mowers, was one hackberry that I was able to save. The black willows that lined the spring creek, tilting southeastward from decades of wind that desiccated their buds and retarded growth, stood as stoic reminders of how the open prairie shapes trees.

It was these trees that drew in the orioles, tanagers, and passing migratory warblers in the spring and fall. Even an occasional goshawk came to my land, perching on the hackberry or ash as it searched for food in the form of rabbits and mice that scurried around the farmhouse and buildings.

Once the farm had been converted to cornfields this small island of trees around the house would have been the only tangible connection to nature. Almost as an homage to these hearty survivors, I worked fervently to nurse them back to health, spending long hours pruning and irrigating all of them. I gave myself the particular challenge of saving a mulberry tree that was near death. It has since come back to life, and I have hung a hammock from its trunk.

Of course buildings stood on the land as well as these trees. My old farmhouse was a reminder of the grit and determination of the settlers. From a distance it looked like the classic simple building with two opposing A-framed rooflines that merge at right angles to each other. The roofs were covered in layer upon layer of old tarpaper. The stubs of a few torn-off lightning rods poked through, still reaching up and providing essential pathways to the ground for the zillion-volt shocks that flash out during spring and summer thunderstorms.

In those early days, I inspected the farmhouse's foundation and found it was made from layered blocks of cut limestone held with a slacked lime mortar, a rather weak glue by modern cementing standards. To add strength the builders had mixed in old pieces of knotted barbed wire, tin cans, broken glass, ceramic telegraph pole insulators, and iron farm implement parts—basically anything they could recycle instead of discard. Twenty feet above the valley bottom, the house had rested for generations on that foundation of four-hundred-million-year-old Silurian Limestone, facing the spring creek that flowed five hundred feet to the west. Both the farmhouse and barn proved to be treasure troves of local history, and lessons in nineteenth-century craftsmanship. To begin with, the wood had been cut using several distinct techniques. The main timbers were pit-sawn oak, cut with saws eight to ten feet long that would have been brought to the harvest site. But others were hewed square with a combination of broad ax and adz. The broad ax chopped vertically while the adz, an axlike tool with a blade oriented to the shaft like a hoe, chopped against the grain, allowing the worker to stand astride the log in order to facet or smooth it. Each method left telltale scars on the posts and beams of the farmhouse: the broad ax's clean, long scars, and the adz's abrupt overlapping cuts.

Unsplit red cedar posts served as columns and supports. According to the original land survey, that kind of cedar grew on the bedrock ridges a mile to the north. The building's main structural oak timbers probably came from those ridges as well. Examining all this lumber, I became very curious about the wood—where it come had from, when the trees had been felled, and how old the trees had been when they were cut. Somehow, understanding the wood of my buildings and its connection to the land seemed essential, so I decided to do a tree ring comparison to learn more.

First I took an increment corer, a hand-drilling tool with a hollow steel bit that extracts a pencil-diameter piece of wood, to both oak and cedar posts in the building. I then repeated the procedure on oak and cedar trees from the ridge where I suspected the timber had been cut. This method provides an immediate and exciting glance at the region's history. Each core shows a progression of annual growth lines, vacillating between the lighter color made by rapid spring growth and the darker banding laid down as the tree's growth rate slows in fall. Lining up the core samples for each type of wood and sliding them alongside each other, I matched together the widely spaced patterns left in the growth rings from unusually wet years and the close, tightly spaced rings from dry years. The patterns were quite clear and aligned perfectly, making it fairly easy to count back year by year from the outermost rings of the trees, which marked the present, to the time when the lumber was cut. It turned out to be just under 150 striations, meaning the trees had been probably cut sometime around 1836. Measuring the core sample from the lumber alone, it was clear that they'd been around 40 or 50 years old when felled. Moreover, the growth ring patterns of the posts and the lumber matched so closely, they confirmed that this ridge was in fact the most likely location where the both the cedar and oak logs were harvested to build this home. The live trees that I cored and used for reference were 210 to 230 years old, starting life at the same time as, and likely close cousins of, the trees that made the house!

As was typical in the surrounding community, the barn timbers were cut from white pine, likely also harvested in the mid-1800s during the heyday of the pineries in central and northern Wisconsin. Some oak timbers in the barn and house were older, likely recycled from other buildings. The original carpenters used irregular, cut-steel nails and pegged-timber joints, both of which contrast with the more standardized building materials used today. I also noted that the large timbers of the buildings created a framework that supported everything else, quite different from modern two-by-four stud construction, in which milled fir or pine boards are held tightly in a framework of similar-sized pieces of wood, and structural strength comes not from the central timbers but from the way the various walls and boards are tied together.

I particularly admired the joinery and the structural elegance in the barn. Fitted primarily with wood pegs, and mortise and tendon joinery, the structure had held together for well over 150 years. The only hardware I could find were the nails used to secure the siding and the lag bolts on the doors used to attach the hinges to the doorframes. This method of joinery used overlapping timbers for strength and inserted tendons to add length. Square-cut pieces of timber were fitted into a mortise, a hole cut to receive the tendon, and the joints were tightened by pounding pegs crafted from fresh-cut hickory, black locust, or ironwood into slightly offset holes with a large wooden mallet called a glug. The woodworkers painstakingly hewed octagonal pegs, because round ones tended to dry out and loosen. I came to appreciate the way that builders of yesteryear had to select the right tree species for their purpose—oak for strength and supports, green ironwood, hickory, or locust for the shaped pegs that were pounded into countering holes to strongly bind the timbers. In contrast, a stud wall of today is created with a very simple formula and no real connection to the properties of the wood or the tree species from which it grew.

The barn had evidently had some additions built, as evidenced by the types of wood and nails used, and the scoring from the saws used to cut the lumber. Cow-milking stanchions and stalls for draft horses were also added, as was a lean-to with newer milking stanchions. A small milk room, which housed a modern pumping unit with suction devices for the cows' teats, directed the milk to a large stainless-steel bulk milk cooling tank, which kept milk cold until a hauler arrived to take it to a local cheese factory. Early on, before the milking machine and refrigerated bulk tank, a wagon would have carted off cans of fresh milk to the local cheese factory. Later large tanker trucks pumped the milk directly in from the cooling tank. These small shed attachments were painted a nauseating pink on the outside and moldy green on the inside, just the kinds of incorrectly mixed paint colors one might find discounted at a local hardware store.

The question of how the house fit on the land had been nagging at me. Gradually, as I determined where the materials came from, and why they were used in certain ways, I came to see that the house was one with the land. It had grown up on this land, and each and every piece of its wood and stone was "borrowed" for a certain period of time from a short distance away. It was really a part of this place, of its natural resources, human culture, and history.

☞

Feeling a bit boxed in by fences, I took some drives to check out the regional terrain. Since the farm rested only one ridge away from the Illinois state line, I headed south first, down the rolling Wisconsin landscape, perhaps along the same route that some of those milk trucks had driven—into the land of Lincoln where the flat midwestern terrain stretched out for miles. Looping westward, I came back through an area of northwestern Illinois and southwestern Wisconsin where plateaus stand unchanged by glaciers since Paleozoic times. This region is called "driftless" by geologists, and was essentially an island that had been encircled by the ice of the most recent glacial periods. Instead of being scraped away by the advancing glaciers, these plateaus stood out, and no drift—the conglomeration of rock, silt, and other materials carried by the glaciers—was deposited around or on them.

Ecological markers proliferated along the drift's periphery. I explored bedrock ridges and exposed cliffs a mile north and hiked down into a fifty-foot-deep limestone canyon a mile to the west, where I found the canyon walls blanketed with bulblet fragile fern, columbine, and numerous other native plants. The

arching fern fronds had made their way down the cliff by dropping small bulbs onto each successive rock ledge, until the whole
cliff face became a waterfall of cascading fronds. Along the bottom of the gorge a meandering rocky stream only hinted at the
former glacial torrents of sand- and gravel-rich meltwater that
had carved through the canyon like fluid sandpaper. The canyon
was prospected during the lead mining days when early miners,
nicknamed badgers, searched for galena, a shiny, heavy lead
ore that formed cube-shaped crystals. It was mined by Native
Americans for ornaments, and used by settlers to make bullets. In
fact, this region was one of the main sources of the lead used
in the Civil War. The mining process had initially involved
hand-digging human-sized crawl holes into the bedrock along
the canyon walls. Just about every exposed limestone area that
I passed was dotted with these badger holes. The University of
Wisconsin "Badger" owes its origin to the miners, not the furry
mammal.

Heading back eastward from the driftless area, I saw how
Stone Prairie Farm was spread over an elevated landform that
included bedrock exposures, springs, and a spring creek. From
here it was possible to see how the different glacial tides had
carved out my land. The earlier Illinois glaciers that covered the
region 120,000 to 200,000 years ago had deposited a finely tex-
tured clay soil whose high moisture and nutrient retention were
still evident in the soils of my farm. On the perimeter of these
deposits, edging right up to the neighboring farm, was coarser
gravel, deposited by the Wisconsin glacier 7,000 to 10,000 years
ago. Apparently this more recent glacier had missed my land
altogether.

These excursions gave me a good perspective on the larger
landscape that encircled my new home. Having grown up on
the low-lying Illinois plain I felt curiously elated to be perched
in the next state, a half mile north of the elevated Wisconsin ridge that formed when the last glacier receded northward.
This ridge delineated the watershed of the area, dividing the

flow of the northern and southern runoff. It would have made geographic and ecological sense to have the state line follow this natural drainage divide. But this elegant detail escaped those who carried out the arbitrary political process of laying out linear state boundaries. In any case I was now a Wisconsinite, living on a unique geological crossroads, where I could conduct experiments that reflected the ecological questions that proliferated in my mind, and in my professional life.

I was becoming comfortable in the area, but a looming problem was pressing on me. When it came to restoring this land, I really didn't know where to begin. Looking at the bigger picture didn't help me decide what smaller steps I should follow. I tried not to worry about it, but I have always hated procrastinating, and that was exactly what I had started to do. I rationalized my hesitation by thinking I had to become familiar with all the issues of ownership and community and history. But I knew I would eventually have to begin the actual work of restoration, and sooner rather than later.

CHAPTER 3

Jump-Starting Land Restoration

Things were shaken up a few weekends after I moved in, when my mom and my three younger brothers, Gary, Ronnie, and Larry, insisted on visiting. They arrived with the best of intentions, ready to lend a hand with whatever needed doing, but I couldn't help finding their presence distracting and annoying. What I really wanted was time alone to continue settling in and getting organized at my own pace. I was becoming increasingly frustrated by my inability to get started with restoration, and their presence would only delay me further. Still, I feigned gratitude as we hugged on the front stoop and I felt the complexities of family relationships descend on my place of refuge.

The oldest of my brothers, I was twenty-six at the time. Larry, the youngest, was then eighteen, in his last year of high school and college bound that year with plans to go to law school eventually. He was a serious, focused kid, and had obviously come along on the visit to help get me settled. He asked Mom and me for a list of tasks he could work on, and then reminded us that he had a concert to go to later that evening and wanted to keep things moving. Ronnie and Gary, eighteen months apart in age, were the "trouble twins," then twenty-two and twenty-three. Both had barely made it through high school and by then had careers working at a car dealership. And while they claimed to be there to help, I couldn't help but be wary.

I gave them a quick tour of the house, followed by glasses of lemonade. Then we began unpacking boxes—and it was good to have the extra hands! Delegating and cooperating, we quickly cleared and organized a lot of space. In fact, I was beginning to feel actual gratitude when I noticed that Ronnie and Gary had disappeared after assembling a table downstairs. *They're just goofing off as usual,* the older brother in me said. I imagined they were poking around the first floor, most likely looking for mechanical challenges. I'd spent my childhood surrounded by the guts of household appliances large and small that these two had disemboweled. While machines were foreign and often intimidating to me, Ronnie and Gary quickly turned into junior whiz kids when they had screwdrivers and pliers in hand.

When I stopped to listen, I heard no sounds from downstairs. It occurred to me that they had probably left the house. My mind scoured the farm, trying to figure out what they would have been drawn to. I settled on the corncrib, the storehouse for what would have been the corn harvest. Parked inside, along with a scattering of old grains dried rock hard with age and covered by a thick coating of dust, were two ancient tractors from the 1940s, an International H and an Allis Chalmers WD. I had no clue how to operate them and, after a cursory once-over upon discovering them, had left them alone to continue their dust collecting. And yet I knew I'd have to face them at some point: they'd be necessary for preparing a proper garden plot. Ronnie and Gary knew their way around just about any motorized vehicle—which, it struck me, was good. Perhaps they could teach me what I needed to know.

Then again, maybe it wasn't so good. They weren't the most responsible young men. Over the years, in fact, they'd accrued a long record of reckless behavior. Growing up, it was common to hear stories about their calamities, sometimes from them, sometimes from angry parents in the neighborhood. There had been several escapades in "borrowed" cars—neighbors' vehicles that would inexplicably stop working one day and just as inexplicably start up again the next—and then there was the mystery of a bulldozer at a construction site a half mile from our home in suburban Illinois that had been set on a course toward the unfinished foundations of a new housing project. (Twenty-five years later I was speaking to a colleague who told me the story of how he'd shown up one Monday morning at the site of a job his company was working on, to find a Caterpillar D8 bulldozer standing vertically on its blade, which was embedded in the concrete foundation they'd poured the previous Friday. The huge diesel engine was still chugging, and his crew was standing about in awe trying to figure out what had happened. He said he thought it must have been some neighborhood kids who'd figured out how to start the engines.) With all this history, I was usually in a pretty high state of alert whenever Ronnie and Gary were around, wary about what chain of events might unfold, with embarrassing, or even perilous, results.

It shouldn't have surprised me, therefore, to hear the explosive thunder rumbling from the corncrib.

"Oh no," said Larry, still inside, gazing out the window.

Exhaust smoke was billowing from the corncrib building. By the time I reached the front door, Gary and Ronnie were racing away on the two tractors, trailing fumes and dust.

Side by side they drag-raced, shouting and waving their arms at each other as they rode around like maniacal rodeo cowboys on bucking broncos, weaving back and forth over the rolling earth. I stood there and watched the dirt kick up, caught between frustration and awe at their skill and audacity. But when they reached the boundary of my land and headed into the alfalfa fields of a neighboring farm, I began to panic and sprang into action. I jumped in my Jeep and sped down the road to intercept them. Seeing big brother closing the gap, they maneuvered away, plunging the tractors straight into the neighbor's cornfield. This was disastrous! It was hard enough to imagine the neighbors accepting my alternate approach to the land, hard enough living out in this rural agricultural world while attempting to promote a different set of beliefs and goals. If my brothers started flattening the neighboring farmers' crops, I'd be an absolute pariah.

As they disappeared into the greenery, I turned the truck around, not knowing what else to do. I was absolutely furious. I ranted to Mom and Larry about all the problems this would cause for me in the future.

"It'll work out," said Mom, placing her hand calmly on my shoulder. "Somehow it always does." Trust me, she seemed to be saying. I've been dealing with these shenanigans for years, and it doesn't help to get too angry.

No doubt Ronnie and Gary knew I'd be angry, and they took their time returning. Eventually I heard a sputtering engine sound from a distance. Soon afterward I spotted them through my binoculars, two troublemakers clambering under the barbed-wire fence on my north boundary line, having apparently ditched the tractors in the cornfield. They crossed the outer field, laughing and running low like guilty hyenas. Only when they started to slip surreptitiously in and out of the various farm buildings did it occur to me that they were searching for more gasoline to continue their joyride. My entire history of frustration with their antics flipped through my mind, and I raced down the stairs and out the front door, ready to ambush them.

As they turned the corner of the corncrib building, wild-eyed glee plastered on their faces, we collided. Our eyes met, then they both stared at the ground to avoid what must have been obvious and intense disdain in my gaze.

"Don't you idiots ever think how your recklessness affects anyone else?" I asked. "I don't even know these neighbors and now you've driven all over their crops. This is not the way I wanted to meet them!"

They both stared at me, bewildered.

"The first time I encounter these people I'll have to explain about my moron brothers. And then offer to compensate them for their lost crops."

Gary spoke first. "We're not morons, Steve. We didn't drive on the corn," he said.

"The wheel spacing straddled the rows perfectly," Ronnie added. "I clipped a couple of plants at first, but I avoided pretty much everything else."

"Show me," I said, shoving them in the direction of the north fence. Once there, we slipped through the wires and wandered into the cornfield. Things there were pretty much as Ronnie had described—just a couple of downed plants at the beginning of the row.

"How was I supposed to trust you guys? You don't know anything about farms. And you've got a hell of a track record."

After a moment Gary spoke up. "We were just blowing the carbon off the engines. Now that they're running all right, what can we do with them to help you settle in?"

"We can use them to pull fallen limbs from the trees around the farmhouse into a burn pile, if you have a location in mind," added Ronnie.

To their credit, they were asking to be put to work, but only on the condition that the job somehow involved the tractors. I stood there considering all of this, and maybe I took just a moment too long to respond.

"Maybe there's a gun in the shed," Gary said to Ronnie. "Let's see if there's a target or something we can shoot."

"Wait! No guns, no bullets! Working with the tractors is a good idea."

I led them to the gasoline tank on the condition that they only do what I requested. I'd already marked off an area as a garden, and it needed tilling. So I instructed them to hook up the three-bottom moldboard plow to one tractor, and a pull-type disk to the other, and get to work turning the soil. This kind of plow has three curved iron blades that slice through the sod. As the soil rides up, it is turned over, burying the green vegetation layer and exposing the dangling roots. John Deere invented this plow just a few miles south of Stone Prairie Farm, in Illinois, specifically to cut through the deep matted roots of prairie sod. Every farm has at least one old moldboard plow, often rusting away behind the barn with other seldom-used implements. Disks are used next in the process. They have rows of round-shaped iron plates sharpened to knife edges, designed to roll along and slice into the soil surface, working up the top couple of inches for seeding. They are also used for breaking up the chunks of sod that come off the plow.

Having explained all this, I led them to the fifty-by-fifty-foot plot I'd marked with red plastic flags, and I showed them as clearly as I could what to do. Then they ran off to gas up the tractors, debating which tractor was stronger and who could roll a line of plowed soil faster, straighter, and deeper. Minutes later a puff of black smoke rose above the cornstalks, and I listened fretfully to the steady drone of those old engines as they approached.

Of course my brothers didn't go straight to work. Instead they began to race around the garden area like teenagers driving doughnuts in a high school parking lot. Eventually, though, they lowered the implements into the working position and settled down into a pulling competition. They pretty much ignored my flags, plowing up a sizable amount of ground outside the marked perimeter. When they were done, my new garden plot covered most of an acre just north of the old barn, nearly a third of my land, and far more than I had intended.

Several thoughts went through my head in quick succession. On the one hand, I didn't need, or want, to cultivate such a large plot. That would basically make me another farmer on the land. How many tomato plants or squash could I possibly plant and harvest? On the other hand, from a restoration perspective, turning up the earth as they'd done wasn't so bad. If anything it would help shake off those weedy upper couple inches of soil, the physical mantle of the farming years, and speed up the process of change. Then a far more pressing, immediate concern hit me: I was leaving early the next morning for a week of working in Nebraska, sampling plant communities in heavily overgrazed rangelands. And I now had an acre of freshly turned earth, on a sloped field that ran right into the creek, with nothing to protect it from the erosion that can happen so quickly with midwestern wind and rain. No straw to cover it, no seeds to plant.

Something had to be done, and quickly. This was a time when some neighborly advice and assistance would come in handy. And despite the fact that my brothers had just demonstrated what a terrible addition to the community I was, I decided to check with Dick, the only neighbor I'd met thus far. I walked across the road toward his house, a little nervous, a little guilty, and Dick opened the front door before I had the chance to knock.

"So, your friends created quite a mess," he said, looking out over the field north of the barn.

"Brothers, actually. Reckless. Always causing trouble, and—"

"Looks like they were having a good old time," he cut me off. "No harm done."

"Well, they got a bit carried away, and now I figure I need to stabilize the soil on the sloped field," I said.

"Yup," he said, then fell silent for a moment, gazing off toward the freshly turned earth. "Looks like they prepared a pretty good seed bed though. Or is the surface still too rough?"

"Parts are ready, most parts," I guessed. "Probably still some areas that need another going over."

"Let's take a look," he said, and started off in the direction of the field. I followed along, trying to keep pace with his long strides.

His solution was quick, simple, and generous.

"I have a bag of oats sitting in the shed out back. If you grab it and get a few of the white plastic buckets next to the bag, this shouldn't take long."

I ran for the seed and buckets and found them just where he said they'd be, alongside what seemed a stockpile of every conceivable supply—seeds, gravel, spare parts, wire, fence posts, you name it. I knew immediately that Dick would be an amazing asset. When I arrived back at the mess, he had already attached the tined drag—essentially a giant rake for smoothing out the rough patches of soil—to one of the tractors and was driving around the field. Ronnie and Gary just stood on the other tractor, watching as I struggled, lugging back bucket after bucket of seed. Larry finally came over and helped me fill the buckets with seed.

Dick stopped driving when I finally got done.

"Your brothers tell me you're afraid of tractors," Dick said.

"Well I . . . I guess certain mechanical things scare me a bit. Mostly because no one ever showed me how to use them," I said, shooting a glance at Ronnie and Gary.

"Well get on," he commanded, motioning with his arm, which sort of swept me up into the driver's seat.

Behind me I heard my brothers snickering. They knew that from adolescence I had avoided mechanical devices, and if something didn't have fur, feathers, or fins, or didn't grow from the ground, I wouldn't be interested. No doubt they expected me to wimp out, which naturally gave me the fuel I needed to get up into the tractor.

Dick climbed up and sat on the large orange fender that extended over the rear tire.

"Now, this is the ignition," he said. "But before you do anything with that," he warned, "turn on the gas." He then touched my shoulder and motioned to the stopcock, a small metal valve on the bottom of a glass bowl filled with an amber-colored liquid that for all I knew could have been Jack Daniels.

"Okay, the gas is on. Now pull out the choke." He motioned to a long, coat hanger–like bent-wire thing sticking randomly out from somewhere beneath the left side of the steering wheel. I stared perhaps a bit too long, so he grabbed my wrist and guided my hand toward it.

"Now turn the key, but keep your foot on the clutch and brake pedals," he said.

Somehow my four limbs acted in concert, and the tractor belched a single abrupt puff of that black smoke before the engine settled into an arrhythmic growling.

"Yup, good," he yelled. "Now the throttle will regulate the fuel to make the engine run more smoothly. And the gears. See the 'one,' 'two,' and 'three' imprinted in the metal chassis? Move the stick shift to these to go forward, and to the 'R' to go backwards," he said, demonstrating the pattern. "Just like a big old car. Stomp the clutch down, shift the gear handle, then ease it out and you're off and running. Your job is to smooth over the rough areas before we seed, and then to lightly rake them over afterwards in order to pull some soil over the oats. Understand? Otherwise the birds will eat it."

"Now," he stated authoritatively, turning to my three brothers, "you gentlemen and I will spread out the oat seed by hand."

He shouted a couple of last-minute instructions to me as I set off, petrified, across the sea of soil in front of me. It pleased me to have him orchestrating the game plan. My brothers seemed eager and willing to follow along, although I'm sure they were secretly waiting for me to fail, so they could leap onto the tractor and take the wheel.

I rolled away on the tractor, aiming for the bumps, driving slowly at first, aware that I was at the helm of the kind of massive bone-crunching machine that I had always loathed. After a few minutes, though, that lifelong anxiety began to ease, and I inched the throttle lever forward with increasing confidence, smoothing the soil. The soil of my land.

When I felt really steady, I looked back to see Dick and my

brothers scattering seed. Each man had his own style. Gary tossed his randomly up into the air, as if they were flower petals, to let the wind distribute them. Ronnie pirouetted like some sort of prancing hillbilly, enthusiastically spewing the seed in all directions. Dick, on the other hand, walked steadily along, grabbing a handful every few yards and gently scattering them, as if he were feeding chickens underfoot. Larry was methodical like Dick. At one point I looked back to see Gary and Ronnie engaged in a seed fight. Seeing them whipping handfuls of seed at each other, I impulsively turned in their direction. When they realized I was heading straight for them, they stopped fighting and stared at me a moment before leaping out of the way. I must have gotten their attention, because when I turned the tractor around they were already back on task. I glanced up to the house occasionally, seated upright in that springy tractor seat, and feeling oddly proud. It didn't take long to get the job done. As I made the last pass with the tractor, all three of my brothers stood leaning against each other, watching me from the edge of the seeded and dragged patch of bare earth. I pulled up next to them and switched off the ignition just as the old workhorse engine was sputtering out on its last fumes of gas.

There was a satisfying moment of calm as we all gazed out over the field.

"That went well," I said. "Will it green up quickly? That's the real question."

Larry said, "With the rain coming in early this week, shouldn't it start to green by next weekend? Light rains are expected, nothing heavy, so the oats will grow and stabilize the soil." I had no idea where he got all this information, but I figured whatever research he'd done boded well for his law school dreams.

Dick looked up at the sky and then smiled and nodded in agreement.

"I don't know how to thank you," I said.

He shrugged and asked my brothers if they'd like to come

over and see his tractors. I told them to keep an eye on the time; dinner would be ready in an hour.

Ronnie and Gary trotted off after Dick. Larry lingered another moment, looking out over the field, and then slapped me approvingly on the shoulder before heading back to the house to continue working with Mom.

⤳

As children, my brothers tinkered with machines, while I became a Boy Scout. Being a scout meant my father, my neighborhood friends, and I could go camping and fishing. I made bows and arrows from branches, then learned how to shoot and maintain a BB gun. When I was old enough I moved up to a .22 rifle that had been my dad's when he was a kid. Finally I graduated to a small shotgun. While my resourceful brothers were helpful to anyone needing a mechanical repair, I focused on learning to repair animals. Bandaging injured baby birds, I learned to help nature heal broken wings, and I marveled at being able to release them back to the blue skies once they were healthy.

For me this youthful exploration of field and forest grew into something more substantial, an uncovering of an organic and even spiritual relationship with nature. I developed what I can only call an ethic for nature, which was linked to personal, tactile experiences. A key awakening moment happened when I was thirteen and several friends invited me to join their hunting excursion. I went along even though I didn't really want to kill anything. I saw no appeal in shooting at birds and animals that I might otherwise have tried to save. Still I was curious, and used the opportunity to get close to wildlife, to uncover their hideouts and learn more about their habits.

Despite my initial resistance, and lack of skill as a marksman, we began going out regularly. Birds were particularly fascinating to me; I stalked them, entranced by their symmetry and their colorfully painted feathers. I watched in silence, patient, spending hours studying the beauty of their flight, often with my gun barrel pointing at the dirt.

Eventually I began going out by myself. I did my first solo pheasant hunt during a heavy November storm. Thick snow had made everything silent and I had lost track of time when a pheasant, practically under my feet, burst into the air and whirred over a hedgerow toward safety. An instant before the bird flew out of sight, I raised the shotgun in its direction and fired. My heart raced as the bird went limp and plummeted into the powdery snow of a lilac hedge. After the punctuated rifle blast faded, the land became deadly silent. I felt exposed and conspicuous as I crept over to the hedge to lift the limp bird and look at its markings. It was a common ring-necked male, a species native to Asia and imported to the States in the nineteenth century as a game bird. In a sense it had now lived out its destiny. Its layered bright brown plumage glistened with snow and blood. I studied its green and purple markings and then folded the dead creature into my pouch and took it home, where I snuck it into my bedroom. The next day I began to draw pictures of it, my first detailed sketches of nature.

I would learn years later that John James Audubon, Aldo Leopold, and many other famous naturalists found themselves taking the path of the gun or bow as a means to find intimacy with nature. Becoming a part of nature requires compassionate stewardship; hunting is a balancing act that offers a perspective on the role humans can play in nature. As far as my drawing went, I wasn't an enormous talent, but over the years my initial crude sketches would become more artful and intimate records of these experiences.

I did hunt some animals, but I spent equal amounts of time and energy on both sides of the line between life and death. I tinkered, tending to injured animals that needed nurturing and care. My medicine cabinet was full of eyedroppers, tweezers, cotton balls, sutures, baby formula, and various nonprescription medicines. I kept screened cages and shoeboxes filled with wood shavings to house the animals in my homemade veterinary hospital. I immersed myself in the role, doctoring and raising these animals until they were ready to return to the wild, or burying them when they didn't recover from their injuries. I was particularly fond of a maimed screech owl that I nursed back to health, and releasing that noble creature was bittersweet.

My brother Larry, though also sharing interests with Ronnie and Gary, participated with me in rearing dozens of little injured or orphaned friends, including raccoons, foxes, birds, rabbits, turtles, and many others. The closeness that I felt for these creatures would persist my entire life—and learning about them would draw me to the land that both the animals and we humans need to survive.

As best I can fathom, my discomfort with mechanical things probably started with a disdain both for their noise, which disrupted the rhythms of the natural places that fascinated me, and for the industrial support system every engine needed. I explored wetlands and wilderness, only to find gas stations dotting the landscape and parking lots covering acres of prairies everywhere. A number of events colluded to convert disdain into fear. Specifically I remember getting my finger caught in a spring-loaded device under the hood of a car when my adolescent brothers asked me to help out by holding something. I couldn't get my hand out and pain, panic, and anger ensued. I must have looked comical—hand stuck in the engine, face turning beet red —and everyone there laughed, only increasing my frustration. I suspect Ronnie and Gary may have also purposely used my ambivalence toward all things mechanical to ward me off, because I didn't like the cigarette-smoking cadre of friends they kept. Whenever they'd get a new junker, there would be a cluster of teenage boys gathered about, a cloud of smoke coming from under the hood.

Our lives took radically different paths, but as my brothers and I aged our values and interests began to converge again. They've had family pets, some of which were neighborhood strays, and I've watched with pride as they have nurtured their yards, even with native wildflowers. As for me, over time I have been forced to become more comfortable mechanically, learning to use chainsaws and tractors and woodworking tools.

After the family left Stone Prairie Farm that day, I went back out to the freshly turned patch of soil. The dirt smelled pungent and rich, and was cool and moist between my fingers. I went over the important milestones we'd achieved. Despite the frustration, the dread, and the near-sabotage of my place in the community, all was really in pretty good shape. Ronnie and Gary's impulsiveness had actually jump-started things on the farm. Whereas I'd been mired in uncertainty over how to actually go about restoring the land, they'd simply turned on the engine and begun digging up the field. I even used my newfound confidence with tractors to rework a small bare patch of soil I had missed. Then, emulating Dick, I walked carefully across it, tossing the remaining seed from one of the buckets. The restoration process had officially begun. There was no turning back now.

And how did the tractor pull play out with my neighbors? I couldn't work up the nerve to go speak with Forest Zimmerman, whose fields they'd raced over. I finally ran into him at the fence line a few weeks later and, to my relief, he was quite calm about the whole affair. He told me he and his wife, Marjorie, had had a good laugh watching the boys race around on the margins and shoulders, but they had become concerned when the tractors entered the cornfields. They'd checked the impact the next day, and found it negligible. I apologized profusely, expressing how angry I was at my brothers for their recklessness, and at myself for not being able not control them. Forest just nodded and told me not to worry about it. We'd be neighbors, he said, for a long time.

CHAPTER 4

Formative Ideas and
Understandings

Now that Gary and Ronnie's reckless fun had initiated the restoration process at Stone Prairie Farm, I couldn't wait to get into the patch between the barn and farmhouse to start a vegetable garden. I had a great assignment in Nebraska that next week, doing the botanical survey of hill prairies and pastured lands along the Missouri River. But it was hard to focus, as I kept daydreaming about what I was going to plant.

When I got back I found the oat seeds sprouting across the north field, just as Larry had predicted. So I fired up the tractor and motored it between the outbuildings to dig up a small area that seemed big enough to keep me busy, small enough to still be manageable. The levers already felt more comfortable in my hands, and I had the ground well turned in less than an hour. I parked the tractor in the corncrib and slapped it affectionately like a trusted horse.

Next I walked into the center of the tilled ground, where I crouched and closed my eyes to let my ears and nose take it all in. The air was pungent with fresh soil, autumn blossoms, sunshine, and the musk of cows and manure wafting downwind from the neighbor's farm. It was one of those thickly comfortable days that muffle sound and make everything languid. I put my palms on the earth and memories flickered by of a younger me crawling headfirst into a childhood bunker, wide-eyed, looking for raccoons. I took a deep breath, opened my eyes, and let the present stream back in. Then I began hoeing straight lines in the soil for the seeds.

I lost myself in further childhood reveries as I fished out uprooted weeds from the ancient clay soil that had once nourished the historic prairie grasslands. The fertile black dirt I scraped from under my fingernails, a mixture of decomposed plant matter and sands, gravels, and clays, had been ground up and deposited by thousands of years of glacial activity. And now I was waking this slumbering soil from its fallow state.

During the previous week, I had devoted my free time to studying up on the geology, topography, drainage, and soil mapping of the area. The soil dynamics were particularly important, because they seemed to me part of an essential puzzle that I needed to piece together in my mind before I could move forward with the physical restoration. And now here I was, with my hands in the soil, interacting directly with these millennia of geology.

What had brought me here, kneeling in reverie on this rectangular plot of land, obsessed with ecology and the untested idea of restoring the land to a "better" state?

⌒

Many of my formative early experiences in ecology were shared with Pat and Rob Dunlavey, twin brothers who were my closest friends when I was at the University of Illinois at Urbana-

Champaign. Particularly influential were the weekend excursions we took to Devil's Lake State Park near Baraboo, Wisconsin. While most of our classmates went to football games, we three couldn't wait to get out of town. While they climbed onto bar stools and studied the effects of alcohol on their nervous systems, the three of us scaled quartzite rock cliffs, lured by the intense view over deep, crystalline Devil's Lake, where we snorkeled, fished, and harvested clams. To satisfy our adventurous appetites, we foraged wild plants, cooking elderberry and strawberry pancakes, steeping staghorn sumac for pink lemonade and sautéing morels.

The twins shared a passion for the outdoors, but their temperaments and abilities were unique. Rob was an extremely inquisitive artist. He was always moving a pencil across his sketchbook, recording and interpreting the natural world around him with quick, easy strokes. I remember watching him draw, seeing a series of owl feathers coming to life under his hand. With a simple sketch he illustrated how all the minute parts of the feathers held together to keep a bird aloft. Pat, on the other hand, was analytical. He took up mapmaking and also did orienteering, a competitive form of land navigation in which participants are given a map and compass and they race to various control points through an unmarked wilderness.

My attempts at drawing were laughable, which may be one of the reasons I turned to science. In any case, the three of us were quite different. Rob would eventually become a highly regarded artist, Pat a professional cartographer, I an ecologist. But for a few years we learned together, sharing formative experiences along three separate paths that converged at interesting points. For example, I was fascinated by Native American uses for wild plants and was set on learning what plants were used for which purposes. This exploration is what led to our foraging for food. Rob and Pat looked at me with skepticism as I gathered my first handful of puffball mushrooms. These plump, doughy-looking fungi seemed a little too foreign at first. But after I diced them, added garlic, and sautéed them perfectly, they looked pretty much like store-bought button mushrooms. The boys relented, tasted, and were won over. We gathered plants and small animals and learned about them in the most intimate way, by tasting and chewing, so that they literally became a part of us.

We were all interested in illuminating nature in one way or another, and we shared the philosophy that nature needed somehow to be preserved as "natural places," untrammeled by humankind. At school each of us was active in efforts to accomplish this. I became the Illinois representative of the Minnesota group Friends of the Boundary Waters Wilderness. This entailed organizing and giving presentations on the current legislative movement to protect once and for all the beautiful 1.2-million-acre wilderness in northern Minnesota. Rob and Pat focused on protecting wild places in Alaska. They helped to prepare graphics and flesh out the nuts and bolts of the arguments used to support this cause.

Our work to protect these natural places was tangible and concrete. At the same time we incorporated the broader value of wilderness into our daily lives. We anticipated the weekend escape not just as a break from the rigors of academic life, but also as an ideal time for physical and psychic rejuvenation. Nothing cleared our overtaxed college student minds like a hard hike and a plunge into crisp lake water.

After long active days, roping our way up the quartzite cliffs and hiking to and from the climbing areas, or snorkeling around the shallow margins of Devil's Lake while foraging for crawfish and clams, we would end up back at camp. Exhausted, we would light a fire and prepare the evening meal—either something experimental, such as freshwater clams (unbelievably rubbery!), or something basic, like macaroni and cheese (perhaps sporting wild mushroom embellishments). Around the campfire we often discussed our course assignments and the corresponding materials we were reading. We brought the occasional essay or poem to share in the deepening stillness of dusk, reading aloud from

Whitman, Emerson, and Thoreau. Their naturalist insights seemed timeless and offered a poetic context to our discussions. But in a fundamental way their ideals reflected a nineteenth-century worldview that couldn't encompass the scale of the twentieth-century issues that we were dealing with in the nuclear age, when the fragility of our earth and biosphere could be measured on a global scale.

One late-autumn weekend in 1973 Rob brought along a book entitled *A Sand County Almanac.* It was written by Aldo Leopold, a renowned ecologist and educator, and published posthumously in 1949. Leopold was revered within ecological and environmental circles, but his work was not yet widely known. Rob had heard about the book from an inspired English professor who spoke of it with a certain ineffable adulation. This professor also told Rob about the Sierra Club, of which he was a member, marking the first time I'd heard of the group.

It turns out none of our biological sciences professors knew about Leopold either. But this was just at the time of a major shift in public awareness of the environment. Soon the mainstream media began to cover environmental problems, particularly pollution in its myriad manifestations: the burning Cuyahoga River in Cleveland, the toxic waste disposal disaster of Love Canal, the lethal impact of the pesticide DDT on eagles and peregrine falcons, whose eggs would break under the weight of the parent bird, even the very notion of endangered species. These all became part of the zeitgeist, together with renewed interest in books like *Sand County Almanac* and Rachel Carson's *Silent Spring,* and the popularity of a new wave of books starting with Edward Abbey's *Monkey Wrench Gang.*

For the three of us it was the *Sand County Almanac,* years after it was initially published, that opened the doors of perception. To me the book was nothing short of revolutionary. It is a candid journal, written in a folksy poetic style, that paints in-depth pictures of the natural world, illustrating it as vividly as Rob did in his drawings. By chronicling the splendor and awe of the changing seasons near his home in southern Wisconsin, Leopold presents a sobering and instructive narrative about land. He posits that our relationship to nature is an ethical question, requiring all humans to expand their concept of community to include the land itself.

But the clarity of thought that I would glean from Leopold's writing did not come readily. The first time I read it I was confused. He pulls from a lexicon that went over my head, and I had to consult the dictionary so often that I regularly lost his train of thought. Nonetheless, it left me with the intense feeling that we humans needed to give nature a much more substantial place in our lives, in our hearts, and in the way we behave. I savor my collection of Aldo Leopold quotes from *Sand County Almanac* as reminders of the influence he has had on my life. Several stick out as particularly important:

> A thing is right when it tends to preserve the integrity, stability, and beauty of the biotic community. It is wrong when it tends otherwise.
>
> Conservation is the state of harmony between men and land.
>
> To keep every cog and wheel is the first precaution of intelligent tinkering.
>
> We abuse land because we regard it as a commodity belonging to us. When we see land as a community to which we belong, we may begin to use it with love and respect.

The more I revisited the book, the more I embraced the pragmatism of Leopold's ideas. Unlike many of my textbooks, Leopold wasn't obscure or didactic. Rather his stories were both poetic and tangible. He spoke of planting trees with his sharp shovel, of burning prairies with a crackling hot fire, and of inferring the history of the land from the rings of an ancient oak as he sawed through it. He revealed the history of ecological changes on the land, because he read the land as one would read a book. According to Leopold, nature saves information, and all we have to do is find out how to interpret its records. I was already well aware of the precepts of conservation, but he was the first to introduce me to the notion of restoration. It was clear that just conserving nature, that is protecting the existing condition, wasn't good enough where the land had been trammeled. It needed more. With each hole he dug out and each tree he planted, he was focused on returning the land to a better state. This notion spoke to my very core and became central to my life.

⤳

Out in nature with Rob and Pat, it was easy to feel a connection with Leopold. Back at school, I struggled to correlate his tenets with my classroom research. At first the scale of our laboratory seemed far too constraining for his expansive ideas. The interconnected natural realms that he described stretched beyond the walls of the world of academia.

After moping about this for a few days, sketching out ideas that were too complex, I decided to create a small, simple, self-contained environment. Working with my professor, I ran a simple experiment that impacted my thinking greatly and allowed me to comprehend the sensitivity and vulnerability of nature. I placed a snail in a glass test tube with some water, a pinch of soil, and an aquatic plant sprig. I heated the open end of the glass tube over a Bunsen burner until it was malleable enough to twist shut, effectively creating an enclosed environment that would theoretically be self-sustaining, like a miniature biosphere.

The test went as I had predicted. As the plant grew, the snail would eat it back, and bacteria and fungi would recycle the snail's waste, thus providing nourishment for continued plant growth. The snail and the plant survived in this microcosm in a kind of circular dance. (In fact this bottled microcosm would continue to survive for more than a decade until one winter night I absentmindedly placed it against a frosted windowpane, killing first the plant, and ultimately the snail.)

Although simple, the test tube model was an excellent microcosm of nature's vulnerability, whereby even minor changes —in this case one small plant—could have grave consequences on mutual survival. Although small in scale, the snail experiment loomed large in my esteem and informed my developing approach to nature, which placed critical value on learning to recognize the differences between healthy and unhealthy environs. Surprisingly this difference is often not always easy to discern.

Also, this constant awareness can be painful. As Leopold said, "The problem with having an ecological consciousness is that we live in a world of wounds." I began to see these wounds wherever I traveled, whether it was the plowed agricultural swath cutting through a prairie or a wetland converted into a parking lot. So I actively sought out areas that were not so wounded, those untrammeled places that Rob and Pat and I cherished—places like the calm stretches of the Boundary Waters Wilderness, the mountains and deserts of the western United States, and many more. Here I was able to learn about healthy wild lands without scabs or scars, to gain perspective on the ultimate ends of healthy restoration.

I contemplated where to focus my ecological efforts. Compared with the natural areas I had explored, saving the fragmented patches of prairie, wetland, or woodland where I grew up seemed irrelevant, if not futile. These patches of land were like scattered organs at the site of a deer kill. Each part still played a role, however weakly, in the life force of the region. They weren't quite dead, but without the thriving corpus of a connected ecosystem, they seemed to me like doomed remnants. The streams, like arteries, still carried the lifeblood from one scattered area to the next. The remaining trees, like brittle lungs, still absorbed toxins and released carbon dioxide. The soil, like a shriveled pancreas, still provided whatever nourishment it could to the vegetation. But how long could one expect those elements to continue to function without a healthy heart? The flesh of the urban centers was gone, leaving only a frail and imperceptible skeleton, and even through the outer reaches of suburbia and into the country, the heartbeat was getting weaker and weaker.

It was a conundrum, but for the time being all I could do was immerse myself in every promising ecology class, undergraduate or graduate. I studied obsessively, learning as much as possible about the different systems and giving myself the necessary tools to do relevant work in the future. The requisite weekend field classes were pure bliss for me, as were discussions on wilderness ecology with Alan Haney, my undergraduate advisor, who shared a mutual passion for wilderness, canoeing, and travel. This fertile period culminated in my graduate research on the fire ecology of the Boundary Waters Wilderness of Minnesota, where I focused on how plant and animal communities reassembled after habitat disturbances such as wildfire.

As small as it was, the garden I planted on Stone Prairie Farm turned out to be quite productive and provided a good lesson on sustainability. How gratifying to walk out the door and pick fresh produce! I planted tomatoes, potatoes, squash, greens, broccoli, and other garden plants. It felt great to dig my hands and feet into the soft earth and work the land. In my zeal I went a bit overboard at first, planting thirty zucchini and sixty-four tomato plants. And while I often ate half of what I picked before bringing the rest back into the house, what could one do with dozens of three-foot-long yellow squash that looked like beached whales? Refusing to let anything go to waste, I began dehydrating everything, slicing tomatoes, zucchinis, and broccoli until two in the morning and laying out the neatly organized slices on trays that I carried down to the basement and placed in a secondhand chicken egg incubator a neighbor had given me. I'd return the next day and flip over the slices, and return the following day to bag the fully dried ones and add more fresh slices. After two weeks of this, I was pretty sick of dried tomatoes.

I continued my little operation, bagging countless bushels of spinach and lettuce, until the giddy satisfaction turned toward a sober reflection on the history of land development in the area, and how it had been so completely converted from wilderness to either agriculture or paved cities and neighborhoods. I thought about the condemned "wild" remnants from my youth in Chicago, empty urban lots where we occasionally stumbled on a sunflower or coneflower. The treasures were holdouts from when the land had been prairie, and it saddened me to think that the current generation of children didn't have even this residual connection to what this land had been. I tried to picture how those empty lot remnants were once part of a continuous flow of natural systems, and lamented the string of ignorant decisions that destroyed the prairies and tree-lined streams in the name of progress.

The empty lots and occasional prairie plant connected me to a place, but most of the connection was cerebral, to a time when the entire landscape was one big empty lot, where the isolation of a lone coneflower wasn't symbolic of the near loss of the entire prairie ecosystem. The connection to the grandeur of intact ecosystems that were large and expansive, and at a remove from the influence of present-day humans, would come during my graduate school training.

"Surviving grad school" had a different meaning for me than for most students. Each year I spent four to five weeks deep in nature, learning how to survive in the wilderness for extended periods. I would pack a canoe with dried vegetables and soup stock, a fishing pole, lures, and a variety of scientific gear— collection forms, measuring implements, and the like. Then I'd launch myself into a lake or river and paddle away from civilization. Usually, other students, assistants, or maybe a friend would accompany me. The first time out it truly was survival, as the rainy and snowy late-May, early-spring weather made it difficult to light warming and drying fires. Worse, the fish weren't biting. Day after day we breakfasted on what we variously called "gruel," "cream of nothing," or "bloat meal," and dined on macaroni and cheese. Eventually we added in a few scavenged vegetables, like fiddlehead ferns and a patch of morel mushrooms. The combination of foods proved unfortunate, as what the gruel had clogged up, too many fiddleheads and mushrooms loosened. So the night was spent with mad dashes away from the tent, relieving ourselves in the midst of a bone-chilling rain.

Regardless of the food, the hordes of mosquitoes and black-flies, and the myriad other distractions and challenges, after each trip into the wilderness I felt spiritually renewed. Nonetheless I kept coming back to Leopold's "world of wounds." No matter how far we travel into untrammeled wilderness, we aren't escaping the existing problems, which keep spreading outward like a slow-moving plague that takes no prisoners. If the globe is a single entity, then clearly the sickness affecting one region will eventually prevail everywhere. I began to think I had made a terrible mistake by avoiding any effort to address urban environments in my research.

Over time this reasoning encouraged me to work with the agents of change themselves, the land developers. I began by exploring strategies to protect and restore deteriorated resources within existing and new developments. Beyond that, however, I hoped to encourage ecological stewardship and protection on the part of the developers themselves—a "teach a man to fish" strategy, as it were.

⟨⟩

It was clear that I needed to get some dirt under my fingernails, to learn what working with land actually involved. What of the soil in which I was making both my new garden and my stand against land degradation in the name of so-called progress? Some historical perspective is helpful.

In 1837 the General Land Office surveyed what is present-day Green County and established section lines on a grid that divided the territory into units of one square mile. Surveyors walked up the middle of what is currently Mill Road, dragging measurement chains and recording vegetation types, as well as wetlands, dry and wet prairies, and timberland. They also distinguished first- and second-rate farmland based on the surveyor's assessment of the quality of the lands and soils for agricultural and animal husbandry purposes. They categorized my property as composed of "first-rate dry prairies" on the ridges and "good and first rate land" across the deeper wet soils and tall grass prairies of the lower areas, which meant the latter were suitable for crops. The surveyor assigned these designations to encourage settlement and agricultural land use on the most fertile regions. The choicest farmland was "first rate ground with little or no tree clearing." But as every settler discovered, farming this land involved tilling the prairie sod, a task more difficult than clearing trees, even for a strong team of oxen or draft horses. It's hard to say whether the surveyors had been intentionally deceptive, coaxing the farmers to backbreaking work on this "good and first rate land," or if they were simply naive and overly optimistic about this golden land. I imagine it was a bit of both.

Regardless, while the spirits of those pioneers may have been temporarily dampened on discovering the reality, their determination prevailed. In the decades since the first team of oxen pulled John Deere's steel plow through those fields, agriculture has broken and tamed this prairie landscape, destroying the thousands of square miles of dense root system that had held the soil together. This has led to soil degradation on a massive scale, most spectacularly in the Dust Bowl of the 1930s. It is no wonder that today meager hay crops, stunted corn, and soybeans struggle to grow in once "first rate" soils.

Thomas Jefferson was the president who requisitioned the national survey and set up the General Land Office process of surveying and subdividing land in the United States into square-mile sections, quarter sections, and so forth. This frame of reference has been absolutely instrumental to the economics of land and enabled an efficiency in defining land for transactions and land ownership purposes, for taxing landowners. Beyond economics, these subdivision procedures have left their mark on the land's ecology as well. By carving everything up on a regular grid, this survey allowed for mismatches, leaving behind myriad small scraps of irregularly shaped pieces of land where property lines didn't conform to the topography of the land, or where rail lines cut across the grid at a diagonal. It is these scraps with uncertain ownership that were often left alone, and where we find remnants of prairies, wetlands, and savannas.

Given the degraded quality of the soil, my success growing beautiful vegetables was quickly noticed by my neighbors. They began to stop by when they saw me hauling produce between garden and house. Dick often appeared silently behind me, like a Native American scout. He didn't say much, but I could tell he approved of my technique by the satisfied grin he wore as he looked over the entangled rows. In particular, Beverly and Bud, neighbors and, increasingly, friends, came by when they realized I was giving away bushels of food. They were dumbstruck by the lushness of the garden and the amount of produce it yielded. I may not have been a farmer, but I obviously knew a thing or two about gardening. For years afterward, when we met at the post office, or when they'd stop by on their Sunday drive, Beverly would interrogate me on the varieties I was going to plant and try to get me to reveal my secrets. As amazed as they were by the fecundity of my crops, they still clung to their old ways, neglecting, for instance, to move their garden into the full sun despite my repeated urgings.

Juicy vegetables notwithstanding, I was procrastinating about my long-term goals for Stone Prairie Farm. I hadn't pursued my education to be a farmer! I realized that I had to break away from all the standard expectations of land ownership in farm country. Zucchini and corn and lettuce and tomatoes weren't meant to dominate this landscape. I enjoyed farming it, but I yearned to see this prairie landscape growing again, with its waving golden grass and copses of savanna oaks that once loomed, ghostly, behind the morning fog, scattered across the ridge tops on sandy and bedrock knolls and secluded slopes.

I closed my eyes again and took inventory of my plot and the surrounding landscape, trying to recall what features existed where, and at what distance. I had spent so much time in the haymow loft that I had a pretty good picture of the landscape in my mind. But now I played another game; I envisioned what wasn't there, and what should have been there, had history taken a different course. I could easily envision sparse scatterings of oak and basswood poking like fingers into the sweeping prairie, and the colorful arrays of seasonal flowers: midsummer's golds, late fall's yellows and drifts of blue wildflowers, and sunlit patches of golden puccoons amid purple birdfoot violets on mornings in early spring. And through this variegated landscape, where springs and seeps coalesced, the meandering brook must have danced through the lush green overhanging prairie with colorful baby brook trout and even more vibrant darter fishes. Then, in my mind's eye, I walked two hundred feet south of Mill Road to the remnant gravel hill prairie that had cast its spell on me during my initial visit. I could see, as clearly as the first time, embedded in the hill, those ancient chunks of bedrock, visibly striated by the bulldozing ice mass, resting peacefully amidst pale purple coneflower and yellow lousewort beneath the shooting stars.

But a scientist can revel in the poetry of his thoughts for only so long before he needs some real data. I knew what the land was like up until the time of the settlers, and I knew firsthand what it had become by the 1970s. What wasn't clear was the progression from unified wilds to truncated farmlands. I needed to learn as much as possible about the recent history of Stone Prairie Farm. I finally went to the county clerk to find relevant historical materials and uncovered the old aerial photographs that I had hoped to find. They were both informative and startling.

A photo from 1956 showed a forested roadway running by an orchard, some outbuildings, and a house with a white picket fence around the yard and scattered horse-drawn farm implements in the fields. It turns out that they had bulldozed those large basswood and elm beauties only a few years before I moved in, backfilling the logs and debris into one of the gravel excavation pits on the hill prairie created when Mill Road was straightened. Going a bit further back in time, a shot from 1937 confirmed the existence of lush cornfields that overwhelmed the pasture and the gravel hill prairie. As with the surrounding farms, the rest of the property grew row crops that typically alternated with hay production. Cows grazed the pasture adjacent to the barn, along a badly eroded spring brook.

A stream is a vivid indicator of changes wrought on the land. Factories and cities have long battled the consequences of runoff. Pesticides, chemicals, and other wastes are a common blind spot in urban planning. Society simply creates more waste than it can handle. Even in a poorly focused aerial shot, the degradation to the stream was clear to me, a scant two hundred feet from the crystal-clear spring that fed it. I was particularly disturbed to see documented erosion going that far back in time. It made me yearn even harder for that idealized image I carried of its once pristine condition, and I vowed that I would find a way to restore the stream from its muddied, eroded, cattle-trampled condition to a rejuvenated state where it would flow again through lush prairies, lacing together restored wetlands between the scattered oaks.

But these bird's-eye views made the task at hand seem even more overwhelming. I found it difficult to see how my farm and the surrounding ones had ever been a unified ecological landscape. Our style of farming, first developed in Europe and further refined on the massive tracts of land in America, and the straight grid-line perspective of the American bureaucracy had clearly overwhelmed the natural evolution of the land. Gone were the sounds of nature, replaced with the motoring drone of tractors plowing and disking soil, the mechanical switching sounds of cutter heads on dinosaur-sized farm combines, and the early-morning buzz of the milking machines and their vacuum pumps. This had become a region dedicated to cheese and beer production and other traditions brought by the settlers.

With hardly any indigenous elements remaining—neither the inhabitants and their traditions, nor the coexisting plant and animal species—how could I really expect to resurrect the past? Perhaps I could repair certain elements, but was it credible to believe that I might restore the landscape to a healthy, functioning ecological system? Was this practical science or foolish hopefulness, or perhaps academic idealism? Besides, my mind's eye regularly trespassed over a broad landscape, but I owned a mere 2.7 acres. And calculating the amount of time it might take to restore the farm on my meager income, it was clear that no matter how much I cared about the land, I wouldn't have time to do everything I wanted.

Rather than become despondent or paralyzed, I focused that first year on definitions: What constitutes ecosystem restoration? What are my targets? How do I balance expectations and actual outcomes? I resigned myself to whatever restoration could be implemented with the available time and, most important, decided to work with nature's tendencies as I embarked on the restoration of Stone Prairie Farm. As inspiration for the future, I continued to dream and scheme about ecological regeneration, while challenging myself to put my scientific training as a plant and animal ecologist to the test. So many of my formative experiences had percolated through my mind during those first months, and they proved to be a wellspring for my evolving approach to restoring nature.

What I did know for certain was that ecosystem functions

have yet to be reproduced by human ingenuity. In fact, efficient ecosystems produce and generate no waste products. Plants process the air we breathe. No industrial process approaches the scale, efficiency, and sustainability of this or any other ecosystem function. Ecosystems are complex. They are not designed for arbitrary disruptions, and cannot always recover. So I had to ask myself if the notion of trying to restore one was hubristic folly, like putting Humpty Dumpty back together again. I used that as a starting point, with the intention of proving myself wrong.

With the characteristics and definitions of a healthy ecosystem as the scientific background for restoration, I next sought to measure restoration success. What would be the indicators of the development of healthy ecological systems? Could they be robust enough to indicate when and where management intervention was needed?

And even if I could recognize the parameters of an ecosystem and knew what success looked like, how could I work toward that success? Could I maintain the work and fund it? Could I develop the relationships required to succeed? I was pleased to have composed a comprehensive set of definitions and goals, but the prospect of manifesting a full restoration was still a daunting proposition.

PART II

What Really Matters

CHAPTER 5

⌒

The Past Revisits and
the Future Begins

During the first year on Stone Prairie Farm I dedicated myself to learning as much as I could about the state of my 2.7 acres. I kept a list of every nonnative species that had taken root, got to know the remaining trees, monitored the soils, and kept track of the ground squirrels that continually chatted while tirelessly collecting seeds for winter. I studied the eroded banks of the stream and tested the water quality. And I tended my garden, the most tangible aspect of my new domestic life. The growth of lush vegetables and fruits from the simple seeds was a constant reminder of the generative power of plants. No bigger than a small pebble, and often much smaller, each seed contained not only the genetic material for a mature budding plant, but also the entire history of its evolution through agriculture. I was pleased to have a garden because this highly productive chore kept my senses aware of the integrated systems working around me. It kept my hands in the dirt and helped put the property's areas of ecological imbalance in perspective.

By the beginning of the second year, I knew the landscape so well that I could have walked around the farm with my eyes closed. I knew the grade of the prairie. I could sense clearings by the subtle change in wind speed, and distance by the sounds of my neighbor's farm vehicles working the crops. The smells alone—nonnative catnip plants and native mints, bergamot, and various types of fertilizers wafting on the breeze—gave me a sense of perspective and grounding, a deep familiarity with the land. It was my home, and I felt elated as I drove or flew back from business trips. Each time I returned, I brought with me new knowledge and widening perspective. My professional work —whether it was studying the impact of livestock grazing on national forest land in Colorado, designing river and wetlands restorations, or exploring the sustainability of nature preserves in Illinois—always informed my domestic life on the farm. And things I learned on the farm certainly informed my work. My only concern, one on which my mother expounded whenever we spoke, was that I was turning into a hermit. I hadn't even encouraged my brothers to visit since their first adventures on the land, confident, I suppose, that I could keep moving forward without their volatile form of aid.

Then one weekend in early autumn, lost in thought while splitting black locust logs with a maul and wedge for a new split-rail fence along the driveway, I looked up from my shaded spot beneath the huge weeping willow to see a dilapidated Ford Ranchero drive slowly into the front yard. It came to a stop beside my pickup. A man wearing a battered straw fedora tilted his head slightly out of the window, and nodded in a cautious greeting. I nodded back. He cut the engine and stepped slowly out of the car, apparently taking a moment to solidify his balance. He walked toward me with an aggravated limp, his age apparent in each step. By the look of his seersucker suit and ragged loafers, I got the impression of someone on his way to a church picnic. Even by farming community standards his appearance was anachronistic, and I felt the slightest sensation that a ghost was coming toward me.

"Hello, sir," he said, in a pleasant tenor that was a bit frayed and short of breath.

"Good afternoon."

He looked around, seeming to take everything in. His eyes finally settled on my freshly cut logs, and he nodded his head up and down knowingly, as though he had just heard a joke that he never tired of hearing.

"My name is Howard. Are you the current resident here?"

"I purchased it about a year ago," I replied. "How can I help you?"

From his tawny complexion and weathered hands I could tell he hadn't spent his working life behind a desk. Even though his belly bulged amply over his belt buckle, his broad shoulders and powerful jaw still gave the impression of someone who had worked the land.

"You know, I was born in this house." He motioned to the downstairs bedroom window. "Right over there."

He paused, as if lost in a powerful memory, and I waited for him to go on. Then his expression changed and his focus returned to the present moment.

"Do you mind if I sit?" he asked, and I cleared the wood chips from the log I used as my splitting base.

"My father, brothers, and I worked the land with draft horses," he began, reaching back into the past. And I listened. "We milked thirty cows, grew corn and alfalfa, and had a big garden and orchard. Our peach trees by the house were darn reliable producers, too. They provided bushels of scrumptious fruit every year. After I retired, I settled a few miles south of here, in Illinois. I drive through this neighborhood and by this farm often to visit old friends in Brodhead and Albany. A part of me remains here, I reckon."

"I was planning to plant an orchard in the same spot. How

long did your peach trees live?" I asked, wiping off some sweat that was dripping down my forehead.

"We had to replace some trees once, about five years in. But we still had a couple of bumper crops with enough extra to give away to any neighbor who wanted a bag." Amused by the memory, Howard smiled broadly, revealing a few missing teeth. "My mother discovered that peach trees planted in the garden south of the house, right by an old garage, lasted longer, sometimes twelve or thirteen years. Not sure why. "

He motioned in the direction of the former orchard, then stood, and together we walked slowly toward it. When we got there he looked around, as if he couldn't understand where the trees had gone. He started to dig his heel into the ground. After kicking around for a few minutes, he found a buried corner of the old garage foundation. At that point, I started digging too. We must have looked like a silly pair of chickens scratching the ground looking for food. But sure enough, after a few minutes of uncovering coal clinkers (the clumps of impurities left over from the coal-fired heating stove in the house), he found a buried peach tree stump.

"These clinkers must have been tossed over the fence behind the garage after the orchard was abandoned," he said, shaking his head. "Now why would someone do that? We used the clinkers to fill in wet areas between the barn and the house, so someone else must have dumped these here. Heck, my mother would have let us have it if we ever messed with the orchard."

By now I was getting curious. "What were the land and house like when you were growing up?"

"Do you have a couple hours?" he asked.

I had planned to finish the entire split-rail fence that day, but I realized that this could be a unique and serendipitous opportunity to learn more about the heritage of the land. "I've got some time," I said.

"Would it be possible to go into your house?" he asked, and I could see in his eyes that this was an emotional request. Even decades after leaving, his connection to the farm was powerful.

"Sure, it would be great to learn about the house and land from you," I said.

After going through the house, with Howard reliving family memories, we sat for a bit in the kitchen. I tried to get him to talk about his experiences farming the land, or roaming it before everything was turned to agriculture, but unfortunately he didn't have much to offer. He remembered catching a few fish in the creek, but he couldn't recall what kind. Eventually he stood and said he needed to get back to the retirement home.

As we stepped onto the front porch, he gripped the banister and tested its strength. While other parts of the house were in disarray, that banister was still solid. He seemed to appreciate that. Maybe he had helped construct it. He lingered there another moment, finally releasing his grip one finger at a time, as if he were playing a game from his childhood, or perhaps trying to memorize the feel of that sanded wood rail before climbing down his childhood stoop for the last time.

"Do you have any old pictures of the farm?" I asked, after helping him into the car.

"I'll look around. If I find anything I'll drop them by. I might also have some records about the land and farming operations," he said, chewing his lip. "Can't really remember."

Howard paused at the street and gave a final wave before driving off.

⌒

The images Howard left with me stayed in my mind as I stepped through the house during the next days. I enjoyed moving about quietly with my tasks, sensing the ghosts of past residents going about their lives: raising children, repairing leaks, installing stoves, huddling around the radio, or drinking and playing cards on cold winter nights, kept warm by the fervor of competition and that leaking potbellied stove.

I found myself hoping Howard would contact me again, in part to solidify a stronger connection to the past, in part, perhaps, to see more of what the future might hold for me. But as the week passed, this hope grew dimmer. It had taken decades for Howard to gather the courage to make the visit. Maybe doing so had opened too many emotional wounds and made him feel as old and dilapidated as the house itself.

Then, about six months later, I returned home from a business trip to find an envelope rubber-banded to the front door of the house. Opening it, I found a scribbled note:

> Dear Steve,
> I finally found that photo. Hope it helps you with your work.
> Thanks for your hospitality.
> —Howard
> P.S. Please return the photo when you're done with it.

There was an aerial photograph centered over the farmhouse and the immediate farmyard. It provided a helpful perspective on the farm. I could see the existing outbuildings and those long gone, the layout of the pastures, the former alignment of the creek, and the presence of a stand of large deciduous trees in front of the house on the east side of the roadway. I could also see the garage he had spoken about and an adjacent grove of lush peach trees.

I had the image photographed and enlargements made for framing. I then composed a letter thanking him: for the photo, for the history lesson, for sharing a bit of himself, all of which had given me invaluable insight into the human element of the farm. I sent more questions and returned the original photograph. And I invited him back.

But I never did hear from Howard again. I figured he'd accomplished what he needed to do in that one afternoon. Where I was hungry for historical details that could put my ambitious dreams in perspective, he was just seeking some form of calming closure, wanting to reconnect one last time to the place that molded his body and engaged his youthful mind and spirit. I hoped he left our encounter feeling the old farm was in capable hands, and that the candle was still burning in memory of all those good people who had loved it before me.

~

I thought for months about Howard's visit. I wished I'd had more time to talk to him. In one afternoon he had extended my own narrative, connecting me to a family and heritage of which I was now a member. I was contributing to a legacy dating back to 1837, and it was my turn now to care for the land, to tend it while I was here and prepare it for the next inhabitants. Although I was only twenty-seven at the time, meeting him made me profoundly aware of my mortality and got me thinking a lot about the fact that I had no family to share this with. I even began to wonder what my own legacy would be. I worried that my efforts to restore the land would be a one-way street to an unknown destination. Someday sooner than I might imagine, I'd be old too, relying on faded photographs and idealistic writings to communicate the struggles I'd faced.

As a single man, I had been both able and inclined to devote myself completely to my work. My career had progressed directly from my childhood experience roaming vestigial swaths of farmland, imagining myself immersed in ever-larger regions of unspoiled wilderness. From that point to the present, the life cycles of plants and animals had held my attention firmly, often more than those of my fellow humans.

Howard's visit made me realize that, as independent as I thought myself to be, I was still reliant on others to make me whole. For instance, my brothers and I had always had a kind of pack mentality whenever we explored old woods and wetlands. We shared that magical land together, like roaming wolves, finding security in numbers. Later, university life bonded me to like-minded young scientists. Like me they engaged in the rigors of academia and utilized institutional resources to train their minds and advance their understanding of natural sciences.

We celebrated our instincts and indulged our spirits in pristine landscapes, proud of having a role to play in the betterment of a society that had lost its connection to the fundamentals of environmental balance.

Work was like this as well. When I left school in my twenties with a master's degree, I was already part of a network of scientists and environmentalists that gave me access to restoration and research projects and working partnerships. In 1975 these projects evolved into a company, Applied Ecological Services, which I formed with several of my colleagues.

Essentially AES started as a research and restoration organization. First we gathered critical technical data about the healthiest remaining intact ecological systems in a variety of regions. Then we sought ways to apply what we'd learned to improve and recover deteriorated landscapes on behalf of clients. The first projects were research oriented, with funding provided for the gathering of data. Then came management and restoration planning assignments where we assessed the ecological condition of the land and prescribed and put into practice land restoration and management programs. Because of our scientific focus and our desire to learn from every job, each land restoration and management project also became a research project, with information to be used in the future.

AES wasn't exactly conceived. It just sort of fell into place, steered by dedicated people who gathered around the beat of the same messianic drum to solve problems through study, action, and education and engage others to live in balance with nature in order to effectively address environmental problems. Individually we brought unique strengths, but only by working together could we have achieved the solutions we reached. Our initial projects focused on everything from planning reclamation projects to storing, cleaning, and supplying native seeds for restoration.

AES's early research projects led to larger, more hands-on efforts. First, a research phase led to a land reclamation project on disturbed military tank training grounds at Fort Knox, Kentucky. There we studied the impact of Abrams and other military tanks and track vehicles on ecosystems. We worked in the midst of mock tank battles, doing plant, bird, and small mammal surveys, collecting water samples, and measuring runoff from streams in both heavily and lightly used training grounds, as well as areas not used for training. We learned quickly that when a track vehicle makes a quick turn, it sends the upper several inches of soil, and the plants therein, spraying off to the side, much the way a water skier sends a wave when turning. This had consequences not only for the affected plants, but for the water runoff and erosion patterns as well. We watched and photographed this activity, then measured the impacts.

Both we and the military quickly came to the conclusion that the current training approach was devastating to land, and that they needed a more efficient type of training ground. Of course we had different reasons for reaching this conclusion: for us the tanks were simply tearing up the ground, loosening the soils, and guaranteeing the deterioration and erosion of the lands; for them the eroded ruts and muddy mess were delaying training, and the repair costs and downtime for the war machines was breaking the bank. Eventually we worked together to develop "multipurpose training ranges" that were contained to minimize ecosystem impacts and optimize the military training mission. We then set about restoring the damaged land, which was stabilizing within a few years.

Other early projects included reclaiming an iron mine that had recently been shut down in central Wisconsin and restoring rare plant and animal diversity in a badly damaged area that became a new Illinois nature preserve. We quickly learned that our applied solutions were effective and that our theories weren't just academic exercises but were applicable in real time.

Soon after I'd moved to Stone Prairie Farm, AES moved

there with me. The growing company required an organizational center for daily operations, and the farm was a logical place to set up shop. Being there, amidst the slowly restoring plants, set the right mood and kept us in touch with nature. I converted the upstairs bedroom in the farmhouse into offices. From the room where I had once watched in horror as Gary and Ronnie raced away on the old tractors, the staff attacked the administrative needs of our burgeoning organization. It was pretty cramped in there, so the hallway served as a reception area, and little by little the organization began to fill my house—first there were six of us, then ten, twelve, and upward to nearly twenty. For a bachelor who dedicated every waking moment to work, it made perfect sense. I was certain that clients who came for a consultation were impressed by our dedication. We didn't just talk the talk of restoration; we also embodied it.

⤳

This setup was indeed ideal for a bachelor. But I increasingly felt that someday I would want to have a family. Meeting Howard had planted a red flag in the comfortable terrain of my bachelorhood. I had a vital career, but I wanted to have a rich life too, and I began to see that a man can do a great deal of important work and still feel empty at the end of the day without someone to share both the investment and the return.

About nine years after moving onto Stone Prairie Farm, I met Susan. I wasn't specifically looking for my mate. I think that's the way it usually works. The Iowa Department of Transportation had recently constructed a highway near the city of McGregor. The road sliced through the Bloody Run Valley, one of the Hawkeye State's most unspoiled and diverse ecosystems. Besides a pristine trout stream, the remote valley contained bedrock cliffs and ridges supporting rare dry prairies and diverse oak forests. Along with this threatened flora, the highway compromised the habitat of an endangered frog species. But the state had cut through this land with little consideration for the ecosystem, resulting in severely degrading habitats. A citizens' committee that wanted to protect this area had devised a restoration plan, and I'd been invited as an expert witness.

Susan was one of the leaders of the committee. She had helped to strategize a compromise plan, which requested that the Iowa Department of Transportation plant native prairie grasses and wildflowers along the road right of way as an insulating buffer to protect further environmental and habitat destruction. The plan looked sound to me on paper, and I happily agreed to attend the meeting. Actually getting there was less happy. I came down with a nasty flu the night before and had to ask my office mate Fred to drive. Why I didn't cancel is a bit of mystery in retrospect, but I'm certainly glad that I didn't. We left in the early morning, in a blinding Wisconsin snowstorm, with me bundled under a pile of blankets in the backseat of his VW Rabbit.

When we arrived I was still asleep and running a 103-degree fever, so naturally everyone mistook Fred for me. Apparently Susan did too, which, had I been thinking in romantic terms, would have put me at a severe disadvantage: Fred was a tall, dark-haired, very handsome dairy farmer, with the muscles and working man's physique that went with the job, and the traditional gold cow earring worn by many of the Swiss dairy farmers in the neighborhood. I, meanwhile, could barely manage to stumble out of the backseat. Sniffling and shivering, I was introduced as "Sicko Steve." Everyone kept their distance.

I washed up in the bathroom and did what I could to prepare for the upcoming presentations and discussion. This did not, however, prepare me for the immediate attraction I had to Susan. I noticed her beautiful smile, the sincere, engaging way she spoke with people, and something in her demeanor I could only call grace. Ultimately the meeting helped the varied factions of the community begin working together to find a solution. Susan and other area residents had spearheaded this project, and perhaps I was also instrumental in its success. Personally I'd lost all focus on the actual project, except as it gave me a way to connect with this woman.

I had no idea if she was available, but I was determined to find out. Having been living alone out on the farm for years, and mostly worrying about work, I'd pretty much lost whatever "chops" I might once have had as far as dating goes, and the fever didn't help. Still, at the conclusion of the meeting I managed to compliment her on the work she was doing. She told me that she lived in a historic building on the Mississippi River with her eleven-year-old son, Noah.

"I also run an art gallery," she said, smiling.

And this is where I like to blame the fever.

"Do you have anything worth looking at there?" I blurted out.

She looked appropriately offended. I tried to recover, to explain that I meant maybe I could come see the gallery sometime. But it was hopeless, and Fred ushered me away.

Embarrassed but undeterred, I left a phone message with the mutual friend who had put us in touch originally. Was Susan single, I wondered? And would she have any interest in such a clumsy foot-in-his-mouth kind of guy?

We spent our first date camping out under a full moon on a small island in the Mississippi River that was connected to the mainland by a dirt causeway. We parked in a gravel lot used by fishermen, walked a couple hundred feet into the woods, and set up our tent. Then we lit a fire and chatted. But I think I really won her over with my barred owl call. I had spent years perfecting that call, a talent honed from a lifetime of raising animals. After a few minutes of hooting, with her looking at me as if I were losing my mind, two owls flew in and perched in the treetops above us. Finally, a truly important use for this skill!

The next day we clambered around the prairies, climbing up the steep bluffs onto dry goat prairies. The so-called goat prairies grew on the steep slopes and headlands overlooking the Mississippi River. It was a rugged climb, and I watched with admiration as she went right up without a second thought. I thought then and there that I could only develop a long-term relationship with an adventurous woman.

For our second date I invited her on a research trip to Illinois, where an ongoing oak savanna research team was studying the decline of ecological systems. Day after day, in sweltering 104-degree heat, she worked as hard as everyone else, and the entire team appreciated her presence. I could see that she could fit into any group.

And so it went. Although we were separated by a three-hour drive, when we could find time in our busy schedules we'd seek out the enchanting places where rare plants grew. We shared our passion for prairies and pristine natural areas. She was attracted by my work and my description of Stone Prairie Farm. We got to know each other primarily in the outdoors, canoeing and hiking and exploring the river region she was working so hard to protect. Besides sharing our philosophical appreciation of nature, we became dependent on the countless discussions in which we used each other to sound out our research ideas, and refine our beliefs.

Finally, our relationship reached a crucial point at which a decision had to be made. The distance between our homes was too great, as was the desire to spend more time together. In 1990 we agreed, enthusiastically but cautiously, that she would move in with me at Stone Prairie Farm. It would prove to be a challenge not only to share my life with a mate but also to include her son, Noah, who was just beginning adolescence. At that time, he was in the middle of the familiar hormone-induced behavioral changes, but his awkwardness was offset somewhat by his physical presence. He was already a strapping Iowa farm boy, both endearing and mischievous, who had a way of getting what he wanted.

For a while any attempts I made to set boundaries for Noah were met with resistance and head games. So Susan played disciplinarian and I just tried to help out. One weekend he returned from his father's farm in Iowa with the ATV his father had bought as a way for them to bond. I was resistant, but we went along, hoping that would serve as a healthy release for him. Instead he rode it around in circles for hours, fueling his anger and frustration instead of discharging it.

Fortunately digging into projects on the farm, both literally and figuratively, allowed us to work together cooperatively. Noah was especially happy if he got to drive the tractor or haul Susan and me up and down trails on the ATV. Ultimately this side-by-side labor allowed us to grow and learn together. It wasn't always easy, but integrating ecology into family life gave us a deep bond.

Susan felt torn at leaving behind the many friendships she'd developed over the past two decades. Nonetheless, her transition into our life together on the farm was more organic than Noah's. She launched a botany program at the University of Wisconsin and stepped right into the work at AES, which by then was a thriving concern. As part of a class project, she constructed an intensive restoration plan for Stone Prairie Farm. Gathering historic maps, original 1837 land surveys, aerial photographs, and soil maps, she presented her findings about the ecological systems. Her strategic focus both contrasted with and complemented my improvisational approach. This altered our approach to Stone Prairie Farm and shifted the way we worked at AES, propelling us to incorporate dynamic planning sessions. In these we discussed planting strategies and seeding mixes that would be ideal to reestablish prairie vegetation and wetlands. We also envisioned the reestablishment of savanna and forest in existing cornfields by superimposing the gathered map layers. Susan was a much better communicator than most of us, particularly in using her art background to create clear visual representations. These skills helped everyone comprehend her larger vision.

It was great to have Susan as part of the team, but both she and Noah quickly grew weary of the continual presence of the company in our home. Soon the lack of separation between work and family life became untenable. Being a complete workaholic myself, there was tension between time commitments for work and for home and family. Whereas before their arrival, I'd think nothing about going back to work after dinner, now I had to learn to be available for the practicalities of family life, such as helping Noah with his homework and making time for fun. This shift scared me at first. How would I possibly get all of my work done? But as I actually started to make time for Susan and Noah, I realized that I enjoyed it immensely. We even found ways to work and play at the same time. For instance during hunting season Noah would lead the hunt for a pheasant or deer, and Susan and I would follow along, doing much-needed botanical study.

To keep from disrupting the flow of both family life and AES work I needed to relocate the team to a place where the office staff could continue the administrative work and the barn crew could operate the seed order business, which had become a critical component of AES. I was pretty nervous about making the move, but the more we discussed it, the more eager the team was to find a place where we could fill orders for the prairie plant seeds that had some insulation and didn't allow snow drifts to come in through old siding and swirl over the floor, as they did in my barn. In retrospect, I was so wrapped up in the work that I overlooked many of the sacrifices we were making as a family, as well as many of the ways that the physical structure of our buildings at the farm was inadequate to our growing company.

So I began looking for another place, an office with farmland for starting a native plant nursery. The process entailed some risk and created quite a bit of anxiety about our future, as change always does. Soon we located a dairy and corn farm that the Farmers Home Administration, or FHA, had recently foreclosed on. I learned about it a month or so before it was to be sold off through a bidding process, and we went over to check it out. It was situated on poor sandy soils that couldn't produce viable corn crops even during good growing years. The two previous farmers who owned it in succession had both failed. I was amazed that they even tried on that rough land. But after we examined the soil, it seemed likely that native prairie plants would grow perfectly well there. The government land sale process was biased against proposing anything but a corn and dairy operation, which was ridiculous after the earlier failures. I assumed that the bureaucrats in charge wouldn't know the difference between a prairie and a football field, and didn't think we would have a chance. But the asking price was reasonable and I knew the land would serve our needs, so we moved forward with inquiries.

I needed not only to prepare a solid bid package, but also to make sure that the farm was worth the debt held by the agency. I had the well inspected, as well as the house, barns, and shop, to make sure that AES could safely operate there. I spoke with inspectors and had meetings with the township to evaluate if they'd even grant me a permit to conduct this kind of business on the farm. Of course, I met with loan agents to make sure the appraisals were in line. And as if I didn't have enough to do already, I had to expedite all these things in less than a month, as the auction was coming up. Fortunately, they were looking to award the buyer with the most economically feasible farm plan. I prepared what I thought was a convincing native plant nursery layout, detailing clear reuse of every building (machine shed, granary, storage building, farmhouse, and dairy barn) as well as the expected startup and long-range costs and profits. And since I wasn't officially a "small family farm," one of the federal qualification requirements for potential buyers, I pushed hard to get letters of support for my proposal.

I had never worked as diligently and rapidly on a project, and as fortune would have it, I received letters of recommendation from a local banker with whom I had a good relationship and from both state and federal representatives and the governor of Wisconsin. I even had one from my mother. I sent everything in, and then began what we nervously called "the hurry up and wait" period. Weeks passed with no decision, and the waiting only aggravated my uncertainty about moving AES and added stress to family life. I was on the phone daily with the agency's receptionist, who would impassively confirm receipt of the latest application attachment or support letter I'd sent in. I must have driven the poor woman crazy as I bombarded their office with letter after letter, in hopes of keeping my application active. I figured that the more times they opened my file to add documents, the more attention they'd give to my proposal.

After what seemed like an excruciatingly long time, the local county review panel called with more questions, which at least showed that they were taking our use proposal seriously. After another unbearable couple of weeks an official letter finally arrived. I was pessimistic, so I didn't open the envelope immediately but rather set the letter aside until the staff left. Only after dinner, with Susan egging me on to stop being such a wimp, did I dare to open the envelope.

Amazingly it said they had awarded us with the farm; they had found the details "logical" and the well-articulated plan "sure to be a success." They sent copies to the governor, the legislators, my mom, and the others who had written recommendations and asked to meet to set up a closing date.

I called the staff into the living room of our house Monday morning. As we sat around the wood stove to take the edge off that spring morning chill, I let everyone know we'd been awarded the farm. We could now have a real nursery—all we had to do was build it. Everyone was so excited we dropped our work and drove over to the farm. We walked through it and began brainstorming dozens of plans and fantasies for this new blank canvas. This was the beginning of a joyous period when it seemed like every week, in spite of the immense energy needed to transform the old failed dairy operation, we were celebrating in one way or another, caught up in the joy of this new beginning.

Within months AES moved—boxes of documents and bins of seeds all schlepped nine miles east to the farm alongside Sugar River. The new operations were next to a protected scientific area right off one of the most beautiful rural Wisconsin roadways. By the middle of that summer, AES was up and running in its new headquarters.

⁀

Back at Stone Prairie Farm, we had the place to ourselves: me, Susan, Noah, and our dog, Max—a ninety-pound blue heeler–German shepherd mix. It took some unpacking and rearranging to figure things out, but soon the commotion died down and I began to remember what it was to relax on this lovely piece of land. Susan and I took several long, delightful walks on the property, together with Max. I felt the return of a contentment I'd been missing without even knowing it. And with our newfound freedom in our own home, now we could be entertained again by the antics of Max, who liked to herd everything that wasn't nailed down. He would gather our socks, shoes, and boots, as well as pieces of wood and sticks carried in from outdoors. Before, his middens had included not just our household items but also the belongings of AES employees, so he was probably a bit disappointed when everyone moved to the new office.

But no sooner had we begun enjoying the quiet than I received a call from my mother's friends who had sold me the original 2.7 acres of land, informing me they'd decided to sell off the remaining 77.3 acres of farmland. In fact, they were calling me on a Friday evening to let me know that they would be driving up the very next day to list the property with a local realtor. They asked if perhaps I would be interested in buying it outright.

"I'd love to," I heard myself saying, and knew it was true. But then I admitted that I had just bought another farm to let my company expand and wasn't sure if I could afford it. They said that they'd go ahead with the listing but would come by the next day to talk further about it.

I slept fitfully the entire night fretting about the situation, my tension fueled not only by my long-standing desire to re-unite this entire parcel of land but also by a profound anxiety about who else might buy the land. I had a dream in which I was counting out huge sums of cash while strange people were yanking the trees right out of the prairie with their hands and armies of workers were pouring cement into the stream. By the time morning dawned I was a complete wreck. I couldn't believe the timing. I had worked so hard to begin the restoration and now I felt like I was being forced at gunpoint to make the biggest decision of my adult life. And yet the thought of another buyer snapping up the land was just too much to bear.

When the knock came the following day, I pulled myself together and opened the door. Instead of the thugs I'd imagined, the absentee landowners stood smiling cheerfully on the front porch. The three Chicago-based brothers, who had invested in the farmland thirty years earlier, in the 1960s, had come with their entire families. Wives, children, grandchildren, and even their dogs spilled out of several large vans and milled about the yard taking in the sights. It was a shock to see so many people roaming about, but all I could do was open the house and invite them in.

It turned out that they had an hour before meeting with their attorney and a realtor to move forward with the listing, so they had no time to waste. I had never felt as vulnerable and emotionally naked as I did at that moment. Buying the farm would be a big decision in itself. But having been through the government land purchase process before, I had to concentrate just to keep myself from weeping.

I composed myself enough to ask what their asking price was. Susan was by my side at this point. I have no recollection of it, but she swears that I looked as if I was going to burst. As they spelled out their terms, which were amazingly fair, I began to breathe again and almost managed a smile.

"The only caveat, Mr. Apfelbaum," said one of the brothers, "is that we ask you to honor the remaining two years on the parcel of leased farmland." This was the cornfield leased by a tenant farmer on a few acres in the southwest quadrant.

They then said that they would take a promissory note, allowing me to make monthly payments.

"We'd prefer to sell you the land, since you own the road access."

"Yes sir," added another brother. "We'd like to see the farm kept intact."

I wanted a few minutes of private time to discuss this with Susan, but her feelings were written in her eyes. There was no time for indecisiveness.

I think everyone was as relieved as I was when the words came out of my mouth.

"I want the farm. I'll take it!"

I quickly gathered my wits and countered that I'd pay the asking price if they compensated me for the land rent of the farmer—either that or pay the taxes during the remaining rental period. They thought that was reasonable, and suddenly we were shaking hands on the deal. Then we arranged to drive up and meet with their attorney in the neighboring town to draft a simple contract with just a few terms, including a $50,000 price for purchasing the remaining 77 acres. I now had the entire 80 acres of Stone Prairie Farm, from the upland knoll down to the riparian strip and across the cornfields that would someday regenerate into the kind of diverse prairies and oak savannas that used to spread across this region farther than the eye could see.

But for now we were mortgage strapped from purchasing the remaining acreage and busy pursuing our careers and raising Noah, so the restoration plan for our land became a low priority. But this didn't bother Susan and me. We needed the time to grow into our new responsibilities, to step back and reassess the situation. Having the whole farmstead required a new frame of reference and we were just too overwhelmed to rush into anything. Besides, we wanted to allow for opportunities to develop organically. I'd wanted the warmth and closeness of family. Now I had it in spades.

CHAPTER 6

Taming the Old House

"There are big gray mushrooms sprouting in the shower, Steve," Noah said. "It's disgusting."

It was true. There was fungus growing between the poorly sealed plastic wall and the underlying framing.

"We love living on the farm, Steve. It's peaceful and beautiful. But it's a bit too . . . rustic," added Susan, as gently as she could. But the point was made, and I knew that it would be wise to acquiesce. I tried to pick my battles carefully, and I was in uncertain territory with this debate. I thought I could take a stand on the size and scope of the changes. Fixing things up seemed fine—a major house renovation did not. I was quickly defeated, and my thoughts of simply replacing the shower were scrubbed in favor of a renovation that replaced the bathroom and also installed a solarium that would serve as an addition to the otherwise worthless kitchen, and as a warm room for eating and growing houseplants. This seemed more or less reasonable to me. But when we called Rick Bott, a contractor friend, to assess the potential damage, his conclusions really raised my blood pressure.

"Why tack on a solarium," he asked, "when you also need a usable basement for your furnace, washer, and dryer? This is stuff a family needs."

He continued his preliminary inspection and came back with the assessment that nothing could make the old basement adequate to serve present-day needs. So, Plan A was a house addition. Just what I needed. With all of our other expenses, I could barely consider this idea without feeling nauseated. Susan, Noah, and my contractor friend kept pushing. And then even the banker went along with the detailed cost appraisal and the loan that would be needed.

Everyone was excited about this improvement in our lives, but to me it seemed like an extravagant change. I foresaw ten months of construction that would disrupt everything and leave us exposed to the record-cold winter that was predicted. And how were we going to pay for all of this? I would never have contemplated any of it were Susan and Noah not living there. But there I was with my new family demanding a shower stall that didn't grow mushrooms, a usable kitchen, and a way to wash clothes at home instead of driving to the laundromat in town. I soon bowed to their wishes for these improvements. What else could I do? But I still wasn't convinced.

I'm afraid I created two monsters by allowing for this initial conversation, one demanding that we merely make the house comfortable, but the other, frighteningly enough, demanding a real makeover. It seemed an addition that included the solarium and new basement just would not do. And this became clear as Susan and Noah's enthusiasm for big changes became more forceful.

"Families don't camp out in their own house, Steve!"

Noah was only thirteen years old, but he was already half a foot taller than me. Somehow that gave him the impression that he was on equal footing regarding household decisions.

"Come on, Noah," I tried to reason. "There is a roof over your head and you sleep in a bed. This is the country after all."

"People don't put on down parkas and snow boots for breakfast," he countered. "They usually put them on to go outside."

I looked to Susan for support. She just huddled, shivering, by the woodstove. I thought I detected the sound of her teeth chattering.

"Do you realize how much energy most people waste?" I said, trying to take the moral high ground. "The average American house uses as much electricity in a month as an entire village in the Third World uses in a year."

I didn't even get a disgusted look after that comment. Noah just sat at the table staring at me blankly, his hands cradling a mug of hot chocolate.

"Steve, maybe we could at least improve the insulation," Susan finally said, after a minute of tense silence. "After all, it's not just the winter cold. In summer it's unbearably hot in here, and there aren't any windows that work. We are clearly outnumbered by the bugs. And when it rains . . ."

She didn't need to finish the sentence. The five-gallon buckets were semi-permanent catchments. The leaks were so bad that we had to toss out two or three full buckets a day during heavy rainstorms. Often enough I found myself mopping up overflow.

I had agreed to the idea of renovations associated with adding on the solarium but was now faced with Susan and Noah pushing for a makeover. I always felt that a rustic lifestyle gave me a deeper appreciation for the inherent luxuries that the natural world offered up daily, such as a golden sunrise, a V-shaped flock of migrating geese, or a clear night sky full of constellations. If you listen patiently, the prairie offers up the songs of birds and toads and crickets, each cadence a reminder of the power of nature to calm and revitalize your spirit. My ascetic outlook has always filled me with appreciation for even the smallest comforts as well as an awareness of the vital interconnectedness of the natural world.

I reasoned that one could still sleep perfectly soundly with a down comforter as protection from the cold. And I saw the three of us as active people for whom a house didn't represent the clichés of suburbia. We were concerned with balance and enduring values. So why invest in these home improvements, which would take time and energy away from the priorities we were committed to?

To me a house was a kind of barrier that separates its inhabitants from the natural world to such a degree that the people inside lose touch with nature—not to mention that contemporary homes are filled with toxic materials such as fiberglass and glue. The construction industry at that time wasn't interested in the kind of sustainable building methods employed when our old farmhouse was built, so any "improvement" would inevitably entail a slew of waste, and a load of chemicals.

But looking at Susan and Noah shivering at the table, leaning toward the stove with their breath icing over like thought bubbles in a cartoon, it dawned on me that family priorities trumped my ecological and idealistic arguments. Heading up a household was still a foreign experience for me. It was just possible that I needed a reality check.

Soon after that Susan and I sat down again with Rick Bott, the contractor friend, and learned more about his specialty of retrofitting timber frame and log buildings. We decided to hire him again to look at the situation more seriously than he had during his first visit. Inspecting the limestone block foundation, he pointed out that it was an accommodating hideout for rodents and insects. The electrical system, installed in the thirties, lacked proper insulation and needed modernizing. There was also a good deal of rot in the structural beams. To my dismay, he revealed that our house was in no way energy efficient. He began to point out the deficiencies: the walls were poorly insulated, with sawdust in the older areas and, in the more recent sections, old fiberglass batting that had been largely dug away by burrowing mice. He also said that it would probably not be possible to hook a usable water heater, washer, and drier up to the old service lines. As he spoke I realized more and more that my idealism had blinded me from seeing real needs that involved not only comfort and function, but perhaps even safety. It was three to one in favor of home improvement well beyond the addition, and even I was on the fence.

As architects and contractors so often do, Rick came up with a more substantial proposal. He sketched out a two-story timber frame addition that used recycled barn beams joined with the same mortise-and-tendon technique used in the old barn. His idea was excellent. His sketch really sold me on the concept, and the initial addition ideas, including the solarium, were abandoned. Like my old friend Rob Dunlavey's sketches of articulated feathers years before, Rick's pencil strokes built the structure before my eyes from the foundation to the rafters, a real testimony to the power of art to inspire change. Within weeks we were ready to go.

It took the county zoning office two months to approve the final architectural drawing, and then we began demolishing the summer kitchen. We found a bulldozer operator named "Big Bud," an experienced guy known for his delicate touch with large machines. Nonetheless, I was very nervous as Big Bud drove around to the back of the house. True to his name, he was a big man with a jutting chin and broad shoulders. When he showed up in his cap and grease-stained coveralls, he looked to me more like a munitions expert. All week I'd had recurring nightmares about the entire building falling down like a house of cards from the mere roar of the approaching bulldozer. Bud's appearance and demeanor did nothing to quell my anxiety about the impending demolition. I was nearly catatonic as Bud positioned his dozer beside the decrepit old kitchen. As he took aim, I could barely watch, thinking that the job required the precision of a surgeon's scalpel, not a contractor's fifteen-ton diesel-powered beast with an eight-foot blade.

But Big Bud swiped off most of the ten-by-twelve-foot room

with a single deft movement of the bulldozer blade. In less than a minute, the attached room ended up in a heap behind the house. I felt emotionally lighter as soon as the dust settled and was surprised at how pleasing it was to see the house freed of that flimsy corrugated cage. When it was my rundown kitchen it was sacred; now it seemed like a wart that I waited too long to remove. Susan and I spent the following few hours separating out recyclable materials.

Removing the summer kitchen definitely knocked down a barrier separating us from the natural world. This felt like a glorious revelation at first. However, it also left us completely open to the elements. Any critter that wanted to invite itself into the house could just waltz right in. And over the next few months they did.

Now, I don't mind a few flies and moths flitting about, but by taking off that rotting appendage we pretty much rolled out the red carpet for gangs of rats. While I had always prided myself on my tolerance for other creatures, somehow rats were different. Once the wall was gone, any morsel of food left on the counter in the makeshift kitchen was quickly dragged off, or consumed in situ. The culprits left behind little turd piles, erasing any possible doubts about what kind of creature was responsible for the invasion.

This added immense stress to the remodeling process. It didn't matter what part of the house we were in, after dark, as we lay tucked tightly beneath the comforter, the unmistakable high-pitched squeak of rats competing for any edible scrap immediately vanquished my tranquility and set my blood boiling. Rats seemed to be everywhere. They found their way into cupboards that I was sure were impenetrable and eventually ventured into our bedroom. That was when they stepped over the line.

Late one night, as I slept huddled under the covers, Susan quietly pulled at my shoulder and whispered "rat" into my ear. She had already grabbed the flashlight from the bedside table and was testing it under the covers to make sure the batteries weren't dead.

"Steve, listen, there are noises in the closet."

Fuming, I slid off the bed toward the closet. En route, like a stealthy ninja, I grabbed the nearest weapon—a long-handled toilet plunger—from the pile of yet-to-be organized things temporarily stacked in our bedroom because of the construction.

"What are you doing?" Susan asked urgently, but in a whisper.

"Shine the flashlight in the rats' eyes as soon as I swing open the closet door," I hissed back. "And keep the light in their eyes. I'm going to get these bastards."

I yanked the closet door open so hard I nearly pulled it off its hinges. Four golden eyes peered out, frozen by the light.

I lost myself in a flurry of plunger attacks as Susan yelled out, "Get 'em!" We had bloodlust. It was cathartic.

"They're cornered! You got one. You got 'em both!"

The rats kept screaming, I kept swinging blindly, and Susan kept yelling as our dog, Max, rushed into the room. Max was all dog, a strong ninety-pounder with black spots on a steel-gray and blue background. As with all blue heelers and German shepherds, the dual lineage from which we assumed he came, his genes were focused on herding farm animals: cattle, sheep, horses. So why not rats?

In an instant he had one in his gleaming teeth. Max clamped down as the rat let out one last piercing squeal.

"The other one is getting away!" Susan yelled.

Suddenly I was Big Bud ripping off the summer kitchen. In one deft move, I swiped at the rat, flipped it in the air, and delivered the fatal blow as it hit the floor.

And then there was silence, and two dead rats.

I tossed the carcasses into the front yard as a warning to any other vermin looking to invade our sanctum.

⁀

Our impassioned late-night rat massacre was both satisfying and disturbing. It led Susan and me to discuss our relationship to nature, and the degree to which we wanted to interact with other creatures. We weighed the sanctity of personal space against our wish to coexist with all species, threatening or non-threatening. After all, we considered ourselves stewards of the earth, and we wanted to be conscientious representatives—not sloganeers who intellectualize that relationship but people who treat their fellow creatures as a part of their community. The rat encounter was a stress test. I decided to retire the plunger, focusing instead on keeping unwanted creatures outside, where they could have full run of the land.

But I had forever turned on rats, and, truth be told, I'm not particularly sentimental about certain bugs either. Most flies aren't dangerous, but they are very annoying, and I kill them for sport. I used to try to impress Noah by using my old karate moves to get two in one swoop—swat the first and then grab the second with the follow-through motion. Then, to lessen slightly the sense of unnatural brutality, I'd return the victims to the food chain, feeding them to the fish in our aquarium—darters, pumpkinseed sunfish, and others that we'd caught in the local creek.

Some moths provoke my ire. They eat clothes, ruin food, and are hard to evict. I despise the ones that lay eggs in my sunflower seeds and my beloved Pendleton wool shirts—but not quite enough to do anything systematic to keep them away. Mosquitoes are ubiquitous on the farm, but I feel no compulsion to kill them. I simply brush them aside—although were this a malarial region I'm sure I'd feel differently. Bees, on the other hand, are good friends. If I knew how to help them in their tasks I would. And spiders are useful and fascinating artisans, a pleasure to watch, and useful in pest control.

We've had many visitors from further up the food chain. Barn swallows would come through and get stuck in the house. Getting these avian visitors out was always a tricky task, with the terrified birds careening into walls and windows in claustrophobic panic. The occasional bat was always a strange presence, a flutter of darkness, swooping and bobbing in and out at dusk but, thanks to echolocation, generally much better than swallows at avoiding collisions.

And there were the snakes. Though Susan always had a queasy feeling when a snake was slithering loose in the house, Noah was usually pleased to see a beautiful red-and-black milk snake, and I always considered snake sightings a good measure of restoration, much like migratory birds that rested a while on their journey. It is a sign of validation when animals congregate somewhere of their own volition.

Everyone has his or her own tolerance level for nature, and I'm sure it mainly has to do with familiarity. I'm comfortable with raccoons and squirrels and varieties of birds because I spent so much of my adolescence nurturing and raising injured animals. Back then I even had a skunk for a pet, a wonderfully curious, waddling creature. Stinky had already been de-scented when I inherited him from a frustrated owner who brought him to the nature center where I worked during my high school years. So he was a more welcome domestic addition than he might have been. But now things were different, and large wild animals were simply too dangerous to allow in the house.

As for the rats at Stone Prairie Farm, I felt a bit of guilt at my brutal treatment of them. Mice are smart and cute, but rats seem to represent a kind of evil, and I was intent on killing them—it was a deeply rooted instinctual response. Rats also have a legacy of danger as bearers of disease, such as the bubonic plague, or "Black Death," which killed off nearly two-thirds of the population of Europe in the early fourteenth century. In a domestic setting, they are unwanted intruders.

⌒

For the few weeks following the rat massacre, I woke quickly at any sound resembling squeaking or scampering. But it was soon apparent that more weren't coming in. With our trusty rat-catching dog on the prowl, I returned my attention to the renovation. We sealed the house more carefully, trying to plug the smallest openings. When the builders poured the new foundation, they attached it to the old rock foundation, which helped seal things further. Then Bud delivered truckloads of sand that we shoveled into the basement and leveled. We had piping installed in the basement slab and the new kitchen floor for radiant heating. Rooftop solar panels absorbed the sunlight and transferred the heat into a glycol solution circulating through the pipes, which ran from the roof of the new addition to the basement cement slab. If you live in a cold climate, heating floors with passive solar is the only way to go.

As the home addition was being designed we became intrigued by green building techniques, well before these techniques were widely known. We simply applied the principle of renewable resources indoors, maximizing insulation and utilizing strategic lighting. At every turn we attempted to reuse materials. The addition was built largely from recycled lumber. Old barn timbers were used for the structure, old siding for ceiling panels, two-by-six beams for exterior wall framing. The nicest touch was the tongue-and-groove flooring sawed from salvaged hickory logs.

One of my favorite additions was the root cellar for storing vegetables and fruit from the gardens and orchard. The cool, slightly moist conditions were perfect for keeping apples, squash, carrots, daikon radishes, cabbage, and homemade sauerkraut for months. They were also ideal for growing greens, and for sprouting shoots from beets or French chicory roots that I carefully dug from the garden beds and replanted into moist sand and sawdust in containers in the cellar. The sprouts grown by this process are a reminder of the summer goodness of the garden—long, white, tender, and mildly sweet.

For heating we eventually replaced the old coal stoker with a masonry oven, which is a wonderfully efficient woodstove with a baking oven. The first times we used it to bake hot, crusty sourdough bread it was intoxicating. We gathered around the hearth, quickly consuming whole loaves without even pausing to talk. The oven provided radiant heat for the house and rapidly heated water, augmenting the hot water contributed by the solar heating system.

Just like the prairie restoration, the remodeling took time. For seven months Susan, Noah, and I lived in a house with three sides, truly exposed to the prairie. Only a few sheets of plywood and some clear plastic sheeting separated our living quarters from subzero wind-driven snow and pelting spring rain. Not surprisingly it was much colder without the buffer of the summer kitchen, so we were vigilant about keeping the woodstove loaded. But Noah and Susan didn't complain about the constant chill, seeing that the new addition was really happening. I have fond memories of our huddling together. It kept us warm and intimate at a time when we were still getting to know each other as a family. Even rugged Max snuggled close and slept on the warm comforter.

As the renovation neared completion, I took time off from AES to help finish the work. With Susan away for a monthlong field trip with her class to Venezuela's national parks, I installed insulation, ran wiring, and painted the interior, hoping to surprise Susan with the completed renovation upon her return.

She was pleased with the state of things when she arrived. Rejuvenated from her trip, she set to work immediately on the interior design, and the three of us threw ourselves into furnishing the new space, excited that our long wait was nearing an end. First we installed a commercial cooking stove as the centerpiece of the new kitchen, which vastly improved our culinary output. I built countertops out of cherry wood from trees along the fencerow, and Susan designed Shaker-style cabinetry that a local firm constructed from recycled barn boards. Working together we applied our blacksmithing skills to two suspended pot racks and then bought ourselves some new skillets to hang on them.

The living room really came together when we found a matching antique couch and chair set, still in great condition, at a local estate sale. Other than those pieces, we made most of the furniture ourselves. Susan's experience in woodworking and joinery was evident in a dovetailed solid oak chest she designed from a bur oak so massive it had set a state record for girth, as well as the harvest table we built from a red oak log found on a neighbor's woodlot. The huge wood slab became a beautiful, smooth twelve-by-five-foot table that stood proudly in our dining room, showing off its mortise-and-tendon joinery to all visitors.

Susan was the sole art curator for our house. She framed a set of vivid watercolors that she had painted on one of our arctic wilderness canoe trips and hung a series of historic Mississippi River photographs and a big topographical map of our area published by the U.S. Geological Survey in the late 1800s.

After dancing around the woodstove like freezing hillbillies all winter, it felt luxurious to be able to lounge comfortably in a thin sweater and socks as spring slowly warmed us. Exhausted after so much activity, the first chance we had we spent a quiet week at home, cooking and drawing and generally playing hooky from life. We savored the change in our lifestyle that the renovation brought, not just in terms of greater comfort but also in sensory experience. The architectural changes created new aural and visual perspectives. There was a striking sense that the timber-framed addition made the old house seem more connected to the land.

This shift was most evident on the sleeping porch. We added it to the remodeling plans during the construction phase after visiting the home of some friends and hearing their captivating descriptions of snuggling under the down comforter while calling to owls, listening to frog orchestras in springtime, and waking to birdsongs.

A sleeping porch is an external room attached to a house by at least one solid wall with the remaining sides screened in. Our room shares two exterior walls with the older part of the house on its southwest side, adjacent to the addition. At night you feel like you're sleeping outdoors because you are exposed to the elements. The sleeping porch creates a permanent sleeping arrangement that protects from bugs and is virtually hassle free: no tents, sleeping bags, or gear needed. I love to go camping in the wilderness because the smell of nature is invigorating and the quiet is calming. I always return home clearheaded and alert. But I don't have as much time to go off backpacking as I did in my youth. With a sleeping porch I wake just as rejuvenated as I would in a tent. My sleep is deep and I don't need as much of it. And nature has its own alarm clock in the persistent early bird responsible for calling reveille. You can't muffle the song of a vociferous robin with a pillow over your head—and by the middle of summer, the cacophony of birdsongs makes it impossible to sleep past 4 a.m.

Out on Stone Prairie Farm, it's a treat to greet the dawn. From the sleeping porch we can see the prairie plants dance in the wind as butterflies flutter by and hummingbirds and yellowthroats hover at eye level. We get to know individual birds and anticipate their arrival. And when I'm up early, I can get a lot of work out of the way before the heat of the day drives me indoors or an appointment puts my truck and me on the road.

We sleep on our porch on and off until late November or early December. It's hard to let go of the feeling of the land swelling up around you, and the fresh embrace of an autumn breeze. Even the crisp slap of winter wind is invigorating. On some frosty nights, we've huddled beneath the down comforter during swirling snow squalls. By morning, snowdrifts press up against the screen and a light dusting covers everything inside. But we stay warm beneath the comforter. And we are out again as early in spring as possible, thunderstorms and all. Max worms his way under the covers because the thunder scares him. Safely snuggled between us, he falls asleep and soon enough is kicking us involuntarily as he dreams of a good chase.

The renovation was a time of taming the old house, which had grown wild and precarious. The previous residents had done their best to improve things, but overall their actions were piecemeal and improvised, creating something of a hodgepodge. By the time it got to us, the farmhouse needed more than repair. Still, not all of our friends and neighbors accepted our efforts. Some thought we were messing with history by building such a modern addition. Others, hanging on to environmental and political creeds, considered our efforts to be a form of land development. They predicted continued commercial development, an absurd charge that was soon forgotten when it became clear we had no such plans. We were simply interested in merging the past with a sustainable future by building around the core structure, honoring each element worth retaining. Yes, we innovated. But we also kept the connection to the original structure by using recycled and sustainably harvested wood, all the while making the house ecologically sound. And to Susan and Noah's gratification (and admittedly mine too), we threw in some much-needed comfort in the process.

CHAPTER 7

Planting the Seeds
of Restoration

Hanging above our porch bed, suspended from a rope and swaying in the breeze, are paper bags with native prairie plant seeds.
After work or on weekends Susan and I tour on bicycles or drive
the back roads through the countryside looking for interesting
prairie plants on uncultivated lands. We seek plants native to the
area whose seeds we can harvest for future planting on the farm
or AES projects. Each year we've wandered farther afield. Often
enough we knock on farmers' doors and ask for permission to
collect seeds for our restorations. Almost always the farmer in
question says, "Sure, go ahead," and we enthusiastically fill our
paper lunch bags with seeds. We always record our discoveries
on a county map, marking locations with pins, color coded to
denote rarity. If we come across a rare plant species that isn't
seeding, we mark the spot, first with coordinates on a map and
later by punching buttons on handheld global positioning devices, so that we can return to gather seeds when the right time

comes. We see it as investigative work, scanning for historical plant diversity that is largely gone. Our search requires a discerning eye, for often enough it is the most unassuming patch of random wetland soil that harbors the richest cache of native species.

We harvest seeds throughout autumn and hang them to dry until it's time to plant them in spring. The number of bags indicates our success in finding new species in our annual treasure hunt. By spring these bags are tattered from wind and mist and bleached from the sun. Shabby on the outside, inside they contain the precious genetic codes of the life indigenous to our region. We cross-reference the seeds we have found with lists we have created containing known historical species.

The seeds within these unassuming bags are transformative. Each year they contribute to the incremental rebalancing of the soils at Stone Prairie Farm. After a controlled burn, which clears the planting area of invasive species that have taken root, we rake these seeds into the ashes of the blackened landscape: wetland seeds go to wetland areas; dry prairie seeds like butterfly milkweed go to the dry ridge tops; and Turk's-cap lilies are worked into the moist, well-drained soil cascading up from the wetlands. Even the tattered, decomposing bags are added to the mulch. In this manner we've grown blazing star, pale purple coneflower, and purple prairie clover. We've also reintroduced fleshy fruits such as wild plums, rosehips, and Iowa crabapples, which grew well from seed and formed flowering islands in the sea of waving prairie grasses.

⁓

The order of events is hard to predict in restoration. The only givens are that it will take time and be accomplished one square foot at a time. Regardless of whether it's one acre or one million acres, there is no way to rush the process.

My start had been serendipitous, an unexpected gift from my brothers and their tractor race. At that time, I was considering only 2.7 acres. After we expanded our land and fixed up the house, there was nothing blocking our progress on the rest of the 80 acres. Nothing except, of course, my own uncertainty over how best to approach it. Again I was daunted by not knowing the proper steps to take. And again someone else stepped in and rescued me from my indecision. This time it was Susan.

She was a good partner for me, her abilities complementing mine and filling in the gaps where I was floundering. She wasn't intimidated by the restoration of the farm, most likely because, at least initially, she had less at stake emotionally. She detailed a comprehensive plan for the AES staff and me that not only energized everyone involved but truly paved the way for the future of the recovery process. Where she took an unemotional and methodical approach, I got bogged down when I confronted the morass of agriculture-induced erosion and the invasion of non-native species on my land. Although I had already achieved some great professional successes with just this sort of work, the solutions to similar problems on my own land eluded me. When I toured the property, I saw deeply eroded crop fields and pastures and gullied, grassy waterways. Were these scars on land of an AES project, I would probably have quickly come up with effective proposals for restoration. Not so on my own land.

I also saw fences in disrepair. These I didn't mind because I was keen to eradicate the existing farm divisions, which were obstructive and arbitrary. I longed for a time when the rolling land would run together into an unbroken ecosystem. Much of this idealism soon faded. I woke one morning to find that the neighbor's cattle herd had wandered onto the farm, trampling a large area that we'd recently reseeded and collapsing a few banks on the spring brook. That damage alone was upsetting, but the cows had also laid waste to the tomato vines, the lettuce, and all the spinach plants in our vegetable garden.

The cattle incident compounded my frustration. As seasoned an ecologist as I was, I found myself obsessing about surface issues. Susan helped allay my aggravation by pointing out that regardless of historical erosion and the existent damage, the restoration was already taking place. Nature had already started the process, and she suggested we follow its lead. For example, I had watched in horror as saplings from the mature fencerow of black cherry trees began popping up across the farm, courtesy of the birds and raccoons that inadvertently dispersed their seeds. I was afraid that if we allowed the saplings to grow into dense thickets, they would shade out native ground plants and deprive them of nutrients. Susan cautioned me not to fire up the chainsaw or spray them with herbicide, pointing out that the plants they deprived of sun were mainly introduced agricultural weeds, not the native prairie plants. As the cherry trees developed into thick copses, it was the invasive weeds such as quack grass and thistle that began dying off. And the trees spread naturally toward the savanna, which aided forest restoration. To counter further invasion of noxious weeds, we pitchforked truckloads of waste savanna grass and wildflower seeds from the AES nursery onto our prairie lands, as well as various native woodland flower, sedge, and grass seeds from neighboring properties. In essence, we used one native but invading species, the cherry trees, to fight the others.

But it seemed as if each turn for the better in one area of the farm was offset by new challenges in another. Eighty acres of former farmland is a sizable parcel to monitor. The ridge tops and slopes cultivated for crops over decades have proven the most difficult to restore. Susan and I began with a concerted effort to kill the remnants of the alfalfa crops that been planted there. We plowed the land up, then disked it. Eventually we resorted to herbicide. However, after each spraying to reduce the dense alfalfa stands, even thicker growths of nodding (musk) thistle (a Mediterranean import) would sprout up. In place of each alfalfa plant, it seemed like we'd get a dozen thistles, or tenfoot-tall growths of lamb's quarters and pigweed, all invasive.

It was a lesson in patience. Over time the perennial grass cover increased and vanquished the musk thistle and the senescent alfalfa. Letting nature take its course was the best solution, and the native grasses were ultimately victorious. Where we had orchard grass, blue grass, and tall fescue, it took four to six years for shading to take effect, and for even these intentionally planted "open-site adapted" forage grass species to decline. Eventually we learned to jump-start the process by reintroducing native prairie grass and broad-leaved forbs, using no-till drilling to drive the seeds into the underlying soil. This requires a tractor with an implement that cuts a narrow slit into which seeds are dropped. The slit is then closed by a packer wheel. No-till drilling works well, we learned, in contrast to disking or plowing up soil, which tends to bring weed seeds to the surface en masse. The slit disturbs soils minimally, favoring the native seedlings that have been carefully placed close to the surface. The native grass and forbs took root as long as we mowed and burned the hay annually, which removed both leaf litter from competing plants and the dense mats of clippings that would otherwise smother the emerging prairie seedlings growing from the slits.

We were also aided by provisions in the lease agreements with the farmers to whom we'd given short-term leases on parcels of Stone Prairie Farm. These farmers wanted to continue growing corn in the fields and, needing the income, I was inclined to let them continue for a bit. That said, I wanted to make sure they began to change the way they went about using the land. For example, one of the farmers, a "flatlander" from Illinois, as the local Wisconsin farmers call them, had a lease before we owned the farm. He was notorious for plowing up and down the slopes, creating significant erosion that filled in the lower margins of the field and was directly responsible for muddying the stream. And if the plowing wasn't enough, his cattle finished the job. They grazed on the 13 acres along the stream in the bottom of the valley, making a mess of everything by clambering up and down and collapsing the banks—not to mention that marvel of coordination, the bovine habit of drinking and defecating at the same time! We continued to lease to this farmer and others but issued year-to-year leases and required them to manage the farm fields in a way that would eventually allow us to plant prairies. We also restricted their access and the locations they could farm. This was fine with them because they still had the best soils and parts of fields available for crop production. Otherwise, with the practices they normally used, we would not have had a successful relationship.

Specifically, the leases required that the farmers remove internal fencerows and scrubby borders of box elders and mulberry trees, as well as stabilize whatever sections of the stream channel passed through their acreage. They also did the soil tillage and weed control, which saved time for Susan and me when we converted the cornfields to prairie land after the leases ended. So upon the return of each field, the farmer would disk and we would plant a dense cover of winter rye. The following spring, we'd plant locally collected prairie grasses and forb seeds to nudge those fields toward balanced regeneration.

Susan's plan called for sustained seeding. On the 25 acres around the house, we spread waste from AES's seed nursery. Pickup trucks hauled tons of waste from the AES seed-cleaning facility at Taylor Creek, nine miles away. Using pitchforks we broadcast this waste in a half-foot-deep layer over the lightly disked soil. The matted material—a collection of screenings, dust, and twigs, not to mention a heck of a lot of dead grasshoppers that had been collected by a combine—smothered existing plants, thus reducing competition for nutrients and fostering rapid growth of the prairie plant seeds from the waste. Seeds made up only about 10 percent of this bulk material, but we'd collected so much of it at the nursery that it turned out to be perfect for our purposes.

The results were delightful. From that mass of waste seed up popped compass plants, penstemon, wild indigo, tall coreopsis plants, and dozens of other species. We had some undesired agricultural weeds, such as foxtail grass, but the smooth beardtongue and golden ragwort (two of my favorite plant names!) were an unexpected bonus, as were horsetails and several varieties of sedge.

⁓

It took a few years, but soon the sections of prairie that had been crop and cattle land began to show promising signs of balance. I then began to address erosion along the brook. Some parts of the banks were so trampled and the vegetation so nibbled away from cattle grazing that sections collapsed as easily as a sand dune. There were also stagnant old wallowing holes and numerous muddy trails that traversed the stream. The soils were so badly depleted that I solicited the U.S. Department of Agriculture to help with stream bank stabilization, because their Natural Resources Conservation Service was offering to share costs with program participants.

After surveying the damage, the agency proposed a plan that involved dumping dozens of truckloads of rocks and doing substantial bulldozing work. While this may have worked to limit erosion, the approach struck me as excessive. And curiously they proposed introducing nonnative perennial ryegrass and Hungarian brome, as well as the invasive exotic European reed canary grass to stabilize the stream corridor. Besides being unnecessarily expensive, their plan seemed at odds with our goal of using native plants to bring the environment into balance.

Instead of compacting the subsoil with heavy equipment and buttressing the slopes with rock riprap, or following their curious advice to seed and introduce plants with documented degrading effects on habitat, we took a more cautious approach, focusing on strategic seeding over the surrounding upland prairie and the stream margin wetlands. Without further cattle grazing in this area, the vegetation began to take hold. And as we predicted, stabilization began naturally in certain parts. Dormant strains of fox and hairy lake sedge, giant blue lobelia, and stands of heartsease, also called red smartweed, took hold, as well as other plant species in the seeding mixes from AES's repository of indigenous seeds and rhizomes that we'd collected along the springs and seeps elsewhere in our southern Wisconsin neighborhood.

We did have to take a more aggressive approach along the parts of the stream bank with severe erosion and fallen box elders. There we were happy to bring in Big Bud to remove the trunks and regrade the banks to create gentler slopes. Calling him "Little Bud," we put Noah to work as Bud's official helper in the compact thirty-horsepower Italian-made tractor loaned to me by my brother Gary. We got a kick out of watching our eighth-grader engage directly in the restoration, working alongside the old master as he dragged fallen saplings and bulldozed wheelbarrow-sized patches of dirt.

As it turns out, Bud had an ironic history with the stream. In the 1960s he'd worked on a crew that was brought in to repair the severely eroded gullies caused by poor farming practices going back to the 1930s and the Great Drought. Essentially, Bud told us, he had "canalized the spring brook by straightening what was originally a meandering stream." He wasn't too surprised to see that those modifications had left it equally vulnerable to erosion. So it pleased him to be able to correct that ill-fated action. I had him backfill the washed-out waterway, restore the meanders back into the stream, and redirect drainage into the abandoned, winding swale that had escaped the onslaught of the 1960s.

At the farm's southwest corner, he constructed three shallow wetland depressions rimmed with gentle landforms that diverted the runoff from neighboring farms, keeping it from entering the spring brook. The lush wetland plants that grew there acted as a filter, cleansing runoff, trapping sediment, and reducing heavy storm flows. He also dug out a pond just below the house. We then found that someone had blocked up a springhead, using it for disposal of a demolished farm building. Water gurgled out but ran off into a murky, eroded ditch. Once Bud cleared the debris away we redirected the flow, feeding the pond and the fringe of wetland around it. It was a fantastic change! Thanks to that new spring we would enjoy countless evenings falling asleep to the lullaby of gurgling water, as if we were camping along a mountain stream.

After the creation of these smaller wetlands, we diverted the grassy waterway along a stretch of the spring brook to revitalize a 2-acre wetland patch. It stayed inundated until late June and became a springtime roost for the blue-winged teal duck and a home to water dragon beetles, swarming water fleas, and crooning American toads and their kin, the western chorus frog.

As Bud removed the remaining internal fence lines, he released the land from the rectangular grip of crop fields and grazing areas. He also removed the buildups of eroded soil that had accumulated behind the fencerows, creating abrupt changes in the topography that were up to a couple of feet high. These discrepancies had hampered the hydrology of the land and altered the vegetation patterns. When Bud leveled those anomalies, he removed the final barriers to a contiguous landscape and allowed the integrated restoration to begin.

Wind is our partner in seed dispersal. It is a tangible force, at once friendly and tyrannical. One windy afternoon I drove to a high prairie location on one of the dry knobs with several hundred pounds of waste seed, mainly little bluestems and stiff goldenrod. Standing upwind of the roughly 2-acre patch, I threw seeds into the prevailing current, planning to use the winds to scatter the seeds. This proved tricky. No sooner had I begun tossing handfuls into the wind than it changed course and blew a cloud of the material back into my face and down my shirt. Those hairy seeds and pointy plant stems rubbing against my skin quickly dampened my enthusiasm for using wind to disperse seeds! But with time I figured out the technique and took pleasure in watching those airborne seeds travel hundreds of feet downwind to dust the soil. Three years later the whole area was covered in lush stands of spiking bluestem grass, blossoming penstemon, and bright mustard-colored goldenrod.

We also get plenty of assistance in collecting and dispersing seeds from other creatures who have helped to restore Stone Prairie Farm simply by engaging in their natural habits. Our dog Max did his fair share of work. Black-eyed Susan and yellow hyssop, among other species that we planted by the house, are now scattered over the land, courtesy of his gallivanting.

Wind is a pure form of energy integral to the return of prairie life. Besides seeds, the wind carries pollen, insects, birds, and dreams. Odors waft from unseen places, bringing the smoky breath of prescribed burns, the sour-sweet smell of rotting apples, and the reassuring whiff of freshly mowed hay. Wind lofts the songs of birds and toads and animates the landscape. Spiders float on drafts, their dewy webs sparkling in the sunlight. I can watch an animated prairie with the same interest I'd give to an aquarium; both are rich in diverse life and constantly in motion.

The wind that powers a cool breeze bringing relief on a summer's day is also the source of winter's driving rain and stinging icy blizzards, and a force that can empower and astound the imagination. But harnessed wind is a critical generative force, pumping water, generating electricity, and grinding grains. On a farm you cannot forgo nature's assistance, which is why almost every farmstead features a tower supporting a water-pumping windmill. My wind generator extends up from the highest southern ridge of Stone Prairie Farm. The turbine unit sits on a 120-foot steel tower. Its blades are similar to the bulletproof Kevlar blades on helicopters, a fine feature if a modern-day Don Quixote were ever to take aim with shotgun or pistol.

As the sun traverses the sky, the shadow of that tower follows it like a sundial, casting long shadows across thousands of dry prairie plantings. Inspired by Aldo Leopold, who had done the same, I installed wooden benches so that passersby could sit along the prairie's periphery and look out over the fields in silent contemplation as sunlight plays off the quietly revolving turbine blades. I had to nudge nature to take its course on that prairie. It was grueling work, but I am still rewarded whenever I see neighbors or random travelers resting under the silhouette of that tower.

⌒

Susan has been instrumental in keeping the restoration moving forward, playing a significant role in most of the decisions made after her arrival on the farm in 1990. And whenever things have been critical, I have turned to her for advice and motivation. But when we turned our attention to the intimate plantings around our home, we had a stark disagreement that stood out in our relatively harmonious life together. Whereas Susan approved of my almost religious zeal to restore the farm to its pristine natural order, she could not understand my displeasure at including cultivated perennials in the house garden. At this impasse, my purist's temperament clashed with her sentimentalism. I was so intent on eradicating introduced species that I could not believe she would want a garden full of the kinds of nonnative flowers and shrubs that salesmen would have hawked to unsuspecting homesteaders in the nineteenth century.

Her beloved heirloom garden varieties were just as incongruous to the landscape as the majestic European larch, catalpa, and Norwegian spruce that loomed over the neighboring farmsteads. Those prairie misfits did not have a place in the agricultural equation, period. But then again, in relationships you have to pick your battles. And I'll admit I did find that the pinks of Susan's peonies blended elegantly with the purples of the Canadian trefoils and the sunshine yellows of the wild senna. I had to root for her underdogs, since the hardy natives would always have to be tamed to keep them from shading out her less aggressive cultivars.

Most important, though my stubborn nature made it hard to accept, this was a small concession. She too was concerned with the bigger picture and constantly kept me focused on key issues such as soil types and preparation and the ever-critical hydrological solutions. And she was no stranger to hard labor. When a nearby prairie was condemned to development, she immediately volunteered to be a landscape surgeon and help me salvage a sizable swath of it. In fact, we dug up and transported thousands of sod chunks to Stone Prairie Farm, enough to cover over a third of an acre north of the barn. We hand dug large divots around rare plants and then carried the sod, one armload at a time, to semi trucks, taking all its weight, water, nutrients, and insects along for the ride to Stone Prairie Farm. And Susan still enjoys contemplating the majesty of the land as much as I do, the splendor of the Turk's-cap lilies, bastard toadflax, wild strawberries, hoary puccoons, shooting stars, yellow stargrass, and their hundreds of cousins as we wander among them collecting seeds for restorations at home and elsewhere.

CHAPTER 8

The Doctor Is In—
Symptoms of Ecological Health

In restoration, as in life, there are continual confrontations. Expectations meet resistance and goals slip backward. The pessimist points at these obstacles and says, "See what I have to put up with!" The optimist says, "So what? I'll find a way around this setback!" The restorer empathizes with the land, identifies with its struggle, and heads straight into the breach, cutting through the weeds and sidestepping the erosion in an attempt to find an acceptable ecological balance that is measurable but, at best, still subjective. Environmental soldiers have different litmus tests and varying thresholds. Their choices are as varied as human behavior, and they often see their fortunes reverse. I've seen some of my finest professional successes turn tragic when clients didn't follow through on the plans we'd laid out together or sold their restored lands to people who were less committed to the health of the ecosystems. Still, there have also been many sustained successes, such as a park in the Glenview Park District in Illinois, where we worked to create a restored environment for native plants as well as the frogs and snakes that have become increasingly rare in the region. The community was integral to the restoration process, and this wave of enthusiasm helped the site evolve into what is now the highly successful Grove National Historical Landmark. Similarly, a family whose farm we worked to restore in Wisconsin invited not only relatives, but many neighbors to get involved. Soon the whole community was intensely engaged in the many processes necessary to promoting healthy prairie—doing prescribed burns, harvesting and planting seeds annually, and more.

Living at Stone Prairie Farm, I try to maintain a restoration paradigm that keeps a focus on the larger landscape and ecosystem. We humans must strive to resuscitate this ecosystem or suffer the same fate as those species and habitats we have already destroyed or imperiled.

When I set up house here over thirty years ago, I became the resident physician for the local ecology. My initial examination revealed a patient wounded from generations of agricultural abuse. The scarred acres had been arbitrarily dissected and rearranged to serve the shortsighted goal of maximum productivity. These ailing, disjointed parcels still functioned independently of the complete corpus. I couldn't call them healthy, but the wounds were not terminal. The diagnosis was grim, but with cautious optimism and the right course of treatment the prognosis was good for a slow eventual recovery. Even over the few short years in which the bulk of the fields had sat fallow right after I bought the land a healing process had begun. And as I measured each year's spring renewal, I found much of the land mending quickly, evidenced by lush green growth. The wildlife and rare plants that returned of their own volition were powerful indicators that this once ravaged landscape would struggle toward renewed health. Nature, with its self-regulating cyclical systems, is predisposed to recovery.

With a human patient it's easy to see the manifestations of

recovery from injury, whether in the healing of wounds or the knitting of broken bones or the regeneration of nerves. But with landscapes, visible improvements such as lush new foliage, although promising, don't necessarily correlate with overall health. Often you really do need to be a scientist to recognize the distinctions. And as with each human, every natural area has unique needs: each restoration project has distinctive indicators to measure recovery. Careful monitoring is necessary to track the way individual systems respond to restoration efforts and to quantify the long-term recovery of desirable native species and their habitats.

With land these careful measurements are more important than any visual indicators, and they require painstaking documentation. Ecologists generally derive patterns from a hula-hoop-sized sample area called a "quadrat." We record the density and variety of species contained within that section and extrapolate to note trends. We then summarize the patterns and index them to identify such key indicators as erosion reduction and forest regeneration and to measure the success of re-introduced animals, fish, and insects and the state of their corresponding habitats.

Aldo Leopold wrote that intelligent tinkerers should save all the pieces. When I first looked out over the 13-acre field at the northeast end of the farm, I saw what struck me as the work of careless tinkerers. The gullies were filled with rocks and the subsoil was exposed. Agricultural erosion had systematically washed away the precious topsoil down to the bedrock, leaving horned coral and scattered crinoid stem fossils jutting out of the ground. The farmers who preceded us hadn't saved all the parts. By planting crops in rows running directly up and down the steep slopes, they'd created pathways for rainwater to wash away the rich topsoils. In so doing they had cast out a critical component and exposed the environment to disease: depriving the land of topsoil is like flaying a body and leaving it raw, vulnerable, and exposed to the elements.

Much of the lost topsoil had ended up downstream along the spring brook waterway as terraced deposits of silt that were obvious to the naked eye. As runoff from row-cropped uplands deluged the brook with mud, sand, and rock, the channel bottom rose up with the influx, impinging on aquatic habitats. And since some hadn't yet made it to the stream and remained just upslope along the lower margins of the northwestern field, it was no surprise to see looming fifteen-foot-tall giant ragweed flourishing in the deposits of nutrient-rich soil. The soil was scattered, taking up residence in all the wrong places while the upper fields were raw and exposed.

How would a patient without vital organs recover? Beyond the loss of a single kidney, a human wouldn't have much chance of an active life. In ecology, however, recovery is a corollary of patience, and nature is inherently patient. It can and will reassemble itself, and I have had the distinct pleasure of watching that process of self-repair. Further, I've be able to help it along, providing supplemental treatments and support. For instance I stopped erosion and stabilized soils in various areas by planting short-lived cover crops such as annual ryegrass, or even the oats in the garden plot Gary and Ronnie had dug up. Eventually I'd replace such temporary coverings with the seeds of long-lived desirable prairie and wetland plants. I've also gone after the noxious weeds flourishing in the scarred lands, hoeing, tilling, and replanting over such areas with native seed stock.

By the spring of 1993, following the farmers' final harvest on the leased fields, signs of recovery were already evident. Had these fields been prepared for replanting, the soils would have been chisel-point plowed shortly after the fall harvest, which wouldn't have allowed any seeds to germinate. Corn stubble fragments would be sticking out of the soil in every possible direction. Instead there was a dense flush of seedlings blanketing the soil. As I sauntered over the cornfields in mid-April, I looked at the newly sprouting seeds optimistically, hoping to see emerging prairie, savanna, or wetland plants. I knew better, but hoped for the best. Instead I found mainly introduced agronomic weeds that had co-evolved with the agricultural crops, such as the green foxtail grass that towered five feet high by midsummer. The transition would take more than one year, I knew. By late summer, the rolling hills offered a picturesque view of golden foxtail stems waving in the gusting wind. With a little imagination I could envision the native bluestem grass and wildflowers of a healthy prairie. And in truth even invasive species like the foxtail are a benefit. Because I let them grow instead of disking them under to prepare for a planting, they acted as soil-stabilizing agents, helping hold the topsoil in place and preparing the field for a next stage of recovery.

⌐

That spring Susan and I burned the fields, replicating a crucial natural process from which these fields had been "spared" during the decades of their agricultural use. We planted seeds of native prairie plants in the ashes. Afterward astoundingly dense clumps of low-growing field horsetail pushed up, a bushy, swirling lime-green carpet that spread over every contour of the landscape like dense fur, overwhelming the foxtail and the giant ragweed groves. Field horsetail, which belongs to the genus *Equisetum*, is a primitive fern relative that is mineral rich and prized in both Western and Eastern medicine. The rapid growth was unexpected and overwhelming, and I was pleased to see a native species taking hold with such vigor.

Abundant dandelions mingled with the horsetail, creating a flowing wave of brilliant yellow that carpeted the fields for two weeks in spring. And for the following ten days, the translucent seed-bearing pappi expanded and floated in tufts and swirls off the desiccated flower heads, coating the field like the winter's first dusting of snow.

The dry, eroded northwestern field would be the domain of the dandelions for the next three years, until the noxious weeds Canadian and nodding thistle took hold as well. And on the highest knobs the thick clusters of hairy aster blossomed until late October, adding flowering rosettes to the landscape.

Different areas recovered at different rates. Some severely eroded sites developed very slowly, while a few locations rapidly developed native plant cover, like the field where I'd let the wind disperse goldenrod and bluestem seeds. And there were surprises. On one field that I'd considered very sick native species emerged miraculously from the first plantings.

In some places we decided to intervene. The 2 acres of prairie around the wind generator were making little progress on their own. I had seeded the area with native seeds, but they were choked out by a thick mat of exotics—quack grass, European brome grass, and dandelion—and had never taken hold. After long consideration and debate, we decided to apply an herbicide. Ultimately it wasn't a terribly difficult decision given that few viable options existed for undoing what herbicides and farming had created. Short of plowing and growing thick cover crops for several years, it was doubtful that we could eliminate these dense growths. We opted for Roundup, the same stuff most of the farmers in the area used, and we sprayed it carefully, with the sprayer head nearly at ground level to prevent drifting of the chemicals, so that we only treated the specific plants we were targeting. We also timed the application to hit the quack grass and European Brome grass as the plants were metabolically active so that the herbicide would be quickly carried throughout their tissues and, most important, into the root system. Once there, Roundup emulates a naturally occurring plant hormone but works slightly differently, causing plants to metabolize without nourishment and die. Fortunately we also managed to avoid the times when the underlying native plants would have been most vulnerable. Soon the invasives died off (effective stuff, that weed killer!), and the sideoats grama, little bluestem, and other prairie plants I had seeded five years earlier began to appear. They'd clearly needed a jump-start to overcome the competition, but once the way was cleared they grew rapidly.

In addition to prairies we sought to reestablish savannas, which are essentially the borderland between prairie and woodlands. They consist of an understory of prairie plants—grass, sedge, and wildflower—combined with trees and shrubs scattered widely enough to allow significant patches of light to reach the ground. A forest, by contrast, has a continuous canopy. We particularly focused on the elevated knobs where savannas would have been historically found, thriving in a region protected from wildfires.

It was the group of black cherry trees that spontaneously sprang up around the perimeter fences the very year after farming ceased that set things in motion, their seeds dispersed by birds and raccoons who ate the previous summer's crop but didn't travel far before relieving themselves. In their trails grew thousands of seedlings, hungry for light and water. Because of their clustering growth patterns—they were far more tightly concentrated than the scattered oaks, hackberry, basswood, and walnut that also populated the savanna—the cherries were highly effective in shading out the agricultural weeds that would otherwise grow below them—the dandelions, thistles, and alsike clovers. This made for a bare understory, a fresh start for introducing native species. Further, my fear of the cherry trees spreading uncontrollably was unfounded, and it proved relatively easy to keep them in check with prescribed burns. The rabbits and meadow voles helped by girdling their bark, and white-tailed bucks in rut scraped the bark from many young saplings.

Susan and I then shifted our seed-collecting work to focus on savanna grasses, sedge and wildflower seeds, acorns, walnuts, and hazelnuts from nearby forest and savanna remnants. With just a little nudge from us, the savanna floor rapidly stabilized with these native plants. Eventually silky and Virginia wild rye and bottlebrush grass started prospering beneath the dense cherry saplings. Next came woodland geranium, Joe-pye weed, Solomon seal, bloodroot, blue cohosh, and woodland trefoil.

To allow time for tree establishment in the savanna restoration areas, I initially thought prescribed burning should cease for several years. A bit of research and discussion with my AES colleagues eventually convinced me otherwise. It turned out prescribed burning done every other year helped maintain gaps for light, thinned cherry saplings and shifted the ground-story vegetation from weeds to native plants. So we began these burns early on.

For the most part, restoration here was the work of the returning wildlife, since 80 percent of the several hundred species of savanna and forest plants found in the neighboring woodlands depend on wildlife—primarily birds, insects, and small mammals—for seed dispersal. Birds nesting in the developing tree and shrub canopy were most active. Occasionally raspberry, blackberry, and even some exotics invaded, including the rosy-fruited tartarian honeysuckle. Fortunately goldfinches and swallowtail butterflies didn't like these noxious weeds. And if the hungry birds didn't do the trick, we diligently pulled the exotics from the ground, roots and all, or zapped them with a spot application of herbicide.

⌒

While the recovery of the land was vividly clear from the plants' growth, the response of animals was the critical affirmation of a broader sustainability. The recuperating ecosystem attracted new wildlife, signaling a growing diversity where monoculture had dominated for decades. Thousands of frogs and toads, more than a hundred bird species, and numerous mammals soon made a home of the farm. We spotted coyotes, badgers, least weasels, several shrew species, white-footed mice, deer mice, meadow voles, and an array of prospering butterflies and moths, katydids, and grasshoppers. The arrival of certain birds was a particularly good omen of rebalancing. We began regularly spotting bluebirds, bobolinks, Lincoln's sparrows, grasshopper sparrows, and long-billed marsh wrens, which proved the abundance of appropriate habitat conditions. And the arrival of rare grassland bird species, like the Henslow's sparrow, which is known to be extremely discriminating in selecting its habitat, proved to me that a truly complex web of life was re-creating itself on the prairie.

Finding snakes was a particularly auspicious sign, as they would have had a much harder journey to find the recovering land. It's a whole lot easier to find enticing land if you're a bird winging your way overhead. But if you spend your time with your eyes an inch off the ground, it must be a lot harder to know what's going on miles away. But they came, and not by simply sliding over from the neighboring cornfields, for there were no appropriate habitats within a day's slither. No, their appearance was unexplained and serendipitous. Some kind of internal compass had caused them to journey many days in our direction.

Unfortunately we discovered the first two harmless corn snakes the hard way. It was the spring of 1995, and Susan and I were grubbing out a walking trail around the house, lining the pathway border with chunks of limestone from a neighboring quarry and scattering wood chips for the trail surface. I was loading and unloading the wheelbarrow with a pitchfork while Susan raked the chips over the trail. Chips were constantly getting skewered on the tines of the pitchfork, causing me to pause periodically and force them off.

I wasn't even looking at the pronged tool when I tried to bang off what I thought was a large clump of wood chips. Instead, I realized, it was actually a writhing snake, impaled on the pitchfork. I quickly dropped to my knees to examine it, and Susan sprinted over. It was a juvenile corn snake, not much thicker than the tine itself. In obvious pain, the snake, with mouth agape, flailed its head and flipped its tail around spasmodically, looking for something to hold on to.

We sprayed water on the dry tine and carefully slid the snake off. Holding it gingerly, we tried to comfort and console it as if it were a loved pet. Seeing no bleeding around the puncture wounds, we figured the snake had a good chance of survival. So Susan ran into the house and reappeared shortly with a shoebox hospital bed. We placed the snake inside the box with assorted dry grasses and set it in the shade under the porch. It felt like a return to my childhood days of wild animal rehabilitation.

Realizing there might be others, we continued our work more carefully. And sure enough, we did discover an additional snake with the same irregular copper, brown, and red patches. When the heat of the day had passed, we walked into the prairie with both snakes. We released them in the twilight by a fallen black willow tree along the spring brook. Apparently the wound I'd inflicted wasn't fatal, and we watched them both slither off into the tangle of tree limbs and bark.

Shortly before the corn snake incident, my colleague John and I were visiting a potential wetland restoration site in northern Illinois, an hour away by car. During our tour of the property we found the large iron lid of an unmapped storm sewer. We hoisted the lid open to find out how deep the sewer was buried, and I jerked backward, seeing a large snake swimming around just below. It turned out to be a mature fox snake, an equally harmless species. Apparently this one had entered through a hole in the iron lid. We snagged the snake with a long stick, lifted it out of the sewer, and dropped it into a spare pair of pants I had in my daypack, which I tied closed at the ankles and secured at the waist with a loop of rope. I brought the snake back to the farm, eager to reintroduce the species into our healing ecosystem. I released it under the backdoor porch, next to garden, so that it could wander out into the prairie at its leisure.

Years later we'd discover that we had misidentified the snakes in our reptile book. Apparently, the names "corn snake" and "fox snake" were interchangeable in the older classifications. According to the updated nomenclature, the corn snakes were baby fox snakes, and the rescued sewer snake was a pregnant female. She eventually chose to raise her brood in the warmth of the composting chip pile. Several years later, Susan and I discovered, with great satisfaction, a grown snake with a healed wound sunning itself near the tomato vines.

☞

As wildlife returned to the farm, the neighbors living in the surrounding community took notice. Many stopped by to look out over the looming expanse of wildflowers and chat about local news. Dick and his wife, Dolores, started coming over to bird watch. Dolores fell passionately for the bluebirds and began painting watercolors of them, and Dick took up building birdhouses as a hobby. Susan and I were pleased to see all the interest, and particularly happy that Dick spent less time on his noisy mower, which had been his Saturday-morning recreation from the time I moved in. Dolores, it turns out, had never cared for that either, so we were all quite happy that it got a lot quieter on the weekend. Soon prairie life began flourishing on Dick and Dolores's land too.

By nurturing the land and restoring its systems I not only overcame my fear of what my neighbors would think, but I was able to engage them in the process and even influence some of their farming practices. One neighbor who had strongly opposed my land use initially was so moved by the transformation that he asked for our permission to hold a family wedding amidst the prairie blossoms. Of course we said yes, and it turned out to be a gorgeous event. We were also happy to allow local grade schools to conduct nature classes on the farm.

☞

After the first fifteen years at Stone Prairie Farm the cautious optimism with which I started had given way to a new level of certainty. We'd followed a slow and steady path toward ecological balance, evidenced in the stabilized soils and the absence of turbid runoff from former cornfields spilling into the stream.

The hydrology had balanced, and the spring brook was running clear and cold year round. Prairie vegetation had matured enough to control stormwater overflow and help it infiltrate the soil and feed new springs that emerged from the banks.

But underneath all the success was a tenuous undercurrent of foreboding that continually whispered about the fragility of this experiment, reminding me not to overestimate my knowledge or rest on my laurels, for at any moment a natural calamity could set the whole process back. There is no manual for restoration, and risk is always in lockstep with the ecologist.

CHAPTER 9

Playing with Fire

I hadn't been living on the land long before I began to realize that this ecological recovery project wasn't only about how the land healed. It was also about me—my desires and my fantasies. And the process brought me face to face with the demons of ambition, impatience, and uncertainty.

In large part this is because the land changes slowly. The story of Stone Prairie Farm has occurred over a period of nearly thirty years. I saw small, incremental shifts during that time, such as the spread of native shooting star plants or the return of the long-billed marsh wren, making its characteristic nocturnal ruckus. These and many other discoveries told me clearly that recovery was under way. Nonetheless, I yearned for faster, more radical transformation. Why this nagging, unsettled, unsatisfied feeling?

Somewhere deep within myself I hoped to walk outside one morning and open my eyes to a pure, untrammeled land, an Eden of sorts—this land, this property, the way it used to be before the conversion to corn. Even then I recognized this pull, for

I've always lost myself in untamed nature, wandering aimlessly, each footstep bringing into view something worth looking at, touching, thinking about. I knew full well that this was a fantasy, but part of me yearned for it, for the mystery of the truly "natural." But the land's recovery takes decades. One never simply wakes up one day to a fully transformed landscape.

Well, rarely at least. One of the most transformative events in nature is also one of the most important in the restoration of some ecosystems, particularly prairies: burning. When you wake up to an area that has recently been burnt, or is just beginning to recover, you may not be looking at a complete restoration to a pre-agricultural state, but it is unquestionably a radical change. And it wasn't long before I began thinking about doing more substantial burns on the farm.

Early on in my studies I'd learned that fire is an essential part in the life cycle of most ecosystems in North America. While we often think of wildfires as a dangerous threat to be avoided at all costs (just close your eyes and remember the image of Smokey Bear, with his stern expression and his ranger's hat), they are, in fact, central to ecosystem health. Many plants, for instance, have evolved seeds that will crack open and germinate only at intensely high heat, remaining dormant until fire passes through their area. Particularly important in the context of restoration, fire tends to favor the survival of native species over exotics, which helps maintain diversity.

I've studied fire in depth, and I've developed a complex, considered relationship with it as a land management tool. But when I was young I saw it as more devilish, more impulsive. Because of its positive effects, burning prairie lands had become something of a challenge among my ecologist friends, a competition to see who could burn this or that prairie remnant first, complete with bragging rights for the one whose match caught fire under the right conditions. But for me these bragging rights carried a hefty price—the guilt that haunted me years later, since lighting such burns was highly illegal and misunderstood by the community at large.

My first burn was an unplanned event. My friend Rob and I were botanizing on a local hill prairie near Chicago during our college years. We parked at the edge of a cornfield some twenty miles out of town early one morning and starting walking, cutting through the corn toward open prairie. Soon we were covered with a light-green goo, the dew-heavy larvae of aphids coating our legs and shirts. When we reached the prairie, we used the vegetation to wipe ourselves off and then looked about. The stretch of prairie occupied a gravel hill that rose 60 feet or more above the neighboring crop fields. Because the soil was so rocky, no farmer had ever attempted to plant crops there. And because of the remoteness and isolation of this hill, the grasses had never been used for livestock grazing. As a result, hundreds of colorful native plant species abounded in this small patch of unplowed land, all swaying in the early-morning breeze. Rob and I planned to catalog them all.

We worked through the morning. Then, over lunch, under the shade of a black cherry tree, our conversation swung to fire. Looking around we saw evidence of fires in the distant past, in the deep scars on a nearby bur oak that, judging by its size, must have been about three hundred years old. Wildflowers flourished all about, except for a bald patch in the shade of a dense, invasive European buckthorn shrub thicket.

"This place would be so much healthier," Rob said, "if it could only experience fire again."

The realization kicked us both into action.

We were both nonsmokers and had no matches or a lighter. But as good botanists we did have magnifying glasses. Within a few minutes we had made torches of dry prairie grass stems and foliage. I focused sunlight onto mine and almost instantly a swirling waft of smoke sprung up. This was the point of no return. I brought the sheaf to my face and, with one puff of breath, ignited a burst of flame. Within moments we were running as fast as we could in opposite directions, each clutching a torch. A horrendous crackling sound sprang up, and flames flicked into the sky, caught the wind, and began to travel. Rob and I circled the 2-acre hill and came together at the far side.

It wasn't long until the wail of sirens filled the air. We ran at full bore back to the car, an exhausting half mile, through corn leaves that slashed at our arms. By the time we got there, panting for breath and smelling of smoke, a crowd had assembled a ways down the road. We got in, cleaned up enough to be perceived as two of the many spectators watching the flames whip into the sky, and drove down to join the crowd. Sheriff's cars from two nearby municipalities and at least five fire engines were soon on the scene. We sat and watched several of the vehicles attempt to drive through the cornfield, quickly becoming mired in the soft soil. The crowd's attention turned from the fire to the efforts at getting the trucks unstuck. Meanwhile the fire grew, unabated, and then eventually burned itself out. We waved goodbye and carefully left the line of other cars that had gathered for this seemingly very new spectator sport— prairie burning. The year was 1975, over a century after Mrs. O'Leary's cow kicked over a kerosene lantern, as the story goes, and started the Great Chicago Fire of 1871—possibly the last time watching flames had been popular entertainment in the region. It was satisfying, and Rob and I drove home high on adrenaline and flushed with the spirit of righteous rebellion.

That was the impulsiveness of youth. At the time I knew that burning would eventually be healthy for the strip of prairie, but I didn't yet know the intricacies of why or how. Instead I began to worry, images of the destructive power of fire dominating my thoughts. What would be the impact on wildlife (one can't help but imagine Bambi)? The wildfires that run amok through western forests annually are serious events, endangering life of all sorts. I fretted about the plants and animals and began to understand the primal fear that we have inherited from millennia of fearsome flames.

Eventually I was able to focus on the good as well. As I learned in my professional training, most of these negatives are in fact fear based and focused on the moment of fiery destruction, not the actual long-term impact on the ecosystems, which have evolved to cope with, and benefit from, the flames.

Attempting to restore Stone Prairie Farm fifteen years later, I had a much deeper understanding of fire. I'd done my master's thesis on fire ecology, the study of the effects of fire, in the Quetico-Superior wilderness area, a 3.5-million-acre region straddling the Canada–U.S. border, encompassing Minnesota's Boundary Waters Wilderness and much more.

Fire is one of the central features shaping that ecosystem. Fire burns through the region in a rotation of about fifty years, meaning not that the entire region will experience a massive wildfire but that for any given point the probability is that it will be touched by fire approximately once every fifty years. To be sure there are specific protected regions—islands, places protected by steep cliffs, and so forth—where the existing forest vegetation is much older, but fifty years is the average. The questions I focused on concerned what happens after the burn, how plant and animal communities reestablish and reassemble themselves, and conversely what happens if areas are deprived of fire.

One of the most important effects of fire is that it releases all sorts of important nutrients back into the ecosystem in usable form. These are nutrients tied up in organic matter, living or dead—leaves, wood, peat, twigs—that are unavailable for use by other life (unless you happen to be a wood-boring beetle, a fungus, or a microbe). Fire causes an enormous release of these nutrients, such as nitrogen, potassium, and phosphorous, back into the system. Immediately after a fire, there is a commensurate enormous response. The conditions for new life are perfect.

First, the blackened earth tends to absorb heat from the sun. And then, when the first rains come, what is essentially a warm soup of nutrients seeps into the soil, bathing all the seeds and traces of life in an energizing wash. Second, there is usually more light available for new life, as the fire has swept away the foliage that hogged the sunshine, creating life-discouraging shade. After a fire, life flourishes. In a recently burnt forest area, there are millions of seeds—many of which may have been lying in the soils dormant for decades, even centuries, just waiting for these ideal conditions to appear. Then, washed in nutrients and given light, they flourish. In many cases these are plants that live for only a few years, until the forest reestablishes a canopy, blocking out the light, and then they go back to a dormant state, awaiting the next burn.

Fire is also necessary to the germination of many species. In Canada, for instance, one of the dominant evergreen trees is the jack pine. The cones of the jack pine, which contain the seeds, are normally glued shut with a dense resin. Only when they are exposed to the scorching heat of fire do they open and drop their seeds. What evolutionary advantage could this offer? The cones themselves are some fifty feet up the tree. So by the time they burn and open, the wind has generally swept the fire past them below. The newly freed seeds then drop to a forest floor that has been perfectly prepared for them: all the nourishing nutrients have been released, the first water will bring a warm, fertile bath for them to germinate in, and the canopy has been trimmed to allow light in. Many other species have a similar need of fire scarification to germinate. As a result there is a bright and abundant display of new growth and flowering plants in the years just after a fire.

There are some great variations on this theme. Among my favorites are the many species with hard-shelled seeds that need to be eaten and pooped out by raccoons, birds, and other herbivores. The digestive acids in the gut of these animals serve to break down the hard shell, and the seeds are then deposited in the scat, which is a similarly fertile pool of nutrients for germination. Most roses on the prairie are like this—and produce bright red rose hips to attract hungry birds and raccoons. A similar wild rose species in Canada relies on moose to do the dirty work.

Another aspect of fire in ecosystem health, and one that I believe has been particularly key in the restoration of Stone Prairie Farm, is its role in leveling the playing field between species. It turns out that many plants actively engage in chemical warfare. In stark violation of the Geneva Convention (which they can't read), they constantly exude chemicals that prevent the germination and invasion of other species. A great prairie example is the ubiquitous goldenrod plant, which produces alleochemicals that actually drip off its leaves during the growing season, creating a toxic rain on the soil below that prevents the germination of competing grasses that would otherwise grow and shade it out. These chemicals are retained in the top couple millimeters of soil, where seeds of other plants drop. These prophylactic chemicals are neutralized by fire, thus knocking down the barrier that prevents other plants from reestablishing themselves. Fire thus nurtures ecosystem diversity, for as you push goldenrod back fifty feet, you may open territory for twenty other species to appear and flourish. For an ecosystem that had been dominated by agriculture, welcoming only the selected crops and the most aggressive agricultural weeds, fire would be essential in restoring ecosystem health and balance.

As fate would have it, while my farm and the Quetico-Superior wilderness area are nearly five hundred miles apart, they are very closely linked, at least in geologic time. In the colder climate of the most recent glacial period, some eight thousand years ago, the boreal forest of Canada and Minnesota grew much farther south, covering the very region where my house now stands. In essence, the years I'd studied those forests could have been spent on my front porch, had I been around to do it eight thousand years ago. Moreover all the prairie land that

I've been exploring, cataloging, and working in at Stone Prairie Farm is really just the ecosystem that recolonized the landscape after the glaciers receded.

⌒

From the beginning of my time on Stone Prairie Farm, in 1981, I couldn't wait to start burns, even on the initial 2.7 acres. My small prairie garden became the site of many experiments. I also burned fencerows, which the neighboring farmers did as well when they cleared the land of weeds each spring. Our techniques differed, however. An efficient and uninterested farmer would generally light the fire and then pay it no attention as it burned into the prevailing winds, working slowly around the farm until darkness, when humidity rose and the fire went out. I, on the other hand, had to dabble and experiment. I'd stand by the flame front, lighting small head fires and practicing with fires that burn at an angle to the wind, called flanking fires. I had the luxury of time—no cows to milk and no fields to disk up for spring plantings. A five-minute farmer's job was a four-hour Apfelbaum endeavor, but eventually I developed excellent strategies and a good sense of how to control fire. Or so I thought.

When I purchased the balance of the farm, my first experiments on a few acres seemed puny. I could no longer easily instigate and control a burn by myself, with a couple hundred extra feet of hose to spray down weeds and create a firebreak to prevent the fire from spreading. Over 80 acres, the front edge of the fire would simply be too long for one man to cover.

So I looked outside for help. When it was time to burn I'd get permission from the local fire department, then enlist the help of my colleagues at Applied Ecological Services to come help burn the farm. It didn't really take much enticement—as burning was part of their work, my farm served as a good training ground for them. Often when the conditions were right I'd get a call from a crew boss saying they were thinking of heading over to light a practice burn, if that was all right with me. It always was, and I'd do my part by racing off to the store for a couple cases of beers and fixings for a massive pot of spaghetti. Sometimes the burn would already be under way by the time I returned, with teams from the local fire departments often joining the AES crew and learning about fire management from them. They'd lay in fire breaks, stretches where there was no combustible fuel to feed the flames, by going to the downwind end of the 80 acres and blackening along this edge of the property, using small fires they'd put out with water. Then they'd burn each edge of the field, parallel to the wind direction. Only after a few hours of running these side fires, which would eventually keep the larger burn from getting out of control, did the real excitement begin: they'd walk to the upwind side of the property and light massive head fires.

Soon intense flames fifty to a hundred feet high would light up the night sky, drawing spectators from miles around. Often these began late on a Friday night, and within hours everyone from teenagers out cruising to seniors from a nearby retirement community would appear out on Shanghai Road, the southern perimeter road running along Stone Prairie Farm. Sitting in their cars, they would watch the flames, listening to the raging crackle, drinking beer, and enjoying the new entertainment form.

In the early 1980s, my first years on the farm, the first plants to grow back after burns were agricultural weeds, those invasive plants that have evolved in connection with specific agricultural practices and are adapted to the same conditions as the crops. My farm was surrounded by cornfields, so what came up were weeds associated with corn—foxtail, crabgrass, velvetleaf, and others. I'd stand out on my porch, look off toward the new green growth, squint my eyes, and pretend these were native prairie grasses, all the while knowing better. But after a few years these weeds thinned out and native plants—initially less aggressive than the invasive weeds—began to thrive. This occurred because most of the invasive plants are short-lived, having adapted to living with annual soil tillage practices, while the native prairie plants are long-lived perennials. While the invasives "waited" for the expected annual tillage, their seeds were shaded out by the native prairie plants that simply grew up once they were given the time.

During this period I quickly learned the meaning of friendship and felt comfortable relying on the help of others to burn the farm. But part of me rebelled inside, a part that, however irrationally, craved complete self-sufficiency. Eventually this desire got the better of me. After several years of securing help with dangled lures of beer and spaghetti, in 1993 I decided that Susan and I could, and should, burn the farm on our own. Why not? After all we'd organized successful burns many times in the past.

Susan was reluctant at first, suggesting we get others to help. But I wouldn't hear of it—I was ready to go right away. At the very least, she suggested, we should prepare the land first, mowing firebreaks on the exposed sides of the property. I had an answer for everything and managed to either convince her or subdue her protests. So together we set out for one of those unforgettable days—a day when we would both come to know the difference between a controlled burn and a wildfire.

Early that Saturday morning I listened as the weather reporter predicted the morning was going to be calm with winds from the west, gentle and cool. But sometime in late afternoon, a 180-degree change was in store, which meant winds from the east. The relative humidity—the amount of moistness of the air and consequently a measure of how moist and combustible the dry prairie plants' stems would be—was also expected to decline. The higher this measure—the more moist the air and the vegetation—the slower the fire. With the wind direction change there was a predicted shift to a very low relative humidity for southern Wisconsin, 13 percent, with temperatures of ninety degrees Fahrenheit. Hot, dry, windy conditions are potentially

dangerous for doing burns even when a full crew is working the
fire, let alone just two people. So we would be in a hurry to finish before the winds shifted.

Nonetheless, I called the local Brodhead police and fire departments and talked with the dispatch officers, letting them
know we'd be burning. I gave them our start time and told
them I would call when the fire was safely out. The woman at
the fire department, who lived nearby and knew us well, said
"good luck" and told me she'd call her husband, also a prairie enthusiast, who would probably show up to watch or even help
with the burn.

That settled, Susan and I began our preparations. We gathered the essential equipment, including "drip torches," which
are canisters full of a diesel/gasoline blend used to ignite the fire,
backpack water tanks that weighed nearly seventy pounds when
full, rakes, and "flappers" or "squashers," which are basically
thick rubber sheets about a foot square attached, like brooms, to
long handles and used to put out flames, much like snuffing out
a cigarette butt with a heavy boot sole. We also had a four-wheel
drive Ranger pickup loaded up with extra water containers and
other supplies.

Susan drove the truck slowly as I leaned from the back of
the pickup truck bed and dripped liquid fire from the drip torch
along the entire inside road margin where the prairie planting
met the dewy, matted cool-season grass. Within a few minutes
the half-mile-long east edge of the property ignited and burned
westward against the morning breeze. We repeated the treatment halfway up the south edge of the property bordering
Shanghai Road. These roads bordering the east and south sides
of the property served as a firebreak. Both edges burned slowly
and controllably, and we felt comfortable that our solitary burn
had started well.

We continued the process of the controlled burn by working
together to protect our home, barn, outbuildings, and some garden plantings that were vulnerable to fire effects. Wearing back-

pack water pumpers, Susan and I sprayed a line to prevent the fire from burning in that direction and guide the burn the other way. We set the fire on a westward course, protected the buildings, and, after an hour, proceeded to burn up the north property line.

The north line dipped down into our creek, which was bordered by a very combustible sedge and native plant fuel. We safely burned through this area, but it cost extra time to control the fire that alternately flared twenty to thirty feet and died down to creeping fires in matted moist plant matter. The weather report loomed in my mind. We began to feel the uncomfortable press of time as the fire flared and morning gave way to afternoon.

I thought a few hours remained before the arrival of the weather reporter's predicted wind change and the humidity drop, and by early afternoon we'd secured the north property boundaries. However, to achieve a 360-degree firebreak, we needed to burn the entire half-mile run of the west fence line to anticipate the wind shift to the east. Then, with the firebreak in place, the fire could wander across the farm. I pictured Susan and myself soon sitting back casually with an iced tea or a beer, taking in the dance of the fire as relaxed onlookers, just like we did when the AES crews did the burning.

As we started to burn the north half of the west property line, I noticed that the smoke rising from the prairie showed signs of the wind shifting. Instead of blowing consistently to the east, the smoke appeared indecisive; it swirled, rose vertically, then momentarily blew westward. My observations indicated the very beginning of the predicted weather change. Susan sensed my nervousness, and I detected the signs of her anxiety as clearly as the change in the wind. "We need to move faster!" I yelled. We picked up our pace to spray water and set fire behind the wet edge.

My heart began to race. The backing fires along the east edge of the property flared up visibly and marched with the changing wind toward where we worked feverishly to secure the west edge of the property. The wind shift and the intensification of the noise made it hard to communicate, and we had to shout to each other. We pushed on, struggling harder to close the remaining gap in the firebreak. But by midafternoon, the weather reporter's prediction hit the mark. Ten- to fifteen-mile-per-hour east winds blew hot smoke in our faces as we fought to finish burning the last several hundred feet of the fire break. We were so close to complete success.

Then a small, lapping flame broke rank from the leading edge and entered our neighbor's cornfield. Only the week before, they had harvested 80 acres of corn that bordered the west fence line. Since that harvest, we had recorded only dew and no precipitation. As the winds picked up and the humidity dropped, the remaining tons of dry cornstalks and leaves dried even more. Perfect tinder for a wildfire. Susan raced up the hill with the seventy-pound water tank on her back to extinguish the burning corn stubble. But as soon as she extinguished one area, another flared up. She ran back and forth, putting out one patch, then racing to another. As the winds shifted, the rebel fire angled toward wooden buildings on the neighbor's farm. Susan was losing the battle and I was out of water. So I ran half a mile back to the farmhouse, through the prairie, over hills, through the creek bottom and tangles of dense prairie vegetation, to get the pickup, more water, and the flappers.

I returned and drove fast into the field, bouncing over plowed ruts and boulders. As I arrived Susan yelled, "Out of water!" She grabbed a flapper and ran back and forth trying to stop the leading edge of fire. Spraying down the stubble also failed to put the fire out. The fire burned into the cornstalks and smoldered internally. We'd wet down the outside of the stem, but minutes later the smoldering reappeared as a new flare.

The fire burned closer and closer to our neighbor's barns and farm buildings. I felt sure we could handle it ourselves, or at least wanted to believe that. But Susan finally screamed, "Call the fire department!" and I acquiesced to reality. This was before we all had cell phones tucked in our pockets, so I sprinted back to the truck to go find a phone—lugging with me my aching pride. I raced across the corn stubble. Then, turning sharply onto Shanghai Road, I missed the edge of the driveway, caught the sharp edge of a culvert, and blew out the back left truck tire. My heart pounded like a fist trying to fight its way out of my chest. I drove fast on the wheel rim and finally made it home to the telephone.

I dialed the seven digits hastily, got it wrong, and then got through.

"Got away, did it?" said the dispatcher, as if she'd been waiting for my call.

"Yes, and it's burning toward the King family's barn and buildings," I told her. "I need to go back and help Susan. Send help."

The tireless wheel cut deep grooves in Mill Road. I could hear sirens sounding from many directions and getting closer. Minutes later, fire trucks from several towns turned into the cornfield. The volunteer firemen went right to work. They drove the tankers along the leading edge and dowsed the fire with hundreds of gallons of water. Two men raked the stubble into the burned zone to keep it from reflaring. We walked the edge with the flappers. Finally, the smoke from the smoldering cornstalks grew dark, signaling the end.

As we gathered up our belongings, the fire trucks converged around us. A dozen guys from the four trucks emerged with the swagger of accomplishment.

"You Steve Apfelbaum?" one of them asked.

"Yes," I replied. "I'm the jerk who started the fire and spoiled your Saturday afternoon."

I abashedly gave them the play-by-play.

"I nearly had a heart attack," Susan remarked. "More than once."

"I'm really sorry," I said and prepared to receive a military-style scolding.

I was totally exhausted. My pride was in shambles, and I thought that Susan had lost confidence in me. So there I stood, circled by fire trucks, firefighters, and my partner in life. For the fifth or tenth time, I apologized and thanked them all.

Finally, one of the firefighters said, "We've been watching you guys do successful burns out here for years."

"Yeah," said another. "It's no problem. It's good practice for the grass fires."

"Got me out of the house," a third said. "And there wasn't any football on today."

Some even told me they'd taken a class I'd taught on prairie burning and learned a great deal from me.

"Maybe I should take that class," I said.

"Hey, this is just a warm-up," said the first guy. "These conditions, there will be more fires today, I promise."

The next evening at a local prairie enthusiasts' potluck dinner, I learned that the firefighter's prediction had proved true. As the dispatcher put it, "There were more than thirty grass fires in the neighborhood yesterday. Yours was different—it was the only one intentionally set." All my neighbors broke into laughter. I wasn't sure if I felt embarrassed or pleased, but I joined in nonetheless. The story of my bad burn sparked other stories of prescribed burns gone wild, and I knew I wasn't the first or last fire ecologist to experience the horror of the wind changing.

Almost two decades have passed, and occasionally my enthusiasm for self-sufficiency still overcomes good judgment. That's when Susan reminds me of our harrowing experience burning the farm alone. Now, Susan and good judgment prevail. And except for the occasional memory of the embarrassing fire that got away, I feel no shame at all. For me, this personal recovery may be as important as the ecological results.

CHAPTER 10

Getting to Know Your Neighbors

The knock at the door caught me off guard since I hadn't heard a vehicle drive up. As I opened the front door, I recognized the young man as the son of a local farmer I'd once met at a chili cook-off. This farmer and his sons worked a pretty tired farm a few miles away that had been in one family longer than most of the other local farms. His son was of medium build with a strong brow and burly forearms. I tried to invite him in, but he declined politely and stood on the porch. He said he wanted to speak to me about my fields.

"That sure is a weedy mess," he said, looking out over the field.

It didn't bother me that he was so direct. I enjoyed these kinds of encounters. They gave me the opportunity to explain my work. So I tried to engage him, as I had done with many other visitors and neighbors those first couple years after planting the prairie, and would continue to do with many more.

"Yes, it's a mess," I agreed, "but it's been planted this way on purpose. Those aren't weeds, actually. They're young wildflowers and other seedling prairie plants."

He looked at me with an uncomprehending smile.

"For the next year or two it will look like that. Random. That's what it's supposed to look like. It's just getting started."

He kept grinning. He looked back over the field nervously and then smiled from ear to ear, as if he'd just remembered a punch line.

"Say, I'm not too clear on what you're saying, but I was just driving around looking for some land to rent and noticed that your fields appear to be fallow and weren't planted to corn yet this year. If that's so, would you rent that land to me for planting corn?" he asked, punctuating "corn" with a broad friendly grin.

"The entire farm has been planted. Those are young native prairie plants and wildflowers," I repeated, pinching my thumb and index finger in his line of sight like crosshairs to draw his attention to the nascent seedlings. "See how they're coming up under those agricultural weeds?"

"So, you'll just let the weeds grow instead of planting corn?" He asked this slowly as if perhaps I was the one who didn't understand the situation.

"Actually, the entire farm is fully planted, and none of it's for rent. Sorry." I had a full day's work ahead of me, and this tutorial didn't seem to be producing much fruit.

"Oh, that's too bad. Well thanks. I just figured that if it was sitting idle, I'd be a fool not to ask."

"Wait a year or two and the wildflowers will be lush and beautiful."

He stopped a second to consider that, as he patted his vest for his keys.

"What good are they? Can't sell 'em, can you?"

"Actually we do. They're a crop. We produce wildflower seeds."

"So your crops aren't in rows?" he asked. "Don't you cultivate and spray to keep the weeds down?"

"Actually, we burn the fields to keep the weeds down. Fire encourages growth of native prairie grasses."

"We used to burn our fencerows to keep the weeds down," he said, visibly pleased to finally share a point of reference. "Well, thanks, and good luck." He shook my hand and pivoted around for one last look at the weedy mess before he walked around the house to his truck.

This was a scene that would be repeated with many variations for years. Neighbors simply don't know what to make of the way we view and use our land.

A weedy mess is what most of them saw in the beginning. But after a few years the mess became so spectacular it couldn't be written off so easily. The green growths of giant ragweed and foxtail grass slowly gave way to big bluestem, coneflowers, and fifteen-foot compass plants. And each subsequent year the prairie showcased its variegated display of wildflowers from late May through early November on par with the most colorful children's kaleidoscope.

As the land changed, so did perceptions. Even the farmers took notice when the wildflowers bloomed. Neighbors, AES clients, and the occasional school group started coming around to take in the full spectrum of color and get up close to the wildflowers. We welcomed them. When we could we conducted informal nature walks. Otherwise we just let people explore on their own. In time we were conducting conservation demonstrations, proposing that interested visitors plant prairies on their marginally productive and erosion-prone farmlands, and showing how this helps restore ecological health and foster abundant wildlife.

⁓

Word got around, not only about the diversity of plant species on the farm but also about wildlife flourishing in fresh new habitats full of foraging opportunities. And where the dubious farmers had vilified the weedy mess, the hunters got excited about the prospect of shooting game. The farm quickly became the largest block of wildlife habitat in the community, so the fields were coveted for their bounteous hunting potential. I recognized the draw. I was no stranger to hunting and had occasionally invited colleagues over for pheasant hunts. But there weren't enough game animals to make the place a hunting ground for the masses. And frankly, I hadn't been encouraging all of this wildlife simply to see it killed for sport.

After a heavy frost, the prairie's autumn hues brighten the rolling hills. At about the time the hay crops and corn foliage fade to tawny yellows and browns, the prairie grasses explode in glowing waves of reddish blue and gold. Like kids in a candy store, neighboring hunting enthusiasts inevitably come knocking on our door, hoping for some of the spoils. Inevitably we'd open the door to reveal a group of men decked out in traditional plaid hunting jackets and modern fluorescent orange vests. Out the window we could see friends and dogs in the driveway, waiting for the affirmative nod that the hunt was on. But I rarely granted permission, because giving someone the green light guaranteed that dozens of friends, and friends of friends, would show up the following day asking permission.

"It's the first hunt for my eight-year-old son" was a typical refrain from a door knocker in a sporty orange vest. "Sure looks like a great place for a young guy's first hunt, what with all the rabbits and pheasants out there."

Sometimes it was coyote hunters coming round, hell bent on lecturing me about predator–prey relationships.

"Neither the pheasant populations nor the Republicans are gonna survive if the predators aren't trimmed," they'd argue.

"Sorry, but hunting just isn't allowed. The ecosystem is still quite fragile," I'd explain. "Besides, the pheasant population doesn't seem to be in decline, even though coyote and fox populations are on the rise."

They'd still try to hunt coyotes in winter anyway. Trucks

would follow a squadron of radio-collared foxhounds. When the radio signals indicated that the dogs had cornered a coyote, the trucks would swoop in, driving as close to the farm fields and yards as possible. The hunters would park on the access roads overlooking Stone Prairie Farm, while their dogs trespassed in search of coyotes seeking shelter in the prairie habitat. Again the hunters would appear at my door asking for permission to shoot the coyotes. I'd always say no, explaining that I'd only reconsider if they needed subsistence food or were addressing a wildlife disease issue that threatened ecological health.

"After all, the coyote and fox pups play with our dog, Max," I'd offer. "I can't deprive him of his friends."

I'd let them retrieve their dogs, but only on the condition that they leave their guns in their trucks.

I didn't like these run-ins. The hunters were usually disgruntled, but fortunately they always honored my requests. I did have one particularly bad experience, though, with the farmer who'd rented my land during the conversion from corn to prairie. He came over one late fall day in 1992 and asked to hunt pheasants. I said no, telling him I'd already invited some colleagues and a neighbor to hunt that same afternoon.

I thought no more about it until he reappeared later that year during deer-hunting season, determined to take advantage of the abundance of game. In an audacious move, he cut a fence and drove onto my land in an all-terrain vehicle, crisscrossing the fragile prairies in an attempt to flush out the animals. Other curious hunters had parked around the perimeter and were poised to shoot should a spooked deer flee into the open. At my wit's end, I called the county sheriff's office. Officers showed up with the game warden, who took photos of the hunters and their license plates to discourage future poaching. To be neighborly I didn't press charges for the blatant trespass. But I did get him to repair the fence, thanks to the sheriff, who facilitated our detente. After this incident the requests to hunt on the farm tapered off.

These days only a few hunters ask. It's gotten around that

hunting is not allowed at Stone Prairie Farm. Susan and I field the calls that do come in and take the opportunity to explain our philosophy. The hunters get detailed explanations of the restoration and are told that our focus is on producing high-quality habitat—and hunting experiences for our family and close friends. We even suggest they could do the same on their farms.

In an earlier chapter I mentioned the patriarch of a local farm family who disapproved of our land use. "A noxious weed patch!" he'd call the farm, only half joking. I met Carl around 1981, not long after moving in, when he was tending to his livestock on a section of the farm that he was still renting. He'd drive through my yard to get to the back pasture where he kept heifers, dry cows, and one large bull. He came twice daily from his farm a few miles south in Illinois to feed and water the livestock.

Occasionally we'd meet on the driveway and talk. He'd sing the praises of his straight, weedless crop rows and the well-maintained habitat-free fence lines. And I'd argue against his policy of leaving no acreage uncultivated, as well as his insistence that the value of every inch of ground needed to be quantified in purely utilitarian terms. I didn't try to insult his philosophy or suggest that one should get nothing out of the land except enjoyment. But I would remind him of specific examples in which farm use damaged the land, as with the silt-clogged streambed and the crumbling, tattered banks where his cows had done their damage.

I think we respected each other, even then. But our debates frustrated both of us, especially Carl. I tried to appreciate the critical reality that every corn plant, cow, or gallon of milk was an asset in a portfolio that he had inherited from his father. He made a clear distinction between subsisting off the land and producing products for markets, as his family did. I'd ask him if there could be no stronger land ethic in the face of market forces, and he'd look at me with a blend of pity and disdain. I failed to convince him, and time and time again we returned to this theme in our discussions.

Despite Carl's distaste for our land use his daughter Patricia developed a passion for wildflowers. When I first met Patricia she was eight or nine years old, shadowing her mother in their garden, carrying a child-sized basket and tending to the vegetables. While she helped with milking chores and everything else expected around an operating dairy farm, she always gravitated to the garden. Then one year when she was in high school I was surprised to find her working as a summer employee at the AES nursery. From that point on she spent a lot of time on the farm, visiting with us and walking the trails, guidebook in hand, to learn about the plants.

Eventually Carl's lease ended and our regular encounters ceased. We lost touch with Patricia as well. She grew up, as they do, and went off to college.

One evening, six or seven years later, she reappeared. She told us she was getting married and asked if they could hold the ceremony overlooking the blooming wildflowers.

"You don't think your father will find that sacrilegious?" I asked.

"Well, first of all it's my wedding!" she said, smiling. "But you know what? He's really had a change of heart over the years. Now that he's retired from farming, he's a different person. I think over time the flowers won the argument for you. Sometimes he'll even stop the car when he's driving by and get out to admire the land."

Susan and I agreed wholeheartedly. We even gave them permission to mow a small plot near the wind generator so that they'd have a clear area after the ceremony for a dining tent. My only complaint was that we'd planned a family vacation then and wouldn't be able to be there!

The wedding took place on a sunny Saturday afternoon and the prairie was ablaze in color. Some neighbors who'd attended got word back to us about the handpicked black-eyed Susans, yellow coneflowers, and bergamot that the entire family, including Carl, had picked the preceding day for the lush bouquets and the wedding party's corsages.

Thank-you letters from the bride greeted us upon our return. In them Patricia and her husband, Mark, waxed poetic about the acres of beautiful flowers and related how moved their relatives and friends had been. It was clear that the landscape had been considered a part of the ceremony.

Years afterward some of their family members were still making visits to walk the trails and learn about the flowers. Carl and his wife, after finally retiring from farming and moving into town, asked if they could collect seeds to grow wildflowers in their new garden. I suppose that besides the meaningful experience of his daughter's wedding, Carl's change in attitude was solidified by his retirement from farming. Now he no longer needed to correlate the maintenance of acreage with the generation of money, or calculate the toil that went into each bushel of corn.

Of course we helped him find the best combination of seeds for his limited garden and offered to be of assistance should he have any questions in the future, or should he wish to replenish his seed stock. We were pleased that he could stop and smell the flowers and enjoy his retirement.

Getting to know Carl and his family helped Susan and me to better empathize with the struggles of the surrounding farmers, some of whom we'd come to see at times as the opposition. Through this relationship, we saw how our experiment related to the larger landscape and how our influence was being felt in the greater community. While young startup farmers were almost entirely production oriented, the older operations began to dedicate more resources toward the care of the land. Older farmers in general seemed to be more accepting of conservation initiatives and took an interest in issues of land use and corresponding productivity.

Our prairie is actually quite cost-effective. With minimal financial investment, it provides something for every season, from roots and berries to rabbits and pheasants, not to mention an abundance of fiber. Granted, the cornfield beats the prairie in a conventional marketplace that measures short-term financial return and sees the land merely as a means of production. However, against wildflowers, or organic vegetable and fruit production, corn actually lags in value on a per-acre basis. In our current marketplace this fact is skewed by the massive government subsidies of corn, but I suppose I can't knock the farmers for playing by the rules that allow them to make a living.

Add in current climate change concerns and the imperative to reduce greenhouse gases, and the prairie wins hands down in its contribution and value per acre. On a per-acre basis, with no fertilization, irrigation, or cultivation, prairies sequester almost five times more carbon dioxide than cornfields. In fact, most cornfields are net emitters of carbon dioxide and contribute directly to soil erosion and impaired water quality. And they provide little or no wildlife habitat value. Which would you rather have next door, a thriving wildlife habitat, or a corn-flake factory?

As our reputation spread, we got a fair number of unannounced drop-ins. Many folks had "windshield" experiences. They were too shy to ask if they could walk the land and just drove slowly by. But some were so inspired that they'd come back yearly to experience the changes.

We received numerous requests from schools for field trips, particularly involving biology classes wanting to collect plant specimens. Around 1996 one unusually articulate sixteen-year-old named Justin demonstrated stunning observation skills for someone his age. We spent the whole afternoon with him on the prairie, helping him identify plants so that he could gather some for class. A week later he came over for supper and told us how impressed his teacher had been with the diversity of species he'd collected. This began a curious relationship.

Justin had grown up nearby on his father's farm. After his sophomore year his folks sent him to a rigorous college preparatory school in Kansas City, so he was only around during the summer months. As a youth I had thought about little other than ecology. In contrast Justin was more of a tech geek who loved music, computer technology, and games. We encouraged him and were always glad to have him over, in part because Noah was already off to college in Iowa by then, and we found comfort in being able to help another young man as he was beginning his journey.

Justin liked to impress us with his growing knowledge of plants. For instance, he could explain the subtle differences between various sunflower species, identifying stem characteristics and flower structures that were not easy to distinguish. Ecology was perfect for his detail-oriented mind. If he wasn't in the prairie or sitting at the table, he'd come over to dog-sit or do some gardening. Naturally, when we bought new stereo equipment, we hired him to wire up the new system.

He ended up becoming a radio station DJ in Kansas City. I'll admit I was surprised that he'd chosen such a physically circumscribed profession, given how much he enjoyed the outdoors. Still, whenever he came home to visit his folks he always found time to drop by and walk the trail. And if we'd missed him he'd leave a note wedged in the door listing the newest plants he'd identified. I was a bit disappointed that he didn't pursue ecology or a related field, but I knew that his experiences on our land had stayed with him, providing a link to the land that endured even as his daily life moved away from the prairie. I believe he'll always carry that love for nature, and share it someday with a family of his own.

⌒

Newspaper journalists also found their way to Stone Prairie Farm. After the local Janesville and Brodhead papers published articles in the mid-1990s, we received wider attention, eventually attracting major outlets like the *New York Times* and the *Los Angeles Times*. These were odd interactions for us. Even though the reporters posed thoughtful questions about the value of restoring prairies, they did so like trial lawyers who think they already know the answers. And like Carl, they tried to narrow the discussion to the question of return on investment, as if that were the only indication of success. They showed little interest in our thoughts on the nonfinancial value of our efforts and the joy we'd derived from the restored farm. But when I explained the economics of native seed production, such as the high value per pound of big bluestem grass seeds or even more valuable species, they took copious notes. Most journalists seemed resigned to satisfying their readership with simplistic results-based reporting.

We did meet some writers and photographers who seemed to understand that it was difficult to convey the scope of our achievements in a short article. Fortunately, the land often spoke for itself, punctuating an anecdote with the sudden arrival of bobolinks, bluebirds, an upland plover, or a meadowlark. When the reporters experienced nature directly in this way, they listened more intently to the pulse of life on the prairie, and their writing was influenced by the wealth of information they absorbed.

After reading a *Los Angeles Times* article, an elderly woman living in a retirement home in California sent a handwritten letter telling us how heartening it was to know that we were restoring prairies. She congratulated us and said that she wished she were young enough to visit the farm, because our work had renewed her faith in the future. It had shown her that restoration benefited both nature and humanity by correcting overdependence on monoculture and creating abundance through diversity. One doesn't have to be a revolutionary to see that the current market paradigm equating financial wealth with happiness is fundamentally antithetical to planetary health. It's common sense. Our elderly friend merely hoped that future generations would be able to enjoy the natural order that had been an inalienable right of humans for millennia. Whether we grow corn or wheat or native prairie plants, we have to recognize that we have the choice.

⌒

We have met many of our neighbors at various summertime community events. We visit the occasional county fair and thresheree, as well as other rural cultural events, such as historical "mountain man" and Civil War reenactments. Among our favorites are the local "Cheese Days," which are much more than a farmer's market. Local businesses display their wares at this festival, but the main focus is the many dairies and cheese makers that provide samples of their products. People come from far and wide to taste regional delicacies, drink locally brewed beer, and generally to celebrate the Swiss cheese-making heritage that defined the culture of this part of America and its relationship to the land.

Neighbors meet to gossip, talk about the pending corn crop harvest, and discuss politics while eating cream puffs and dancing the polka. A percentage of the money raised at these events goes to scholarship funds. For weeks afterward, the local newspapers and club newsletters run stories on the lucky scholarship winners, the overall financial success of the event, and the prize-winning parade float. AES has even joined the fun by putting together a mobile prairie display. One year, AES employees and their children decorated a truck-drawn trailer filled with thousands of pots of blooming prairie plants for the Cheese Days parade in Monroe, Wisconsin. No one had ever seen such an eco-friendly float, and it was a big favorite with just about everyone.

Overall our relationship with our neighbors and the broader culture is complex and ever evolving. The social ecosystem and our position within it change with time, finding one point of equilibrium, shifting as new factors are introduced, then establishing another, much like any natural ecosystem.

⌒

CHAPTER II

Globally Connected

Wilderness is fragile yet hearty, ever striving to reestablish itself. The persistent weeds springing up on the edges of cornfields are only a small indicator. As we cleared out some real space for wildlife on Stone Prairie Farm, much more exciting shifts began to occur. Before restoration began, we occasionally found the tracks of coyotes, Norway rats, and rabbits, but most of the tracks we saw were those of white-footed mice and meadow voles. Within a few years there were also tracks from weasels and mink dotting the spring brook after a fresh snow, not to mention the occasional badger. And soon the birds made themselves known.

Early one Sunday morning in April 2005, I received a call from my neighbor Brad, a local bird club member and avian enthusiast. He reported that one of the whooping cranes from a returning migratory flock of seven on their way back from Florida had spun off from the group, perhaps because of injury, and was lounging in the Sugar River bottoms a few miles east of my farm. It was a rare opportunity to see this endangered bird species. Brad was pretty excited, and he said that Susan and I would be able to observe the large bird without a scope as it strutted tall among the winter wheat and soybean stubble.

We dressed quickly, grabbed our binoculars, and rushed out the door. We followed Brad's directions along the backroads, and twenty minutes later we were scanning a tilled soybean field trying to locate the bird. It eventually emerged from behind a scattering of shrubs along the far fencerow, a large white bird with black wings sauntering slowly along, lowering its head intermittently to feed. Word must have spread quickly, because within minutes others began showing up. Soon we were sharing the experience with a family of churchgoers dressed in their Sunday finest, a farmer and his wife in flannel shirts and work boots, and a Department of Natural Resources employee dressed in his official uniform, who drove up in a state vehicle. He greeted the farmer, who it turned out owned the land, and joined our crowd watching in silence as the crane made its way through a patch of tall grass.

In his excitement Brad apparently had called everyone he thought would be interested, regardless of the early hour. For bird enthusiasts, Sunday is just another day. Ironically, he and his family drove up last. He parked, got out, and started motioning for help unloading several spotting scopes. Susan and I helped set up the tripods and everyone started taking turns viewing the bird up close. Personally I enjoyed watching each person's reactions to seeing the bird through the scope as much as I appreciated bird itself. One by one they seemed mesmerized by the regal, prehistoric creature. And there was yet another level of appreciation at being able to share the moment together as a group.

"Well, I guess I can't disc up the soil today," the farmer finally said, breaking the silence. "Not while that beauty is visiting."

Moments later he gazed through the scope and added, "I guess planting my beans will have to wait too."

This evoked appreciative chuckles. But what he went on to say next amazed me.

"If I could help guarantee that this bird would regain its health, I'd think about making some land available so it had a place to come back to each and every year. Maybe my farm should be planted to those prairie grasses and wildflowers you got going on your land, Steve. If I removed my tiles and levees, the lower ground could flood and restore to wetland."

It was shocking. I'd never heard a farmer make a statement like that. I was so intrigued, plotting out and picturing the results of his unsolicited suggestion, that I didn't even notice our viewing party had swelled to over twenty people. I stepped a few yards away to have a better look at that crowd. Everyone was standing shoulder to shoulder, jockeying for a chance to look through one of the scopes. That ancient bird had everyone's undivided attention, and they seemed to know how rare an opportunity this was. Here they were at seven o'clock on a Sunday morning, unconcerned with anything other than that solitary crane.

Naturally I was pleased that day. But I was also puzzled. Why does it take the threat of extinction to rally humans to the side of endangered species? I think it has something to do with active involvement. There I was standing with a group of enthusiastic folks, all inclined to birding, in the presence of a rare species only recently coming back from the brink of extinction. This would be a case of preaching to the choir, except that the bird had also charmed the farmer.

It's no wonder that people take little interest in things that exist beyond their range of experience. You have to enter into the natural world if you are to appreciate it. If the kind of collective mentality that swept over the birders that morning had prevailed a hundred years ago, this species would never have become imperiled. The population of this endangered bird, once abundant in midwestern prairie and wetland ecosystems, had dwindled globally to a low of sixty-four birds, victims of rampant habitat destruction, the brutal effects of pesticide, and inadvertent hunting. Their comeback story is famous. Dedicated groups began captive rearing programs, that is, capturing wild birds and getting them to complete their life cycle in pens. Their caretakers, concerned the juvenile birds would imprint themselves on their human caretakers, dressed in crane puppet suits while feeding and grooming the babies. Scarcely a hair away from extinction, and still vulnerable because so little genetic stock remained available for the captive breeding, flocks of these reared cranes followed humans across miles of inhospitable developed and agricultural lands from the Wisconsin breeding site to a wintering ground in Florida. While still endangered, and rare in the wild, there are now several hundred whooping cranes, including the fellow we watched that morning. But it could have gone the other way and they could have disappeared forever. That fate befalls many other species each year.

I'm not sure why more people care now than before, but I'm glad for it. Years ago species preservation was a non-issue, a fringe cause for a dedicated few. Now the scale of human concern is larger than ever. Perhaps with the advent of modern telecommunications, the Internet, and globalization, more and more people are finally seeing how interconnected everything is. Concern for one species reflects concern for every species. Endangered species still concern only a minority of us, but somehow now that things are literally heating up, the trend is toward action.

Brad roused me from my contemplation of that farmer's epiphany that morning, motioning me to join him and a few of the others. The soulful proclamation had fueled a small group discussion of what it would take to actually restore the hundreds of bottomland acres and create a permanent future home for the cranes. The farmer had apparently been brewing this idea for a while. With Brad and the DNR official listening attentively, he told us about other sightings he'd made in recent years, and said that he'd really like to follow through with this restoration. We all agreed that we would like to help him do that and committed on the spot to working with him to achieve this goal.

When the churchgoers decided it was time to go, there was a sudden mass exodus of children being ushered away by parents eager to eat brunch or get on with their day's agendas. After Brad and the DNR official left, Susan and I stayed a while longer to watch in silence with the farmer and his wife until the whooping crane strutted behind some shrubs and disappeared from sight. At that point, I worried aloud that perhaps it had simply vanished.

"I hope not, Steve," the farmer said. "I'm counting on him coming back every year and bringing his kin."

"Well," Susan interjected, "you're rolling out the red carpet. He'd be a fool not to take the invitation."

He laughed at that and said that he looked forward to hearing what the group would come up with. It was clearly a relief for him to put his idea out for others to hear. I thanked him for his inspiration and courage on that fine morning. On the drive back to the farm for some brunch of our own, I couldn't help wondering if that crane knew exactly what he was doing when he broke off from his flock.

In October of the same year, ultralight planes guiding a juvenile flock of whooping cranes flew south over Stone Prairie Farm. This was part of a program in which the cranes were being trained to fly new migration routes. The innovative intervention has been quite successful, and it has strengthened and protected their numbers by diversifying the flocks.

Two of my AES colleagues were pheasant hunting that morning when the two ultralight planes flew a hundred feet overhead, trailed by seven cranes in formation. Susan and I, unfortunately, were reading and buried in preparation for a busy upcoming week. We did notice Max racing to the window to look up at the sky; at least he got to appreciate that unusual sight.

We were confident that the birds had looked down at our prairie and considered stopping. Our farm ecology would have reminded them of Wisconsin's Wood County and the Necedah National Wildlife Refuge, where they first summered. I believe animals have excellent memories. I hoped that this anomalous prairie regenerated here in the middle of corn country had made an impression and provided the cranes with hope that for the first time in over a hundred years, the land was being readied, for them, and not exclusively for humans.

The following fall I finally got to see the ultralights guiding the next migrating flock of juvenile whooping cranes. From the living room window, I watched them soar low and slow over the riparian strip. I could clearly see the cranes turning their heads from side to side eyeing the prairie. That moment further reinforced my belief that the cranes were cognizant of this valuable habitat. And presumably they would have been equally aware of other, bigger projects, such as the 7,300-acre Kankakee Sands restoration in northwestern Indiana. This is a restoration AES was hired to design and help construct for the Nature Conservancy.

Ours is not an isolated effort. Stone Prairie Farm is a stepping-stone. Our 80 acres are a small but vital part of a process of recovery with global implications, and there is no time to waste. In my lifetime, I have witnessed few recoveries of endangered animal species—most remain on the endangered species list or, worse, join the untold thousands of species forced into extinction by the onslaught of humanity.

Later on in the afternoon, after the ultralights cruised over, Louis, one of our on-site restoration specialists at AES, phoned. He was beside himself and could barely get his words out from the excitement. He was calling to tell us that the same cranes we'd watched just hours before had landed in the new prairie and wetland plantings we'd developed in the Kankakee Sands project. As it would turn out, the pilots let the cranes remain there for a few days. This was another confirmation that the stepping-stones were real. I later learned from Louis that the pilots of the ultralights told him it was the cranes who decided to land, not them—and that none of the cranes were eager to leave the restored landscape days later.

Ecosystem and animal health are inseparable. Each needs the other to survive. Besides restoring hydrology and plants, AES and some of our colleagues had been laboring with other groups such as the Michigan Department of Natural Resources, the nonprofit Peregrine Fund, and others to bring back populations of the elusive minklike pine marten in the Upper Peninsula of Michigan, as well as increasing peregrine falcon populations across the midwestern states. We've given a boost to the wolves as well, but they get most of the credit, coming back on their own in parts of the Midwest.

We have contributed to this wildlife recovery by planting tens of thousands of acres of prairies, wetlands, and forests with indigenous plants that are otherwise becoming increasingly rare. These habitats attract the wildlife, which feeds the regenerative cycle of these plant species. Since endangerment is the direct result of habitat alteration, contamination, and loss, restoration of habitats promises that wildlife populations will rebound within integrated plant and animal communities. The benefits of such projects are far reaching, and the interconnection of multiple projects is essential. Well coordinated, we can truly reconnect nature on a large scale. Each one us has the potential to do more than he or she thinks. This reconnection with the land, and of the land, starts and ends with a heartfelt commitment. Success depends on a generosity of spirit. The return on that kind of personal investment is more rewarding than that of any retirement funds backed by financial markets.

All it really takes is people like the farmer who wanted to do his part to save a whooping crane. In his case it ended up taking a year to get the wheels rolling, but eventually the State of Wisconsin ended up buying the property for restoration. Now the farmer's dream will become a reality.

PART III

Preparing for the Future

☞

CHAPTER 12

Gone

Susan and I have had many great successes in the restoration of the farm. Nonetheless we have reason to fear for the future of this land, and to look skeptically at methods of assuring its sanctity over the long term. Despite the best of intentions, the devastation of fragile ecosystems can happen swiftly, often without warning or resolution.

In late spring of 2004 I was on the road helping Trust for Public Lands evaluate a potential greenway plan for Camden, New Jersey. While I'm away, which can be a couple days each week, I try to call Susan nightly to discuss meetings, to report progress on projects, and simply to hear her voice. This particular evening I hadn't even managed to say hello when Susan blurted out that something bad had happened.

"Catastrophe," she said. "Across the street. All the trees. Piled in a heap." It was all she could do to get out these few words. I could hear her breathing, feel the struggle for language.

"Don't go out there until I'm back, okay? We'll go together and check out the situation."

After hanging up, I pictured how the prairie had looked that first afternoon I'd come to the farm, back in 1981. My mother had been poking around the house, clucking her tongue at its dilapidated condition. I wandered off, drawn across the street to the gentle rise above the prairie. As with the clear-flowing spring by the house, that spot had struck me with a sense of mystical and historic significance. There was an undeniable energy, as if the land remembered the elk and bison that grazed there and the spirit of the Native Americans that had hunted them in the tall grasses for many hundreds of years before the European settlers' arrival. The ancient boulders and the trees couldn't have been laid out more harmoniously. It was a rare glimpse back at the historic nature of the larger landscape, a place of solace. Just knowing that that sanctuary existed provided stability in my life.

In my worldview, the hillside prairie across the street was a special place, a symbolic extension of our land because of its interrelation with our farm's ecology. That hillside was a major highlight on my first visit to the farm and a powerful influence on my decision to move there.

After agonizing briefly, I shook off my reverie and managed to concentrate on the work at hand in New Jersey. I didn't give any further thought to the conversation with Susan until I'd flown back from the East Coast and was driving home from the Madison airport, my heart racing, fearful of what I'd find.

About a half mile from the farm, as I drove south on Mill Road, I actually started shaking and had to open the car window for the slap of fresh air. Coming over the hill, I saw immediately that the magnificent hill prairie had been bulldozed. Not just the trees along the perimeter—the entire north slope up to the hilltop had been flattened. Just a few days before, the north slope was pristine and ecologically diverse, having somehow escaped ever being plowed or grazed by livestock. It was a showground for scores of blue-eyed grasses, lead plants, sandwort, dozens of shooting star plants, and a few pasque flowers, as well as hundreds of birdfoot violets and at least seventy other plant species. Now it looked naked, raw, the way land does before construction begins.

My thoughts turned immediately to Larry and Dory, the neighbors who owned that swath of land. We'd always had good relations with them, and they knew how much we cared for the land. I couldn't believe that they had suddenly decided to sell off the lot. I was overwhelmed by sudden deep despair. In my shock I drifted past our driveway and pulled up to the edge of the destruction. It was a massacre, a slaughter of uprooted plants and exposed glacial granite boulders. Torn plants lay bare and exposed, with root systems shriveling and vital moisture escaping into the atmosphere. It appeared that the earthmovers had scraped the upper few inches of topsoil and pushed it down to the lower north face of the prairie to cover a gravel extraction pit that had been created twenty-eight years before and left open. This was the only evidence of hope—that the assault had been shallow, the bulldozer appearing to have snapped off only the tops of many plants, leaving the root systems relatively intact.

I couldn't imagine getting back into the claustrophobic car, so I walked back to the house, where I found Susan, equally distraught, ranting about her unbearable day at the office. Depressed as we'd ever been in our time together, we walked back silently to the devastation to make a detailed assessment of the damage and determine what level of recovery was possible. We actually crept on hands and knees through the dozer-flattened plants to see what remained. The experience was far more primal than any other investigation I'd ever done, more personal and pressing. I wanted to know everything, inventory every root. By the end we'd decided that at least the south, east, and west slopes were largely recoverable, with many patches relatively intact.

These findings gave us cause for optimism. But my fury with Larry and Dory was overwhelming, and I couldn't wait to confront them. I had particularly admired Dory's love of flowers and bluebirds, and of prairie life in general. I couldn't fathom that she and Larry could be a part of this destruction but was so frazzled that I knew I couldn't talk to them in my present mood. I kept asking myself why, as images of bison and elk and flocks of passenger pigeons ran through my mind. Their prairie occupied the promontory directly above the perennial springs on our land and had played a central role historically in the larger landscape.

⁓

When I started the restoration of Stone Prairie Farm in 1981 I was young and energetic. There were immeasurable amounts of work to be done, but any lack of financial resources was offset by my determination, patience, and creativity. Like most young people, I didn't know what aging meant, so I didn't care that recovery would take years to accomplish.

Nearly three decades later, age has crept into my step and my eyes, and forced me to stop and consider what the future will be like when I am incapable of continuing with my work. Ironically, as my visions have become realities, my once birdlike eyesight has weakened and blurred at the edges, making me more dependent on binoculars to track the flight of birds and the movement of deer. Without glasses I can't tell whether the ten thousand white flowers on the horizon are *Baptisia* or penstemon. I can still tell cows from buffalo, but in time I'll just be guessing.

Susan and I are by no means old, and our achievements are not meager. We are nonetheless concerned about what will happen to Stone Prairie Farm when we are not there as stewards of the land. Time and again I've seen how land that has been transferred to public conservation agencies and nonprofit groups by well-intentioned owners often ends up run by individuals whose enthusiasm wanes under financial or political pressure, or whose focus shifts to other pressing priorities. The missing element here is the presence of knowledgeable and compassionate people in these organizations—people with the experience to build the cooperative relationships needed to cope with the evolving issues of science-based land management. This combination of flexibility and resoluteness in restoration management is essential and cannot be achieved simply with well-crafted legalese, or by a roving ranger charged with protecting property boundaries from trespassers and arranging burns every other year.

Certainly there are real success stories of lasting commitments by those who will steward the land into the future. But these lasting commitments are typically in regions that have visually breathtaking mountains or panoramic shorelines, and where rare species dwell in unusual geologic settings with clear historical narratives. I know that an old farm field converted back to a native landscape cannot generate the same excitement, and this is terrifying. Restored farms like ours should not have to be the proverbial "baby in the basket" left on the doorstep of humanity like a needy orphan, forever dependent on the beneficence of institutional management. But I fear that is the likely fate of our little paradise, regardless of what we do before we pass away.

Indecision and discord have derailed some of the most promising and well-intentioned conservation initiatives. The experience of our friend Betsy is an example. She is one of four siblings who agreed a generation ago to a considered plan for maintaining their family's lodge and land in the Adirondacks. The plan was carefully laid, with a clear financing strategy and long-term philosophy. Scant decades later there are now sixteen owners (the siblings and their children), who haven't had an easy time and ultimately don't see eye to eye on what should be done in terms of ecology, recreation, and their financial realities. Meanwhile, of course, the land has suffered.

Even on the Leopold Reserve near Baraboo, Wisconsin, to me the most sacrosanct of landscapes, there are problems. It is designated a national historic site and has a strong board of directors in addition to familial oversight. Nonetheless it has endured years of turmoil as management, neighboring landowners,

and various state agencies have promoted their different agendas
for the land. Having seen such projects pushed to the breaking
point—whether by family infighting or the siren song of eager
land developers—I cannot bear to compromise my life's work,
despite the assurances and safeguards that an institutional char-
ter might provide.

So Susan and I make every effort to analyze each imperfect
scenario for clues that will help us find that operational balance.
What I do know for sure is that I'd fret less if Stone Prairie Farm
were part of a larger, healthy ecological system. There is strength
in numbers, and expanding our efforts beyond the farm to a
broader campaign of recovery could place Stone Prairie Farm in
the middle of tens or hundreds of thousands of acres of restored
lands. This larger landscape wouldn't necessarily need to be a
wild place, but landowners would have to support it by encouraging healthy ecosystems and maintaining biological diversity.
This goal could manifest itself in numerous ways, some of which
are discussed in chapter 15 on ecological reserves. In the mean-
time, Susan and I will keep doing what we are doing. We will
discuss strategies with friends and colleagues and solicit funds to
build a financial endowment for the future upkeep of the land.
We will continue to seek out like-minded allies and staff who
share our specific vision and will generate more ideas and enthusiasm toward our lofty but essential goals. Just as diversity rules
the day in nature, we will corral our eclectic and flexible human
resources, who never tire of integrating new information and
strategies as the future unfolds. If nature truly abhors a vacuum,
then we will fill the voids with unwavering compassion and
commitment.

⌒

The destruction of the prairie across the street was particularly
frustrating for me, as I had spent two years trying unsuccessfully
to convince Dory and Larry to sell that acreage to me. I even
tried to entice them with the promise that they could continue

enjoying the land because I would be preserving it as a prairie. But whenever I brought up the subject, they'd deflect the proposition with incoherent concerns about increasing taxes and land costs and the higher cost of living. I even asked Ron, the general manager at AES, to meet with them to try and negotiate a lease-purchase agreement. Besides my personal feeling for the land, my goal was to protect the prairie and the larger farmscape by circumventing any future threats from regional development. I didn't want to push too hard, but I had to be persistent, particularly in light of an upsetting talk with Larry, who was showing interest in the subdivision strategies of a local realtor. Hearing him even consider this possibility left me uncharacteristically speechless, and so nervous that for months I had recurring nightmares about a housing complex being built next door.

Several weeks after the bulldozing, while I was away on business, Dory and Larry called and had a long talk with Susan. It turned out that they had been out of town visiting their kids when it happened and were as surprised as we were by the bulldozing. They found out that some young municipal clerk, without notification, had acted on a twenty-year-old request to the township to clean up the old gravel excavation pit on the north slope. The clerk had sent notification only after the fact, as if he were simply announcing that the city had performed some tree trimming, and offered consultation should they have any concerns regarding erosion control or cover cropping. So after all that internalized frustration, we discovered that in fact Dory and Larry shared our despair over the damage to the prairie ecosystem.

Knowing how distraught we must have been, and with the hope that our relationship was not irreparably harmed, they invited Susan and me over to explain the extent of the demolition. The four of us walked slowly up the graded slope and discussed the ramifications of the township's actions. The most upsetting fact was that it only took about three hours to destroy that twelve-thousand-year-old landscape. All we could do at that point was agree to move forward with restoration techniques. So the following week we reconvened with a few dozen pounds of local native prairie grass and wildflower seed from the AES nursery and hand seeded the exposed gravel substrates, as well as dispersing some of the seeds using the wind.

After what had happened, Dory and Larry dropped their evasions and had some frank conversations with Ron. Perhaps because the three of them were all in their sixties and had discovered that they were all suffering from similar medical problems, the couple was able to cut through their apprehension and talk honestly about their future and the land's fate. About six months later, Ron finally managed to negotiate a lease-purchase agreement.

As it turns out, their discomfort with our proposals had not stemmed from a disagreement with our vision for the land, or from some nefarious plot to sell the land to developers. It was nothing of the sort, as Ron confided to me later. Just the most human of concerns—pride and the fear of aging. Dory and Larry had been uncomfortable talking about their health issues with an energetic youngster like myself (although at forty-five I was no longer feeling like a spring chicken!). They were proud people and felt that any straight talk about departing from their farm was akin to giving up on life. It would nudge them a step closer to assisted living in a retirement home, which they weren't ready to accept. They couldn't see themselves living anywhere other than on the land. They had once hinted to me that with their children grown and independent they were worried about the quality of emergency attention available in the countryside, but I guess that I was so focused on the sale of their land that I failed to recognize the significance of their fears about mortality.

Remarkably, several years later the hill prairie did rebound as remnant species reemerged from the remaining root systems, but overall there was a diminished diversity of native prairie grasses and flowers. Susan and I continued to hike around the unaltered prairie slopes to the west, east, and south, gathering seeds of pale purple coneflower, sandwort, blazing star, puccoons, and shooting star that were ripe for collecting. We continued to disperse the seeds in the wind, attempting to replenish diversity on the embattled northern slope.

Perhaps the tragedy on the north-slope prairie would have been even more traumatic had it been my first. Though certainly no consolation, earlier experiences had alerted me to the possibility of such loss and prepared me to accept such land catastrophes and do my best to counteract them.

The first of these experiences was on another stretch of hill prairie called Healy Road, in the western Chicago suburbs, the same hill my friend Rob and I had set fire to all those years ago. In the early 1970s a rare comet was passing through the night sky. I set out with some friends and members of the local Sierra Club chapter to find a campground that would offer an unobstructed view. We looked at a topographical map to determine the highest elevation of land with a southern exposure. We found a rocky hill in the middle of some cornfields along the Fox River, just East of Dundee, Illinois. We obtained permission from the landowner to enter his property. So, carrying telescopes, sleeping bags, and food, we passed through his field by flashlight to the hilltop, where we settled in for a night of comet gazing. As it turned out, I vaguely remember seeing only some blurry and unremarkable wisps of light in the sky, which everyone said were the comet, before falling asleep in my down sleeping bag.

When I awoke the next morning to the dew-covered landscape and started rolling up my sleeping bag, I realized that I was standing amidst a brilliant display of wildflower species, including birdfoot violets, puccoons, and many others I didn't recognize. And underneath my bed, I'd flattened a patch of shooting stars (but no comets).

Enchanted by the prairie, my Sierra Club friends and I proposed to the owner that we remove the exotic shrubs in order to revitalize the still vital prairie. He was amenable to our plan, so I embarked on my first restoration project. With bow saws, we cut back box elder, buckthorn, and honeysuckle and girdled larger invading trees, which we then felled and dragged to the margins of the surrounding cornfields. For several years, I visited what became known as the Healy Road Prairie weekly. To celebrate the restoration, we returned in the winter to light a bonfire with our trimmings. Entranced by my prairie experience, I shifted my career aspirations from wildlife and veterinary medicine to native ecological systems and botany.

The crisis came twelve years later when the once welcoming owner succumbed to economic pressures and the enticement of some local developers. Rather than bulldoze the prairie with no warning, he let us know what was happening, and we were able to save a portion of prairie in the most excruciating of ways. With help from the Nature Conservancy and more than four hundred volunteers, one of AES's clients, who owned an excavating company, was retained to dig up the Healy Road Prairie chunk by chunk and replant it on the site of an abandoned gravel quarry four miles south in Elgin, Illinois, which was adjacent to a similar native prairie landscape. This salvaged sod extended the existing prairie, helping to begin the reclamation of a part of the quarry. The ordeal made the January 1990 issue of *National Geographic*. Even though the newly created Elgin prairie flourished, the project lost its allure and mystique for me. Each time I visited, a weary despondence cut short my walks.

The other project that ran aground was the 80-acre Chevy Chase Country Club prairie in Wheeling, Illinois, which had deep black soil and contained stunning remnants of wet-site prairie communities, packed with rare wildflowers and an abundance of wildlife. Similar soils in the surrounding area had long since been drained and plowed to grow corn, yet somehow the Chevy Chase prairie had been spared.

I first saw the site during my third year in college, when an old friend called to ask for help identifying some very unusual plants. I drove up from Champaign in late April of 1976 to find my friend standing among hundreds of blooming shooting stars. There were also clumps of white lady's-slipper orchids in pre- bloom (one of the specimens gathered by my friend), as well as thousands of Indian paintbrush plants. After a month spent in- ventorying, we produced a detailed plant list with photographs and a summary memorandum.

Around this time we learned that the landowner intended to destroy the entire prairie, and was in fact starting to bulldoze areas of it to accelerate drainage in order to effectively clear the prairie for sale to a developer. We frantically contacted every- one who we thought could intervene. The first person I called was Alan Haney, a professor and close friend of mine at the University of Illinois, who had been recently appointed by the governor to the Illinois Nature Preserves Commission, which was charged with identifying and securing such endangered landscapes. I sent a memorandum to Alan and also contacted two influential local naturalists and taxonomists, Floyd Swink and Ray Schulenberg, at the Morton Arboretum. This process resulted in a very aggressive campaign by the County Forest Preserve District to acquire the prairie. Sadly, during the nego- tiations, the owner continued to bulldoze the prairie without permits for land clearing. By the time the community filed an injunction for the owner to cease and desist, the prairie had al- ready been destroyed.

Still, we tried to rescue thousands of plants, and in May of 1977 I sent a letter to the Nature Preserves Commission and key local officials in a last-ditch effort to halt the destruction and protect what little remained. But my appeal went unheeded, and soon afterward a grid of roads and development displaced the prairie, leaving only a sliver of the original land protected by a power line easement.

⌒

Susan still grieves over the destruction of the north-slope prairie overlooking our farm. I can empathize, as she may never get over the trauma of her first prairie-loss experience. Years later on a fine spring morning, she gestured toward a neighbor plowing his field and exclaimed that the prairie had looked as bare as his beaten fields seeding to corn. It had healed quite well, but the scars remained. We sat in silence as the green John Deere tractor droned and plowed on its linear path. She gets emotional anytime she finds herself recounting the story of that infamous day, as if she were talking about the untimely passing of a loved one. I too find tears easily welling up in my eyes. For those who love a prairie, its passing leaves little room for a weak constitution.

⌒

CHAPTER 13

Exotic and Invasive Species

Besides the dangers presented by bulldozers and developers, there are other significant threats to the prairie. Various exotic plant species mount one of the most persistent assaults at Stone Prairie Farm. These invaders from around the world make me tense and angry, since they often present serious risks to the health of the local ecosystem. The alien species that thrive often dominate native plants and animals, depleting both soil stability and biological diversity, the very things I've struggled to heal. They use a variety of tactics, such as the chemical warfare described earlier, or growing faster than the natives and thus stealing their sunlight. One would think that such a lush green wall of vegetation would benefit soil stability, but often the reverse is true. The successful invasives tend to have shallower root systems that don't hold the soil well. As the deep-rooted natives decline, the soil becomes subject to easy erosion. I have to work quickly to counterattack and weed out these invaders that deprive the indigenous plants of their soil nutrients and light or they will take hold and overwhelm the prairie.

The migration of aggressive, invasive species is accelerating worldwide as the demands of global trade and an expanding international commerce system facilitate the unintentional spread of seeds and insects. In addition, the nutrient enrichment of the landscape from airborne and land-applied fertilizers has elevated levels of nitrogen and phosphorus, which tend to favor invasive plants. Stone Prairie Farm is a representative microcosm of this global phenomenon, which has serious implications for human and ecosystem health, implications that promise diminishing returns for world economies, particularly in the agricultural sector.

We have developed tactics to deal with this dynamic on our patch of land. Realistically it is impossible to prevent invasion, but I make informed decisions that help neutralize unwanted change, and sometimes manipulate it to my advantage. To do so I must consider many elements when fighting back against exotic or invasive species.

⌒

At daybreak, one mid-May morning I awoke to the melodious call of an oriole beckoning me to come watch the sunrise. I stumbled into the front yard just as the uppermost branches were igniting in the glow of golden morning light. The first oriole of spring, orange and black against the tattered bark, always gets my attention, even when I'm sound asleep. Max heard me and made it known that he was ready for his morning romp, so I let him out. Startled, the orioles took wing, landing some distance away in the branches of the weeping willow tree by the spring.

We followed, and soon I stood marveling at the spooky dead branches hanging from the willow tree's scarred, spire-shaped trunk. The former main section of the trunk was practically a cadaver, yet the tree still stood, splendid in the sun. A downy woodpecker poked out from one of many holes in the barkless trunk to warm itself in the morning sunlight. A few feet below the woodpecker, the head of a chickadee appeared from a silver-dollar-sized hole that was partly concealed by the young lime green leaves of a willow branch. Squawking grackles flew into the upper branches, chasing the orioles off for good. The grackles jostled the branches, staging for a short glide down to the nearby blue spruce that housed their nests. Blue jays rolled in next, addressing all assembled with their raucous clatter.

The willow is an introduced species that has become invasive in some locations of the country, and my general response would be to cut it down and plant a native. But this tree is so beautiful, and such a hub of animal activity, that I've let it stay, year after year. Originally it was a cutting that the previous owners of the farm had planted. They'd stopped at a garage sale on their way up from Chicago sometime in the early 1970s, and along with a couple of cast-iron skillets they'd been given a willow shoot. They'd dug a shallow hole and stuck it in the ground where it now stands. Artesian springs run a few feet beneath its root system; otherwise it's well drained and dry at the surface. A looping gravel driveway meanders beneath its outermost branches, and Susan and I must be careful to park well beyond the distance that a respectable wind might carry falling limbs.

Death has often seemed imminent for the willow. It is constantly shedding parts of itself, a branch here, a limb there—once a twenty-foot section of the main trunk crashed down in a fierce windstorm. I can't remember how many times I've dragged away the wreckage chained behind the tractor, thinking that this time it was surely a goner. On the cusp of death, however, the tree always revives, with green buds sprouting new branches. This persistence has reinforced my compassion for the willow, and I have allowed it to grow amidst native plants because I feel as if it has earned the right to be there—and, most important, it lives in peace among the other species on the farm.

Scarred where limbs have fallen off, it is not a perfect specimen by any means, but from our porch it complements the landscape. Susan and I relish its organic twisted form, comparing it to a nonagenarian with a teenager's flowing mane because once the numerous new branches grow, a supple curtain of young, elongated yellow-green leaves hides the gnarled and stalwart hulk. Beneath all that virgin growth, it's amazing to see how long dead rotted limbs remain on the trunk, especially as willows are not known for the strength or durability of their wood. I often wonder if it's immortal, able to continue this cycle of decline and regeneration indefinitely. It falls into the category of "living dead" that I assign to places or things that are hovering in the shadow of death.

Overall, I have been a reluctant lumberjack because the farm had few trees to start with, and they are important resting spots for migratory birds. They also shade the house on hot summer days and protect the woodland wildflowers that grow beneath it, such as phlox, jack-in-the-pulpit, and bloodroot.

Some exotic plants, such as this willow, remain innocuous and are content to stay put. Others become invasive, and it is still possible the willow might someday begin to spread. Though I have accepted this individual tree, I remain wary of making hasty decisions on other loners and misfits trying to call the prairie their home. Once they cross the line and start to colonize, all sentimentalism is vanquished because of the harm they are able to inflict on the ecosystem and the economic damage they might cause. I meet the challenge head on, with whatever tools are called for—shovel, herbicide, or chainsaw.

The possibility of exotic species developing aggressive habitats is a real threat. Because of this unpredictability, I can get terribly distraught by the appearance of exotics, regardless of how charmed I am by their beauty. And since continual waves of exotic plant and animal species are still intentionally circulated, there are ongoing invasions on the land.

The pioneers started the process, introducing many species and their corresponding diseases, which tested the limits of the adopted environments. The common English plantain, or "pioneer footstep"—an oval-leaved plant that looks like a smaller-leaved, flattened hosta—is an introduced plant from Europe that has been found growing in former canoe portages as far away as the most remote North American wilderness and in pathways around log cabins and the few remaining prairie sod houses. This European perennial is only mildly invasive. Many other exotic plants are nearly untamable. As a result some native plant communities once thought to be impenetrable because of their dense and long-established root systems are now being overrun. One of the new threats on our farm is reed canary grass, which as an invader is the equivalent of a malignant cancer. When it first appears in moist floodplain soils along the spring brook, it initially seems harmless, establishing itself only in small isolated colonies. Then, in a sudden rampage, these disparate patches coalesce, and the native sedges and wildflowers are consumed.

Not only have we brought in invasive species, we have also inadvertently laid the groundwork for the invasion in many ways. Before the exotic species even arrive, many native plant communities have been weakened through livestock grazing and the particularly devastating effects of agricultural runoff, which infiltrates the soil with high levels of herbicide, fertilizer, and sedimentation. Natural immunities are thus undermined, and sadly there are no effective antibiotics for the plant and animal communities in developed, agricultural, or other altered landscapes. (On the positive side, it is worth noting that some native plants resemble exotic species in their propensity to fight back, invasively counterattacking after environmental disturbances. Black-eyed Susan and evening primrose, for instance, are biennials that cannot be controlled with fire. Like garlic mustard, they effortlessly reseed themselves and persist despite focused management and against all odds. Transported to another ecosystem these might be dreaded invaders we would fear. On their home turf we cheer their resilience.)

What is the process of invasion? Reed canary grass provides a good example on prairie land. Recognizable by its broad leaves and coarse growth, reed canary grass is unlike any native plant. Once established it disregards environmental gradients and habitat distinctions and establishes itself easily everywhere it can reach. It manages this rapid spread in a number of ways, reproducing with rhizomes—underground root systems—as well as seeds. Its growth pattern generally follows nutrient-enriched surface waters and sediments, but it will also invade well-drained soils. We have even witnessed canary grass invading from downstream into the upper reaches of our spring brook and into adjacent uplands. This unusually diffuse pattern led me to ponder its mechanisms for seed dispersal. Wind seemed unlikely, and the stream ran in the wrong direction. Then one day I saw Max tromp through a patch of ripe reed canary grass. The following week the house was littered with the shiny grayish-black seeds that he had scattered everywhere: in our bedsheets, rugs, couches, anything covered with cloth. And adorning all my clothing, of course—a couple weeks later I had a project interview with the City of New York. I became so irritated by a prickly object in my shirt that I couldn't focus on my notes until I excused myself and retrieved a seed fragment with a strand of Max's hair. All of this gives me a much clearer understanding of how important raccoons, opossums, foxes, coyotes, and deer are in disseminating the canary grass, as well as other exotic plants.

None of the fields of Stone Prairie Farm, or the neighboring farms on this side of the drainage divide, contained any canary grass when we arrived. However, an isolated individual plant, perhaps seeded by birds or coyotes, will occasionally sprout along game trails that parallel the stream margins and spread radially from the nexus. I'm hypervigilant in combating this invader as soon as I notice it. First I'll pull the plants up by hand, or mow the patch if it's large enough. This prevents it from reseeding but doesn't kill it. To do so I'll return at the right time of year and spot spray or brush the intruder with herbicide.

One spring morning Susan and I drove to a farm a few miles to the north where we thought there might still be some patches of wild prairie, with the concomitant profusion of native species. We'd spotted this land from the road some time before, intrigued by the prominent bedrock cliffs we could see cradled back in the dark recesses of the valley. When a chance encounter with the landowner allowed us to ask if we could hike the land, his "yes" was a welcome invitation to explore. We began our hike at a sandstone outcropping faced with draping ferns. On the ridge top we discovered a tall, dense planting of crown vetch, a purple flowering species commonly seeded along highway embankments. It grew in a dense dark-green profusion, spreading out over longer distances than most other plants with running root systems do. This plant forms billowing green foliage with telltale purple flowers, sometimes looking like soft, cushy, gently-mounded green snow drifts.

We walked along the ridge for about a mile, stopping to peer through the occasional breaks in the monotonous wall of crown vetch. On the other side we hoped to locate patches of the dry prairie community that historically grew on similar south- and west-facing bedrock bluffs. We spotted numerous plants there—remnants of little bluestem grass, clumps of northern dropseed grass, and Indian grass—the seeds of which we had in abundance back at AES. Then, unexpectedly, we spied something remarkable, a lone birdfoot violet plant, peeking out between a few clumps of grass. It was a marvelous and bittersweet discovery, as this plant was the sole survivor of a species that had likely been prevalent across this shallow bedrock landscape many generations ago. The crown vetch, it turns out, had been intentionally planted by the farmer in the 1970s to help stabilize fields in areas where heavy cattle grazing had resulted in serious erosion. But now the vetch had completely overrun that patch of prairie and choked out the violets altogether.

Federal agencies have routinely introduced plants like canary grass and crown vetch, European brome, multiflora rose, pine plantations, and numerous others—with utter indifference to their effect on the diverse native plant communities. And as we had seen countless times, the exotics had flourished, mercilessly dominating the native flora. Susan and I realized that if we left the violet in place it too would be overrun, so we dug it up and moved it to Stone Prairie, where it could be assured a more certain future. The decision to dig it out of its natural environs was difficult, but we felt it was the only choice in such a hopeless situation.

Even exotic plant species that are introduced inadvertently can sweep across the land with ease. Popping up sporadically, individual plants such as wild parsnips have steadily marched down road margins as their small waferlike seeds are carried forward by the whirl of passing cars and trucks, spawning thousands upon thousands of siblings. In addition to animals, the wind acts as carriers, allowing the plant to invade neighboring hayfields. Only the annual soil cultivation in corn and soybean fields and the shade of dense woodland environments has foiled the parsnip.

Other than the garden vegetables and orchard plants, and a few cover crops such as winter rye or barley, we've reduced avenues for invasion by exotic plant species on the farm. This cuts down significantly on the proliferation of species like white mulberry, multiflora rose, and tartarian honeysuckle, which were originally introduced to North America as cultivated ornamental plants.

When multiflora rose and honeysuckle shrubs display their telltale red fruits, it's a signal that they're going to spread across the land, since the birds are only too eager to comply by ingesting the fruit and dropping the seeds far afield. One October afternoon I found a large honeysuckle bush and two multiflora rose shrubs laden with bright red fruit growing in the middle of the prairie. I returned immediately to the barn for the tractor, my leather gloves, a lopper, and paper bags. Using the front-end loader on the tractor, I hooked the bucket onto the base of the honeysuckle's thick main stem at the soil surface and pulled the six-foot-tall plant and its entire root system out of the ground. After the fruit was removed from the rose shrubs, these too were yanked from the ground, roots and all. It took a few hours to collect the ripe rose hips in paper bags, but Susan and I enjoyed burning them in the woodstove along with the honeysuckle. It takes great vigilance to repel the invaders, and one must celebrate every victory!

The economic impact of exotic species in the United States totals hundreds of billions of dollars annually. If you want to find a career with excellent job security and an opportunity to be outstanding in your field, take on invasive species management. Most restoration projects require large investments for the control, reduction, and management of invasive species. The costs for this service are rising rapidly and expected to skyrocket in some parts of the world, where invasive species management may require Herculean efforts for decades to keep land available, even for economic uses such as farming.

In part this is because we as a society have ignored and underestimated the global impact of invasive plants, bacteria, and certain viruses, so we have been slow to guard against them. Many invasive species are even welcomed in, with no thought of their potential threat. They lie low as their populations grow and spread until reaching a point of critical mass, when they are capable of exploding over the landscape. For example, reed canary grass was widely distributed to farm owners by U.S. farm agencies without consideration for the consequences. Rather than turning to local native species, they simply provided this nonnative species to stabilize waterways. For a few decades the stream courses looked stable at first glance. But where the rubber meets the road is at and below the soil surface. There reed canary grass is problematic. Its shallow roots bind only the top couple inches of soil rather than extending down for many feet. It also has very few stems per square foot compared to native grasses and sedges, which have much denser growth patterns. So the land looks lush and green from above while soil is actually being swept away beneath the stems.

Managers of natural areas eventually began to recognize that this species was lying in wait, multiplying, and ready to explode. In the mid-1980s I published the first detailed account of the ecology and management of the grass, predicting that it would become a serious threat to biodiversity in nature preserves, national parks, and private lands. Reed canary grass has since invaded sensitive alpine meadows in Washington State's Olympic National Park and elsewhere. Waterfowl and other birds and wildlife are declining in national wildlife refuges and other public and private lands in direct proportion to increases in this invasive grass. I now receive over a hundred pleas for help with this problem from farmers and land managers each year. I have made countless phone calls offering to provide the results from our studies on how to manage this rampant species. I've copied and forwarded a barrage of the letters and e-mails I've received with people's personal stories of exasperation. Still the agencies are slow to react.

Restoration has its critics. Many question our ethics and even accuse us of "playing God" by determining which plants and animals are desirable. But as we study in detail the effects of ignorance, it is clear to us that we have to make intentional decisions to restore plant and animal communities and reduce invasive plants and animals. Any decision about land use and crop selection favors one species or set of species over another. But bringing in an exotic set of crops always entails the risk that they will become invasive and have a major negative impact economically. So our definition of ecosystem health clearly prioritizes ecological settings with a prevalence of native plants and animals, both because it seems right to be in tune with nature and because it has long-term economic benefits.

⁓

Not long ago, I participated in a tour to educate corporate executives and municipal officials on the ecological changes they could make in their communities with regard to property management. When the buses parked in front of the corporate headquarters of a Chicago-based concern, everyone got out to admire a new project that replaced lawns with wildflowers, which has become the rage for so-called trendsetting corporations trying to revamp their images.

Instead of an expansive lawn, we stood before a 20-acre planting dominated by dame's rocket, a European import in the mustard plant family, which was blooming in shades of purple, pink, white, lavender, and blue. Very colorful indeed, but I became quietly furious as I stood there among the assembled group listening to their exclamations of approval for the "lovely wildflowers" and the pitch of the representative from an esteemed local landscape architecture firm responsible for the design. True, this was a remarkable turnaround—the planting replaced expanses of expensive lawn that had required ongoing care and management to deal with environmental impacts ranging from fertilizer runoff to air pollution generated from weekly summer mowing. But while I was pleased to see this attempt to change direction and adopt progressive policies, they had failed in the details. Dame's rocket was a horrible choice that wouldn't fit the environmental intent of the design.

I didn't want to say anything negative in that setting, where environmentally conscious and civic-minded citizens were trying to demonstrate how concerned corporations could be leaders in ecological stewardship. But it's not always easy for me to withhold my thoughts when I'm impassioned about something, and I couldn't manage to keep quiet.

"I really don't intend to chastise or embarrass anyone, but beautiful as this all seems, it raises real concerns for me."

Things got very quiet. There was a sense of brows furrowing.

I'd opened my mouth and there was nothing to do but continue in a steady, friendly manner.

"This is a wonderful redirection we are witnessing here, to switch out unsustainable lawn for lower-maintenance flowers. But the details are seriously wrong. You've planted dame's rocket, which is beautiful, and appears to be a healthy wildflower that fits the environment. In fact it is an exotic plant that has invaded state reserves and critical conservation areas around the Midwest. There's an inherent conflict here. While huge efforts are ongoing to control its rapid proliferation, projects such as this one are encouraging its use by getting people to like the way it looks."

Dead silence ensued. Finally a businesswoman broke the silence, and a productive discussion began.

"So you are saying this successful planting may have used the wrong species?"

"Exactly. And I'm sorry if I seem aggressive, but I've just spent the last three weekends surgically removing each and every dame's rocket plant in a southern Wisconsin scientific area, where its invasion is associated with the steady decline of rare plants. It's agonizing work! So I'm a little riled up."

"I'm not sure I understand the problem," ventured another one of the spectators.

"This plant has been a traditional farmstead garden flower for over a hundred years, which is why it probably looks familiar to you all," I said. "Just in the last decade or so it has become unruly, even ambitious. It has begun invading our most precious and important midwestern natural areas."

"Why would it suddenly start spreading if it's been around all this time?"

"We're not entirely sure why this happens, but it does. So a species may seem sedate and well behaved for decades. Then all of a sudden, within a few years really, it seeds into adjacent landscapes. Presto, it's coming up everywhere. My best guess is that nutrient levels of nitrogen in the soils finally reach a tipping point that favor this plant."

"And they kill the native species, Mr. Apfelbaum?" the businesswoman asked.

"Let's take garlic mustard, for instance, which is a common invasive relative of the dame's rocket here. The mustard family produces a number of compounds that act as what we call biofumigants, killing off many organisms in the soil and altering its microbial communities. Once the soil chemistry shifts on a large enough scale, the native plants species begin to decline and the invasive mustard takes over. This is clearly contributing to the decline of native plant diversity."

"I'm not alone in thinking this is a problem," I continued, scanning the crowd for skeptical expressions. I looked to the representative on hand from the U.S. Fish and Wildlife Service, which was a co-sponsor of these corporate efforts. "Many scientists believe that this is just the beginning of a greater assault on our ecological systems. I hate to be so blunt, but the truth is that this planting is a clear example of good ideas and bad details."

The government official nodded in agreement with my concern over the invasive species issue. But he clearly had a more political agenda. He told the group how pleased the Fish and Wildlife Service was to have this level of corporate commitment to this project and reiterated his organization's intention to make it successful. Perhaps he was simply being more tactful than me by portraying this corporate shift as setting a good precedent. To him, it seemed, the invasiveness issue was a secondary consideration in this preliminary stage of the project, and he may have simply assumed that in due course the details of the process would be refined as things moved forward.

Conversations broke out on the side. One between an executive from the host corporation and their designer was a bit tricky, with the corporate executive commenting on the apparent beauty being undermined by the larger problem. "What can you do to fix this situation?" the executive asked.

I didn't hear the designer's answer, but his body language looked very defensive.

I was somewhat sorry that my lecture had embarrassed well-meaning people trying to create beautiful landscapes in a well-intentioned project. But I didn't really mind opening that can of worms. It would have been unconscionable to remain silent. This was another clear example of decisions being made with little thought as to the obvious consequences. And what made it all the more infuriating for me was that design professionals had initiated this, and they should have known better.

⤢

Susan and I seized on an opportunity to convert a monocultural landscape into a small paradise teaming with hundreds of native plants and animal species. It took vision and a great investment of time and hard work. But once aided, nature itself joined in the effort—for instance prairie ants have returned and they help in the restoration process by transporting the seeds of the violets across the landscape, so we are beginning to see the greater landscape bobbing with the spring blooms of thousands of birdfoot violets.

But nature can't undo all of our devastation alone. We must act, helping it regain the ability to take care of itself.

Like other parts of the world, North America has experienced many invasions of animals, molds, and viruses as well as plants: the European earwig, the West Nile virus, chronic wasting disease in deer, and canine distemper in indigenous gray and introduced red foxes, and in timber wolves. Starlings have displaced red-headed woodpeckers and other cavity nesters, and carp have muddled the waters once used only by native fishes. There are countless nonnative earthworms in the soil. The list goes on and on: houseflies and house mice, the voracious European green crab, and the Chinese mitten crab. And let us not forget the ironically named Norway rat, originally from China, which has spread throughout the contiguous forty-eight states since its unintentional introduction as a ship stowaway in 1775.

Both these invaders and exotic plant species, brought in by

the world's incessantly mobilizing and globalizing societies, have had profound effects on our native ecosystems. How can the land withstand the invasion or ever recover from the resulting changes? According to fundamental ecological and population dynamics theories, it cannot. If societies don't show vigilance against exotics, nature won't get a second chance.

CHAPTER 14

The Invading Humans

As concerned as I am about invasive plants and animals, their combined impact doesn't hold a candle to the damage and disruption of the single most invasive species, Homo sapiens. Human expansion has affected the entire global ecosystem. Even in our remote rural neighborhood, its progression is relentless. Large stretches of natural habitat are decimated in mere hours to make way for the new homes that sprout like poisonous mushrooms across the woodlands each year as families relocate to our area, where the houses are cheaper and surrounded by natural beauty.

Madison spreads out southward, Milwaukee westward, and Chicago and Rockford push to the northwest—all, essentially, in the direction of Stone Prairie Farm. Woodlots spring up with a new house as farmlands become subdivisions, and new roads trace the pattern of human progress. The footprints of these new developments are never meager, and as each new housing complex strips the landscape of trees, the streams turn brown with sediment. For years I have been trying to cope with my anger at these small but significant invasions. What is essential is that we learn to temper such systemic assaults and create conscientious communities that will commit themselves to alleviating the damage they cause.

I clearly can't stop this flood of people "returning" to the land; the politics and economics are insurmountable. Instead Susan and I try to invite newcomers to our region to join us in pursuing ways to both sustain the land and allow for economic development. We have wooed land developers and policymakers, and spoken with newly arrived neighbors deciding what to do with their land. We use our revitalized prairie as an example, hoping to inspire others to respect the natural beauties and limitations of their own lands and restore them for posterity. This has helped the surrounding community change in exciting ways. There are now many of us working together with shared goals, each person aware of their potential contribution to the larger conservation project.

Most communities, however, are eventually divided and conquered by the lure of development. Sadly, the battles between those concerns coveting real estate investment and those skeptical of unchecked development disrupt both human communities and natural environments. Thus our conflicts become nature's problem, inevitably becoming our problem again in the long term. Perhaps humans need to experience the clear effects of environmental destruction firsthand to take notice. Perhaps cooperative efforts will only be spurred when living standards decline noticeably, not only in the poorest nations but in the richest: when coastlines are saturated with toxins and freshwater sources are permanently soured; when particulate levels in the atmosphere become unbearably high for human habitation, and nature's built-in filtration and humidification systems break down to a shocking degree.

Our species is quick to act, but slow to learn. Where human enterprise prevails, whether in rich countries or poor, examples abound of nature losing ground. Even where we haven't literally paved over the land, our destructive tentacles reach far and wide, strangling the natural systems. We pluck trees for wood and pulp without hesitation and bore into the earth for our mineral needs in an ever-widening radius from our population centers. One need only view the landscape from above to see the creeping battle lines. Through the lens of time-lapse photography what might seem like slow and innocuous change is actually exploding in front of our faces. Our environments are theaters of war, and humans are destroying not only the habitats of other species but poisoning their own wells.

What will people do when what we have always been able to take for granted is gone? No technology can replace what nature generously provides free of charge: climate regulation, the production of food for life forms at every level, and the enrichment of the human spirit. Although the health of the planet hasn't been completely compromised yet, we must deal with the implications of our trajectory now. We are losing traction and time with each passing day. Certainly some of our clever technologies may facilitate renewal, but the real problem, and the prerequisite for solutions, is human accountability. As Homo sapiens continue to debate the severity of pollution and global warming, arguing over what constitutes adequate scientific proof, other species continue to lose their habitats and die out, and native plants disappear in the path of invader species.

Never has a species been so keenly aware of its environment and its own fate, or had the tools to prevent its own demise. We cannot eradicate the human footprint, but we can mitigate the damage. The journey will entail a huge reversal of course, which will steer us into uncharted waters. If we are to do so, sustainability must become the global mantra. It must flourish at the local level to allow restoration efforts to take hold. Our species needs to show contrition but remain optimistic so it is possible to develop collective strategies for reconciliation with the land.

How do we get there? Well, if you've heard the phrase "Think globally, act locally," then you have the basic direction you need to get started. The trick is that people must actually act. Polls suggest that the vast majority of Americans think of themselves as environmentalists. If we were all to truly act that way, we could make enormous changes, on our own lands and in local agencies. The increase in this environmental self-identification is one of many great strides that have been made in the past two generations, strides that are necessary to counter the relentless march of corporate "progress," and its reckless conversion of natural resources into consumer goods.

Social consciousness needs constant stirring up, for we live in a culture of convenience, and convenience breeds apathy. Once started, however, we can achieve great things. The Internet is an invaluable tool, allowing the rapid dissemination of information and facilitating the creation of networks of concerned individuals. Thirty years ago, we had to take the process one project at a time. Now we can coordinate many simultaneous efforts. Ultimately we must educate those around us and inspire them to work for change. This change happens with each individual who is inspired to act.

The few woodlots that remain in our neighborhood belong mainly to retired farmers. Two of the closest ones were sold some time ago and partially razed for oversized homes. The environmental devastation was significant. One house landed directly on top of the second-largest local population of goldenseal, a threatened plant in the state. The European lawns obliterated large populations of yellow lady's-slipper orchids. It seems to me there is a paradox here, or at least a misunderstanding of motives. The people who move to the country are generally seeking, for whatever reason, to escape towns and cities. They want more space, more connection to the land, and perhaps to a community spirit. Given a choice, I imagine many of the new residents would have preferred native wildflower gardens to high-maintenance lawns and hedges.

Susan and I met one such couple, bright young professionals who'd abandoned apartment life and high-paying careers in downtown Chicago once they were expecting their first child. They had wandered around the rural Midwest looking for the ideal place to start their family, finally locating a small tidy farmstead not far from us. We invited them to dinner and showed them the farm after hearing how intent they were to learn about alternative energy choices. They specifically admired our wind generator. As Susan and I saw it, they were experiencing an impulse similar to that which drove people to reconsider their lifestyles during the back-to-the-land-movement of the 1960s. Like those modern pioneers, they wanted to become more energy independent and self-reliant. They wanted to grow organic produce and live simpler lives in rural communities. They had grown up confined by their surroundings and wanted their kids to have more immediate access to nature. And yet they weren't moving so far away that their old city friends couldn't converge on their place for celebrations or holiday getaways.

I understand, even admire, these impulses. And it is likely that instilling the value of nature in future generations will require that people continue to move to natural areas. So stemming the tide of humans from the cities may not be possible, or even warranted, given the status quo.

Instead Susan and I have sought ways to influence how development is done, making cities and suburbs more desirable in natural terms. We stay active in the community, and our broad professional networks have given us opportunities to counsel certain open-minded developers on how to design projects that are more ecologically friendly—clustering the housing more densely, for example, while creating larger swathes of restored wilderness. The network of ecologically aware builders and developers has expanded significantly since I first came to Stone Prairie Farm.

That the path to significant change is a difficult one was apparent from my very first AES project. In 1979 we were working

with a developer who owned a 500-acre wetland along the shore
of Lake Michigan, as well as another hundred acres of surrounding uplands. He envisioned building a marina abutted by
condominiums and single-family homes. In our research, we
discovered that most of the existing wetland was once a ninety-
foot-deep lake area that had been filled with millions of cubic
yards of sediment from deforested lands during the settlement
of the tributary watershed in the mid-1800s. So the wetland we
were all interested in preserving wasn't even a natural landform!

We wanted to be cautious, so we talked to the developer
about the threats to the landscape inherent in conventional development and convinced him to visit other endeavors that
successfully integrated and protected nature. We suggested his
project could be a regional role model, and after we visited and
further designed his project, he agreed to include protected natural areas that would serve as the fabric that wove the entire
community together, rather than some "green stuff" at the ter-
mination views along the axis of a roadway.

We had won the developer and the financer over to protecting sizable areas, giving up on a proposed marina, and restoring
the wetland. But then the developer fell ill and abruptly passed
away. The decisions were left to several family members who
hadn't been involved and simply wanted to be done with it. They
sold the land to another, less visionary developer. It now sits idle,
overrun with various invasive species.

Moving forward, we realized that we'd need to piece together
a network of exemplary projects to influence people and help
generate enthusiasm for both the aesthetics and economics of
sustainable design. Not long after that, we were inspired by one
of the only regional developments that was using some ecological design principles. Located in Kalamazoo, Michigan, the development featured homes that were nestled organically into
predominantly forested terrain. Apparently the developer's market research showed that people yearned for a closer relationship
with nature and were willing to pay more to live near it. Thus

the abundance of trees improved the profitability of the development. Could ecological and economic value be created simultaneously? I sought projects that would test the value of adding a forest, wetland, or prairie to developments.

As new restoration jobs came through AES, I focused on analyzing the economic factors. It was quite common for adversarial parties to contest the use of land containing important ecological resources. In such situations I would often be brought in to identify which areas would be suitable for development and in which ones it would be not only unadvisable, but detrimental ecologically and economically. These studies nearly always revealed a deterioration of natural resources in both urban and rural neighborhoods resulting from years of land use changes, hydrological modifications, and exotic species invasion. When attention is drawn to these problems, developers can be given a clearer picture of the potential opportunities provided by restoring parts of deteriorated ecological settings. Once they are aware of the benefits of restoration they can become part of a growing solution and be allies in conservation.

By assessing the impacts of many such projects and other research I compiled a sizable data set. Analyzing the data, it is clear that nature is inherently more cost-effective than even the most cleverly engineered strategies or solutions. For instance, compare the data on stream discharge levels (how streams handle water flow) from the U.S. National Archive for the Chicago area from the late 1800s to more recent municipal records. Prior to development of the Chicago metropolitan region, most watersheds had up to 75 percent less surface stormwater runoff, meaning the native landscape could absorb four times as much water, and almost certainly maintain a much greater amount of topsoil. Flood event peaks, the maximum flow during a flood period, were 60 percent lower than the present ones, and thus far less damaging. This all demonstrates that the historic natural ecosystem managed stormwater quality, rate, and volume far better than the extensive and expensive manmade solution of pipes, curbs and gutters, and detention ponds ever could. As water management is a substantial consideration in development, this saving in implementing nature-based systems is significant. Additionally, home buyers are willing to pay a premium to live in a more natural environment.

Using this kind of data I was able to explain to clients that protecting, restoring, and using natural resources in developments would, in the short and in the long run, be more cost-effective—that by including open space to manage stormwater, they could actually add value to their land both on a practical level and in terms of improving aesthetic and recreational opportunities.

I developed some loose development guidelines from this data. Then in the mid-1980s my approach was put to the test. In 1985, David Hoffman of the prestigious Red Seal Development Corporation in Northbrook, Illinois, contacted AES for a consultation on a parcel of land in Highland Park, harboring a small population of federally endangered prairie white fringed orchid. It was an exciting and daunting project. We prepared extensive field inventories of the flora there, as well as many maps and reports. As I reported on the findings, I watched the development team shift nervously in their seats. After taking it all in, the team leader asked if development could occur without destroying the ecosystem irreparably. I confirmed that it would be possible with a set of provisions including alternative stormwater management designs, ecological buffers, and protected land that would need to be set aside. The development proceeded and was a success for all of us. Named Hybernia, modified from the scientific name of a rare orchid, it was one of Illinois' first dedicated nature preserves with a stewardship program integrated into the development, and a financial endowment for the perpetual management of the preserve. Ultimately there were nearly one hundred homes on the 132 acres, nearly a third of which was set aside as a protected preserve. Ideally the preserve would have been larger, but we found ourselves fighting zoning regulations intended to keep the population density low. Ironically, this leads to bigger yards but smaller expanses of nature!

Nonetheless Hybernia was a great success, and the first of many such projects. A larger development, known as Prairie Crossing, took me to a Chicago skyscraper. I arrived early for the initial team meeting and was ushered into a corner conference room on the fiftieth floor overlooking Chicago's waterfront and the long horizon of Lake Michigan. From that height the view is amazing. The lake appears as big as an ocean, but you can't even open the window to feel the breeze. As the participants assembled, I stepped away from the view, sat down, and watched the action as people popped in and out, making quick introductions, all obviously very busy.

In my experience, engineers drive the design of most developments, leaving little room for input from landscape architects or ecologists. Fortunately, it was clear from the beginning that this project was going to be different. I remember getting excited when Vicky Ranney, one of the developers, had first called to inquire about my interest in their new project, particularly when she mentioned that she had written a book about Frederick Law Olmsted (often referred to as the father of American landscape architecture). She spoke about her respect for his keen focus on designs that utilized and honored natural landscapes and native plants, and I could tell that she had a long-standing connection with nature.

As the meeting was coming to an end, I spoke with Bill Johnson, the world-class landscape architect with whom I was going to be working. He was pleased by the proceedings and said he looked forward to this project, in which the underlying metaphor was to design an integrated development as a functioning ecological system. It was extremely unusual to be paired up with such a like-minded colleague on such a monumental project. Prairie Crossing proved to be a fine example of collaborative vision and set national standards for ecological design and development strategies. The homes were energy efficient; local water quality was maintained and restored; stormwater drainage alternatives were utilized. There was open space integration and native landscaping. By melding ecological and human systems, Prairie Crossing made clear how achievable sustainable development could be, accommodating both comfort and economy under the umbrella of environmental ethics. This project protected nearly 70 percent of the land by developing much smaller lots and narrower streets than was possible at Hybernia. By urging the establishment of train stations on two rail lines that crossed next to the site, the development also provided mass transportation for new residents in the four hundred homes. Over 400 acres of former agricultural lands were restored to prairies, wetlands, and lakes that were accessible through a labyrinth of public and private trails. A working organic farm was integrated within the project, localizing a great deal of food production. Finally, this plan and "conservation community," a term new to the development industry, would be a model to demonstrate values far greater than the conventional developments springing up in converted farm fields all about.

The unusual success of Prairie Crossing was due largely to the fact that the owners, unlike most developers, clearly communicated an inspired vision to the contractors and consultants. We acted as a team, working from a shared set of principles and dedicated to providing environmental protection and stewardship; multiple modes of transportation; lifelong learning opportunities; and racial, cultural, and economic diversity. From its inception, the project looked different from other sizable suburban developments, which often intimidate surrounding communities with the fear of eventual expansion onto their lands. In contrast, 2,500 acres of farmland and trails surround Prairie Crossing, creating a buffer. It has become a regional anchor, a place for environmentally thoughtful and community-oriented persons to live. Residents converge at markets for fresh organic produce; they swim, fish, and canoe in a clear lake; and a wind generator produces some of their electricity. The residents appreciate these amenities and understand that they made a choice not to build on top of rare plant populations or cut down dwindling woodlots. They did not have to move to the country and start from scratch. The country met them halfway there.

On New Year's Day 2003, the *Christian Science Monitor* praised Prairie Crossing, using the new term "conservation community," and profiling it as one of the few projects nationally where the bulldozer did not plow under farms. They reported that Prairie Crossing integrated agriculture and nature and, most important, provided a high quality of life in an environment that functioned in and of itself as a healthy ecological system.

When Aldo Leopold wrote that intelligent tinkerers save all the pieces, I believe he was envisioning a future in which people would rejoin the natural world and their communities. Decades later, projects like Prairie Crossing have demonstrated that these aspirations can be realized. The success of this approach has sparked the interest of other progressive builders on the "who's who in conservation development" list. Some of their developments have become shining examples nationally—such as Wild Meadows, a Minneapolis-area project that has preserved over half of its 345 acres as a restored ecosystem with connecting trails for the residents. The stormwater management at Wild Meadows was based on AES's Stormwater Treatment Train design, and the community there has dedicated itself to a level of stewardship above and beyond what typical homeowners commit to their communities.

Inspiration, another Minneapolis-area project, has over 200 acres of restored lands that include a protected state scientific area and rare American Indian burial mounds. Inspiration also uses the alternative stormwater management approach and encourages long-term stewardship and land protection commitments. South Village, a South Burlington, Vermont, conservation development, actually held their formative planning sessions in the farmhouse at Prairie Crossing. They also embraced restoration on more than 100 acres, as well as stormwater management treatment methods, communal food production, gardens, orchards, and an agricultural teaching extension through the Intervale Foundation (an organization in Burlington started by Will Raap, the CEO of Gardener's Supply Company, the largest gardening equipment supplier in the United States). Noisette, in North Charleston, South Carolina, is using the same design principles to redevelop and restore a 3,000-acre navy base on the coast. This project includes the vast Noisette Reserve and its extensive trails and salt marsh, as well as the coastal forest community restorations, which include an exhumed stream that will resume the historic route from the development out to the coast.

Many projects have come through Applied Ecological Services. Whether they are large or small, complex or relatively simple, Susan and I and more than 140 associates work with clients to transform degraded natural areas. Our work style is collaborative, and we draw from our broad pool of different skills and knowledge bases to create the appropriate team for each project. Both developers and residents can attest to the success of these experiments. To see the levels of commitment at Prairie Crossing and the other developments after years of struggling to raise awareness is immensely rewarding. It was worth the wait to finally see developers embrace the economic and public relations benefits of sustainable design principles. The projects that result offer desirable living spaces to the general public, excellent financial return for investors, and sustainability for the ecosystems—a win–win–win scenario.

Perhaps with this kind of vision the public will learn that urban and suburban areas can be more attractive and alluring without trampling over rural woodlots and other natural resources. Perhaps with pristine environments at our doorsteps, people might opt to stay at home during vacations instead of escaping the cities and suburbs for seemingly urgent two-week trips in their campers and sport utility vehicles. After all, the lake in Prairie Crossing has the quality and clarity of more remote ones in northern Wisconsin. If people could derive the same enjoyments locally, the numerous private cottages springing up along pristine habitats in northern Wisconsin and Michigan's Upper Peninsula lakes might no longer be so coveted, or necessary. Such conservation-oriented development may also be a solid strategy for stimulating sustainable economic development and population growth in rural towns. Instead of spreading out through the countryside, inevitably destroying valuable habitats, housing could be more centralized, allowing development to expand while still preserving the calm and beauty of nature.

The social fabric of rural culture is often based on long-standing family ties. Newcomers are usually welcomed, but they rarely contribute to the community with the same commitment as the locals. City folks often retain old social patterns, accustomed, perhaps, to living in a kind of isolation in their anonymous urban jungles, or behind their suburban fences. Their urban ways help unravel the fabric of local communities and work against preservation of rural history, traditions, and wisdom. Of course, Susan and I are relative newcomers ourselves, and we have been striving for many years to modify aspects of traditional land use to enhance biodiversity. So perhaps some recent arrivals and their ideas aren't all bad. But many rural communities are teetering on the edge of an uncertainty that will only intensify as generational landownership transitions continue and cities creep closer.

CHAPTER 15

Ecological Reserves

I cherish having easy, regular access to open space that incorporates wild and functional landscapes. From our farmhouse door, the trails on our farm connect with those of our neighbors' lands. I can follow the forest's edge along the Spring Creek tributary that originates on Stone Prairie Farm and explore the land between the creek and the adjacent agricultural field. I usually let my neighbors know when I'm going out on these walks, and they always welcome me. I often report back to them with the observations I've gathered as I wander the banks of Spring Creek through old black maple woodlands and oak savanna remnants to the fern-draped cliffs bordering the stream. This walk takes me through a farm producing goat milk and cheese, and another with a third-generation fruit orchard and well-tended vegetable garden. Each time I pass this route I am struck by the beauty of the historic farmsteads, with their nineteenth-century barns looming red or white and old granaries and vestigial smokehouses spread out along the winding rural roads.

Even with the intervening farmlands, the landscape and its ecology still try to cohere.

I wonder if a somewhat more formalized version of the access and freedom my neighbors grant me could be the kernel of a new model for structuring rural land ownership and use. After all, there are limited public-use trails for biking and hiking. What if a gentle hand could magically create more places for visiting, hiking, fishing, and hunting? What if landowners allowed others to experience their lands? They could benefit from new relationships that would connect them to their neighbors, and from their own increased relationship to nature. And, perhaps most important, they could benefit financially if others were willing to pay for access.

This is one of the underlying principles for ecological reserves, a model for future sustainability that I think could have an enormous impact. Such a reserve concept could start small. Imagine a handful of neighboring landowners who cooperate to make equestrian or hiking trail access across their adjacent properties available by permission. Even at this scale it would have great benefits to a diverse group—all of the owners and those who might pay a fee to use the land.

And there are other potential beneficiaries as well. For example, by working with existing landowners to retire and restore a few thousand acres of farmland upstream of a metropolitan area one could help reduce costly flooding and improve human safety and health in the city. This could create a brand-new revenue stream for the farmers—establishing their land as a storm- or floodwater management landscape.

That same land could also be used to clean up the quality of the water in that river. As the river water flowed through the biological filters of restored wetlands and prairies, nitrogen and phosphorous levels would be reduced. Such strategically located ecological reserves, lying in the right watershed, and on the right channel, could be very valuable conservation-based projects. The benefits listed above are always needed, and already paid for in one way or another—through tax payments or the fees necessary for water utilities to maintain pumps and filtered water for drinking. There are many ways these fees could be shifted to pay the landowners whose land provides some of these services.

And there are other reserve types less directly attached to cities that could supply organic food and fuel—fruit, vegetables, meat, biofuels, and fibers—to local communities. These could be produced in one portion of a larger reserve and create another revenue source. This would help diversify rural agricultural land and, most important, give measurable value to rural ecologies.

Great potential rewards await those willing to work together to build a community based on a shared vision of ecological and human health, because even the process of restoring land health in itself consoles and inspires the human spirit. This would be a wonderful collaborative opportunity for like-minded persons, who could address spiraling property values by pooling resources and preserving nature. This could be done directly by inspired visionary farmers. Or, for instance, if ten people each purchased 80 acres, together they could establish an 800-acre restored, working ecological reserve. Entice another forty of their friends to follow suit, and the whole group could enjoy 4,000 acres, or about six square miles. And imagine what would happen if each person purchased 400 acres!

Imagine this becoming a new model for diversifying and localizing food production systems and drastically reducing the distance food travels to reach your plate. Currently, most of our food travels some 1,500 miles from where it's produced to get to you. This just about guarantees it is not really fresh when it gets there and has lost much of its nutritional value in transit. From an environmental perspective, the cost is much higher. The pleasant road trip this food takes in getting to your plate has enormous ecological, environmental, and social impact. If total accounting were done for the Californian, Floridian, Mexican, or Chilean food on your dinner plate in environmental impacts alone, we'd realize that the dollar price we pay at the checkout counter is only a tiny portion of the real cost.

Our apparent "savings" will ultimately be paid for by each of us, and our children, as we address the climate change that is bolstered by carbon emissions from trucking lettuce to your plate. There are social impacts as well. Not knowing where your food comes from is a significant loss—for me there is nothing so pleasurable as seeing your food growing in a garden and knowing its origin. Food quality, flavor, and the human relations that evolve from knowing those who produce your foods are all benefits that are lost in the dominant food production system. Reserves could be a fundamental new way to localize food production, linking farmer and consumer to healthy lands.

Yet another advantage is that well-managed ecological reserves with an agricultural component could help significantly in managing much of the environmental degradation of food production. Healthy soils have higher levels of organic matter and thus higher carbon content. This both sequesters carbon dioxide and helps grow healthier food.

And energy as well as food production could be localized through a reserve system, with enormous benefits. Our current decentralized power plants are less than 40 percent efficient, meaning for every ton of coal 60 percent of the contained energy is lost to heat, literally going up in smoke. What a shamefully wasteful system! And believe it or not, each of us pays not only for the actual energy we receive from the electric company but also for the waste intrinsic to the system we have in place. We pay the operating costs for each ton of coal, but we get less then 40 percent of what we pay for. And we are going to pay double as climate change continues and we must fund efforts to clean up the mess our energy production system has released into the atmosphere. Reserves could contribute to the localization of energy production—be it wind farms, solar farms, production of carbon-neutral perennial oil-seed crops, or harvest of perennial native grasses for later combustion in small-scale power plants.

This doesn't mean you will necessarily drive out to the farm to buy cut firewood grown as a biofuel, but it could mean that native prairie grasses will be harvested by the farmer, then pelletized and added to nearby conventional power plants, replacing fossil coal and oil consumption with annually renewable "grown" fuels. As all members of ecological reserves could be co-owners in such a venture, perhaps financially structured around a utility model, this would create steady long-term revenue streams that could ensure the restoration and stewardship of the land in the reserve. With continued success, revenue could be reinvested in enlarging and diversifying the reserve program.

The ecological reserve model would allow everyone to know exactly where their food and energy comes from and give them the choice to involve themselves in this scheme as members, innovators, or entrepreneurs working toward a cooperative future. I am fascinated by the potential of this concept and believe the model is tenable at all scales, based on a balance of personal needs, market demand and access, and the enthusiasm, commitment, and courage of the participants.

The unifying outcome of an "ecological reserve" approach would undoubtedly lead to revitalized ecological systems, with each reserve designed to attain measures of health corresponding to those we have achieved at Stone Prairie Farm. By working toward this outcome, farm by farm, we could reassemble a sizable landscape and assure the commitment and success of its ecological, economic, and cultural future.

One summer weekend in 2002 our Chicago-area friends joined Susan and me at Stone Prairie Farm. Their visit included side trips to view idyllic properties, some of which contained flowery prairies, trout-laden streams, shaded forests, and craggy cliffs. Touring these landscapes, I pictured them with refurbished farmhouses for my retirement-age friends, who were undoubtedly intrigued by the idea of retreating to a tranquil location, perhaps near our farm. As we traveled through the countryside, inspecting farms with our friends' stated priorities in mind, Susan and I referred to aerial photographs and maps of each property to give them a more distinctive picture of the region. They enjoyed learning that the region was tucked into the east edge of the driftless terrain whose condensed biological diversity included fire-vulnerable mesic forests (black maple, red maple, basswood, and ironwood) nestled next to fire-tolerant bur and white oak savannas, dry to wet prairies, and scattered rock outcrop ecosystems. But agricultural land use over the past century had transformed the land into a façade of patchwork farmsteads. Because the underlying ecological settings were diverse and included elements such as wetlands and trout streams, Susan and I laid out a compelling and comprehensive picture of the restoration potential.

Many of our friends, although intrigued by the idea of a move to the country, could not relocate so far from their urban employment and commitments. But their potential investment could be vital to the rural economy, particularly if they were to help fund the establishment of an ecological reserve. By transferring a portion of urban investments to the countryside in the form of land stewardship ventures that support the efforts of experienced local stewards, such a reciprocal relationship empowers both city dwellers and their rural counterparts to work together for the land's future.

Of course investors like assurances, particularly those that spread the risk. I figure that if urbanites, including land developers, were willing to financially link their urban livelihoods with rural investments, then the ecological reserves could be marketed to potential homebuyers in urban developments through a membership that included time-share retreat facilities, cottages providing hunting opportunities, and other revenue-generating strategies that would finance the reserve and additional user services. The incentives need to be clear, or people will continue to do what some of my colleagues have done, which was to jointly purchase 1,000 acres that they have used primarily for hunting. Such projects neglect the local community—they simply supplant local involvement with outsiders' needs, which do not emphasize land restoration or necessarily support biodiversity short of land management for prime deer habitat.

Therefore Susan and I make a clear pitch to our interested friends that the establishment of an ecological reserve must pool the resources of both investors and local residents to protect the patchwork of farmlands. It has long been our fantasy to entice friends through a collaborative process to invest in acreage that includes our farm and adjacent farms, many of which are owned by aging farmers whose children have little interest in moving back to take up farming. Through such a collaboration, we could even develop creative purchasing arrangements to retain farmers as members who could assist in restoration and land management, and perhaps also in food production. With such arrangements, farmers could even secure life leases if they choose.

⌒

Scale and placement of reserves are essential considerations for their success, especially for those designed to help solve costly social and infrastructure problems. To think at a meaningful scale in ecological terms, watersheds are often the place to start.

What exactly does that mean? A watershed is an area of land that shares water runoff and drainage systems. Ask yourself, if rain falls in one location, where does it run to? Eventually, through tributaries, streams, brooks, arroyos, and raging rivers, it travels to some destination—a lake, a much larger river, an ocean. The watershed consists of all the land that feeds water to these drainage features across and through a landscape. In some low-precipitation watersheds there may be no runoff, as the water sinks into the ground and evaporates back to the atmosphere or is used by plants growing within the area. In any case, a watershed is a very useful area when thinking in ecological terms.

In thinking at the scale of a watershed there are many details to consider. How the land is used affects not only the amount of water running off the land but also its quality. If your watershed was all a "paved paradise"—a sea of asphalt parking lots stretching across the entire region—just about every drop of precipitation falling on it would theoretically run quickly off the land into whatever was below it. And because there is little resistance to water flowing over a sea of pavement, the water can have a lot of energy, so things of varying sizes can be swept off the land— from bubble-gum wrappers to cars and houses. Significantly, in less paved areas, soil nutrients and contaminants also are swept from the land and into the rivers. This doesn't bode well for the river channels downstream, which have only so much capacity to carry water. With the addition of more and faster-moving runoff they become unstable, eroded, and a threat to the economies, health, and safety of the downstream communities. Healthy watersheds and the ecological systems they comprise, as described early in this book, are stingy, meaning they hold water and nutrients in soils and vegetation and filter them down to deeper underlying ground water. Thus it's important to understand how much of the local watershed is paved—with asphalt, rooftops, compacted, heavy clay farm soils, impenetrable bedrock, hardpan soil, or caleche—compared to how much has intact ecological systems, healthy water-absorbing soils, and vegetation that creates the desired stinginess.

A watershed offers a good way to think about the scale of an ecological reserve, if not a specific size. Depending on the specifics, successful reserves could be tens of acres, or tens of thousands of acres—formulated in many sizes and shapes to meet specific market opportunities, local demands, and ecological outcomes that can be achieved without impairing the land or the community. Some reserves may need to be large enough to handle the volume of water needed to relieve flooding impact. A local food-production-based reserve, in contrast, might be a central growing area together with a patchwork of smaller restored ecological areas that harbor native pollinating insects and predacious birds and mammals that eat food crop pests. These food production centers, whose actual production may take place at a site within the larger reserve, may also be designed to protect water supplies for growing food, watering livestock, and maintaining healthy streams, lakes, wetlands, and ponds.

What may be most important is the shared philosophy of the participants and their willingness to embrace the responsibilities intrinsic to restoring the land and creating a diverse economic foundation. Individuals or partners, acting as trustees, could reassemble the land by collectively buying parcels and building or renovating individual homes or cabin sites. Each reserve could have a single unified plan that addresses unique restoration needs, overall land management guidelines, and a monitoring program to ensure compliance. Unlike the situation of the recreational hunters, who maintained autonomy and put self-interest first, these reserves could share resources and be dedicated to land stewardship. This level of cooperation could help transition recreational hobbies into centers of profit such as Stone Prairie Farm's commercial syrup operation, or facilitate tool sharing, particularly with larger expensive items such as tractors and specialized gear like seed-planting equipment. There would be opportunities to establish cooperative enterprises like breeding and reintroducing prairie chickens and other native wildlife. In fact, near Stone Prairie Farm some neighbors are already breeding elk.

Even an ambitious plan must be developed in increments. Just as we restore land one square foot at a time, we need to build reserves one relationship at a time. Friends who have shown interest in finding a meaningful balance between a return on their investments and the quality of their environment may be the best candidates to launch land protection projects, using simple measures that are at once profitable and environmentally sensitive. In all cases it's essential to consider geography. As they say in real estate, "There are three rules: location, location, location."

The steps in establishing a reserve include territorial map-making (to denote not only property boundaries but also contiguous soils, historic vegetation, types of ground cover, topography, drainage, bedrock geology, and even cultural history); charting a clear reserve lands restoration concept; devising a land assemblage strategy; and preparing a firm but flexible business and financing plan. Financial elements to consider putting in place include nonprofit corporations, which can help provide tax and estate planning benefits, and an endowment fund to guarantee restoration and continued stewardship in perpetuity.

As illustrated by projects like Prairie Crossing, Applied Ecological Services has experience designing ecological restorations that help integrate development strategies with a more expansive ecological reserve paradigm. Models like these, if applied to reserves, would allow true partnerships with the land and expand the potential range of social and economic benefits. Projects would be judged on how well they link ecology, economy, and culture through the reassembly and restoration of functioning, healthy ecological systems.

Farmers would be great partners in ecological reserves, given the right support. Many farms are in transition. Their aging owners reap less and less from the land and they are falling deeper into debt without retirement security. Let's help vulnerable farmers wean themselves from federal subsidies and avoid selling out to developers and agribusiness just to survive. They can be part of a new system that gives them flexibility in how and what they plan, allows them to play a vital part in the future regional and local economy, and creates opportunities for institutional support in critical estate planning decisions. If farmers are brought into the reserve concept, long-term agreements could compensate them for any land use changes, pay for their land restoration, and provide a guarantee of financial solvency better than any the federal government can offer. Buyout agreements can be designed that don't compromise the farm families' cultural ties and history, or their commitments and allegiances to their communities.

Forming a cooperative of privately held lands is another approach to establishing a reserve. For example, one of our neighbors suggested setting up a cooperative to restore and maintain privately held parcels of land and establish cottages for lodging or second homes available to rent or to lease for retreats. Community members and even visitors would participate in some element of restoration through internships or stewardship programming. Old farmhouses could be donated and converted for learning and residency programs that celebrate the restored landscapes.

LandKeepers was originally established by AES and several partners to help reserve and conservation projects. It partners with another organization called Conservare, which is focused on creative conservation developments as profit centers that will finance further land conservation. Most conservation organizations focus only on land protection. LandKeepers and Conservare deviate significantly from this approach by delivering not only conservation and restoration planning but also the implementation of perpetual plans and subsequent monitoring, as well as financial planning, training, and event coordination. Using this model, the ideal reserve ranges from a contiguous protected landscape that links adjacent lands and has a single coordinated restoration and management program to patchworks of restored farms over a larger landscape with a coordinated stewardship organization to see that the future needs of the land are met.

By linking protected farms it may be possible to achieve greater ecological benefits. Again, the coherence of this configuration could be mapped through aerial photographs that illustrate the connection of landscapes with waterways and drainage routes, arguably the sutures holding the patches together. And since most farms include drainage ways, it might be possible to build reserves that integrate farm programs and water quality outcomes. Linking waterways and protection buffers with other natural resource areas might be the practical framework needed for enlisting voluntary participation and for leveraging financial cooperation.

⌒

The reserve ideas here have focused on working with farmers. This is in part because they own the land. It is also the case that dealing with individuals and even groups of people can be much less challenging than working with governmental agencies and jurisdictions when it comes to these things. Simply put, the natural world and the political world don't relate well. Watersheds, for instance, rarely follow political boundaries. Instead they cross them with total indifference and abandon. This is one reason that water management policies generally don't work very well.

It is inconceivable that the states of Wisconsin and Illinois do not cooperate in addressing water quality and flood management for those rivers and watersheds that start in Wisconsin and then boil up into flooding problems to the south, in Illinois. But they don't, so poor water management practices in Wisconsin have dramatically negative effects, exacerbating the even poorer downstream water management practices in Illinois, a scenario repeated around the country and the world.

Perhaps the ecological reserve concept could be useful in transcending ecologically arbitrary jurisdictional and political boundaries so that our local, state, and federal agencies can actually begin thinking and operating in watershed terms and address issues and opportunities at the scales that matter. The State of Wisconsin could alleviate flooding and, if it were concerned about the cost, charge its downstream neighbors for this service. Consider the potential of several thousand acres of wetland restoration in each of the flood-prone Chicago-bound rivers that originate in southern Wisconsin. The natural benefits of publicly accessible open space, which would serve to regulate these waterways, would be enormous. Instead, for political and jurisdictional reasons, the agencies for that part of the Illinois watershed created a flood management plan without taking a comprehensive look at the upstream watershed.

What's to be learned from all this? From now on the safety of our drinking water may depend on each of us demanding that our public agencies invest at the watershed scale, and look upstream, downstream, and below our feet for ways to turn problems into opportunities. Ecological reserves can link rural and urban needs by connecting the health of the land and its ecosystems to the physical and economic well-being of human communities, and perhaps rebuilding time-honored networks of interdependence.

⌒

Implementing ecological reserves is not without its challenges. However, it may be the best chance we have to stabilize our rural lands and their economy, and to ensure a continued supply of the products they provide. And it is essential at some point early in the process to think in terms of profit, for establishing and expanding reserves takes significant funds. No matter how beautiful the land is, it must produce a supply of services and products that can be linked to revenue streams. And there are many different ways to establish this kind of profit flow, including those discussed earlier in this chapter.

Imagine tens of thousands of acres in every rural county networked together, following watercourses and crossing over the uplands to corresponding protected landforms. Picture being able to follow walking trails passing through each watershed from one side of the county to the other, or just walking across your state through a network of public and private reserves. If you're lucky you might even be able to stop and pick local apples, or encounter a trailside food stand serving great burgers and locally grown salads!

Such integrated reserves would not only support local and regional markets but also become a fundamental unit of our national economy. Each reserve would be a building block in the construction of durable and profitable relationships between people and land. And let's face it—this relationship is long overdue. Imagine an earth ethic that unites all communities so that all life forms can once again thrive on our interdependency. Even urban dwellers, removed from the vast countryside, can participate in and enjoy the solace of nature's boundless beauty and production. Perhaps this involvement and access to reserves would restructure land developments altogether and relieve the pressure to build in woodlands, which have become the bull's-eye on the landscape for new homes.

The idea of ecological reserves is not new. For instance, in 1995 Prairie Crossing set up a 5,800-acre patchwork of adjacent lands called the Liberty Prairie Reserve, initially established to protect open space against land development. Now a community-supported agricultural system within the reserve produces organic food for some five hundred families. Moreover this food production takes only up a few dozen acres, and as there is a large unmet demand for organic vegetables, fruit, and other foodstuffs in the surrounding Chicago metropolitan region, plans are afoot to convert more acres to this sustainable agricultural use. The reserve successfully generates revenue in many of the ways discussed above, including mitigation credits for developers elsewhere. It also provides hiking, biking, and equestrian trails that allow the public to travel throughout the reserve.

Liberty Prairie Reserve is a great success, but there are still few other examples of working ecological reserves. It is clearly possible to have functioning reserves that are self-financed though environmental services and products produced from the land, and to my mind, this approach may be the most important new idea for the future conservation and restoration of land.

⌒

CHAPTER 16

A Healthy Earth Ethic

I began my restoration project inspired by Aldo Leopold's concept of a land ethic, first described in print in 1949 in his classic book *A Sand County Almanac*, which I consider to be the environmentalist's bible. After nearly thirty years on my land, I believe that I too have become a steward and a conservationist in the Leopoldian tradition. But with each rereading of his book it becomes clearer to me that because times have changed, bringing new challenges and ideas, his vision needs a similar update. Keeping the same foundation, it must respond to the magnitude of our current level of globalization and exploding conservation needs. Some of the differences aren't so great, but the imperative he suggested as far back as the mid-twentieth century requires us to reaffirm our collective position and spread the word far and wide. To have a sustainable future we must engage every willing person to join in creating a healthy vision of the earth.

Aldo Leopold started us down this path. At the end of *A Sand County Almanac* he clearly documents a vision for an ethical relationship to the land, which he elevates from its status as a mere setting for human activity, and one that is often taken for granted. He speaks instead of honoring it and fostering a bond based on love and respect.

In today's consumer culture, by contrast, the land is nearly always seen as a commodity to be bought and sold by the acre, divided into square feet and parceled out as lots. In this process of commoditization it is easy to lose sight of the role land serves. A schism exists between the perception of the value of land and its aesthetic and nurturing significance for humans and all other life forms. The streams don't calculate human needs. They would flow regardless. Birds and wildlife disregard our boundaries and our concept of ownership, as do weather patterns (until recently) and soil systems, wildfires and insect infestations. Mortgages and land contracts are arbitrary deeds, written for humans. Nonetheless they infringe on the rights of all the plants and animals that call the land their home.

Could you live without your kidneys? Healthy soils and vegetation are the ecosystem's kidneys. Without these filters, stormwater runs off instead of seeping down into ground water, and land health declines. Erosion leads to an inevitable depletion of biodiversity and decreased productivity on the land, in freshwater systems, and in the oceans, all of which adversely affects the ecosystem's potential for recovery.

Leopold eloquently argued for bestowing land with ethical rights. He didn't mention legal rights, and we can only assume that his concept of ethics transcended policy and law. In the years since he made this argument, our society has succeeded in expanding social justice for women and minorities, recognizing the rights of pets and farm animals, protecting scientific and wilderness areas, and beginning to legislate the protection and rights of citizens of the earth to decent water and air— almost inalienable rights that should be available to each human. We are making strides, although many questions of race and social equality are still unresolved. We are even more ambivalent toward biodiversity and ecosystem health—to date we have given it passing consideration at best.

One framework for determining what to do with land is a guideline present in numerous land policies, that the "highest and best use" of a particular stretch of land should be the basis for determining its value, a use that may or may not be the current use. This "highest and best use" is a somewhat vague standard to a layperson, but not to a lawyer or realtor. It is essentially defined as the most financially profitable use of the land. In practice, reliance on this standard is very troubling. After attending many meetings and participating in many debates over how many acres of nature and open space should remain in land developments, I find that the decision for more or less nature is usually contingent on the orator's persistence, not on the facts. In the end, unless some consensus is struck, an overstated economic argument usually prevails, with the result that nature is carved up into ever smaller and more isolated remnants.

Under its current definition, the "highest and best use" of land does not take into account the health of the earth and its inhabitants, including us humans, who are either too frightened to read the writing on the wall, too helpless in the face of corporate will, or too proud and deluded to reject our own fallacies and accept the consequences of our actions. Economies are powerful forces, and societies are hotwired into market-based value systems that trump the real highest and best use of land.

Unfortunately, with exception of a few nations, the rest of the industrialized world is trailing close behind America in ecological failures. European ecosystems are in dire straits. Business interests in the developing world—Asia, the Middle East, South America, and Africa—are also promulgating this no-win environmental doctrine, mainly because no objective criteria exist for judging ecosystem performance. There is no central database for environmental impact, nor agreed standard for the value of healthy functioning ecological systems. This lack of global stewardship and cooperation has accelerated decline. The conferences in Kyoto (1997) and Bali (2008) are steps in the right direction, because we do need broad consensus on global climate change and emissions caps. It is also a good thing that these climate change negotiations provide a forum for discussions regarding the value of nature. But people at the grassroots level must not wait for governments to solve environmental problems, even if they are chiefly responsible for allowing them. We also must not wait around for a certified consensus on standards or on the value of nature. We must take it on ourselves to work together to rebalance and restore nature.

We must view the health of the land from an ecological systems perspective analogous to the way we view human health. In this manner we can make the land ethic more tangible. Nature is largely self-regulating, just like the human body. Both require proper nutrition and sunlight to maintain well-being. Humans think we are taking care of the earth, but nearly always we are damaging it. Our species is invasive, colonizing, and overbearing; we must modify our behavior. If not, we will simply continue to bite the hand that feeds us. In contrast to our behavior, consider the valuable services a healthy planet provides at no cost: fresh water, purified air, and nearly boundless foodstuffs. It filters wastes and sewage, attenuates flooding, provides raw materials and fertile soils that grow lush vegetation, and offers habitats that afford us material, aesthetic, and spiritual luxury. A conservative estimate of the value of these services in human terms between Leopold's era and our own amounts to more than three trillion dollars annually.

The value of these ecosystem benefits and services makes for a strong argument against the doctrine of "highest and best use" in the narrow, profit-centric way it is generally interpreted. As we can now calculate in economic terms the reciprocal worth that an acre of prairie, desert, wetland, forest, or ocean provides for our health, we can no longer deny the value of ecosystem benefits. By extension, many seemingly absolute rights we have bestowed upon our species, however nobly intended, are not cost-effective; for instance, if we promise each family a home, we should be careful not to negate the value of the land it is built on. Every acre scarified and covered by manmade structures reduces nature's contribution, because the sum of all parts working in harmony is substantially greater than the value of the individual tract. "Highest and best use" considers only the parcel, not its intrinsic connections, including the multiplier effect of these contributions to greater global ecological function.

~

I was introduced to valuing nature early in my career when AES was hired to determine the value of a 500-acre coastal wetland on Lake St. Clair in eastern Michigan, just north of Detroit. The landowners had wanted to develop condominiums worth many tens of millions of dollars on existing landfill areas, but the development proposal was denied by state and federal agencies. The attorneys representing the developer decided to sue the regulators, claiming their decision to deny the permit for the condominium was arbitrary and capricious. They requested a valuation of the land to develop a rationale for suing the regulatory agencies. It took a year for the team of which AES was a part to measure the tangible wetland products in order to evaluate them. Besides seining and surveying the local fish population, we measured fish captures by fisherman in the wetland and tallied the hunters' duck and goose harvests. The fish were valued using the average price fetched at the local food market. AES also tallied the money spent per capita by the fishermen to fish and by hunters to transport themselves to and from, and hunt within, the wetland. Just considering the fish and duck populations that were hunted there, we concluded that each acre of wetland provided a tangible net benefit of over $20,000 annually in 1978 dollars. Furthermore, the flood control and water quality benefits provided by the wetland contributed a combined net value of over $100,000 per acre annually. The courts agreed that the federal and state agencies were arbitrary and capricious in their denial and directed the agencies to buy the land as part of a court settlement agreement. The court settled on the $20,000 figure, and the wetland had to be purchased through an inverse condemnation process by the agencies.

But if an inland freshwater wetland were to go on producing

$20,000 to $100,000 in ecosystem benefits annually into the future, then the ecosystem values would far outweigh the sale and resale value of the land. And although the individually purchased lots and the condominiums that were sure to spring up on them would continue to accrue value, the value of the destroyed resources and services would be lost forever. So in reality the governmental agencies got a great deal when they were forced to purchase the land. Taking ecological processes and functions into account, each year the land produces value far in excess of what the normal "highest and best use" valuation would have suggested. After all, this was nothing but swampland by most appraisals.

Ecological valuation can cut both ways. By increasing the actual recognized market value of healthy ecological areas, it can lead to better policy decisions about land and open space protection, although it may also drive up land prices, making land protection more expensive for conservationists. Still, if we know land has ecologically based economic value that may pay perpetual dividends once protected, compared to some comparatively short-lived tax base contribution if the parcel were developed, maybe market forces will begin to influence the way land is used for the better.

If not, if open acreage continues to disappear and ecological quality continues to fall, then both the health of humanity and its ability to use and enjoy the earth will become further impaired. The vast scale of the planet and our short lifespan on it prevents us from understanding the long-term impacts of our actions in any great depth. But at the very least we must take on the short-term impacts. Farmers, for instance, have to deal with the immediate cost of topsoil erosion, the contaminants included in that soil, and the effects downstream when it gets into our waterways, lakes, and estuaries. Because of our history of poor soil management, farmers are forced to invest thousands of dollars annually in soil amendments, primarily fertilizers to boost productivity and pesticides to combat pests. These stop-gap measures are expensive, and yet they will not save the soil culture in the long run. We cannot continue to prop up ecological systems through the application of chemical surrogates because, like invader species, they don't respect the harmony of the ecosystem. Why should food production pollute our environment and threaten the health of our wildlife? That it pollutes us, through the high contaminant content of our own foods, is bad enough.

Unfortunately our economy is increasingly stressed from our having to clean up our own mess. When will this tired agriculture-based economic system get tossed? Hopefully it will be before the sediments and chemical contaminants washed from agricultural lands have completely fouled our rivers and lakes and coastlines. Once they have, once the capacity of these ecological systems to assimilate them is exceeded, the lakes will become unsightly, unsettling places. The only recourse then is to dredge and treat the water, a massively expensive process. In these situations we will begin to learn about the true costs of the inept "highest and best use" politics.

Our economies need to be shaped by our environmental policies. Perhaps someday we will measure our "best use" decisions against a gross environmental product (GEP) indicator, a kind of macro accounting that adjusts for all land-use decisions and takes into account human happiness and quality of life. Would people take these issues more seriously if they could reference "real use" costs on a wall-mounted ecosystem health indicator in their kitchens? Hopefully we don't need that kind of barometer to guide our ethical relationship with nature, but well-informed people do become better community members. As Leopold entreated us, let's make the land part of our community.

In some ways it is very difficult to define what it means to have a land ethic. Developers who strip 90 acres of forest but save a dozen trees could view themselves as having a land ethic. So, too, might an individual who shoots one duck less than legally allowed by the bag limit. Is it ethical to use the latest and best management practices in farming if the erosion of soil continues, or streams still become spoiled? We must develop a new land ethic, a way to understand our collective impact on global ecosystem health and to make decisions about our actions in light of this impact. Ethical means what is morally right, not what has been successfully lobbied, legislated, and regulated. This is a critical period in evolutionary history. Our own survival depends on being as cooperative and adaptive as nature.

⁀

Land Community Membership

For nearly three decades at Stone Prairie Farm I have redefined my relationship not only to the land but to the land community. As global ecological systems deteriorate all of us need ways to understand the larger context of our relationship to the earth.

Most people, not just farmers and gardeners, feel they're part of the land community and already treat nature with honor. Our neighbors felt they celebrated being land community members by installing a bird feeder and keeping birds alive one cold Wisconsin winter. After their planted 80-acre prairie restoration matured, however, Dory and Larry's land became the bird feeder. They realized, as did we, that one's contribution and membership in the land community can change. What makes us members of the land community, or gives us a land ethic? Is it the number of acres dedicated to nature preserves or conservation easements, or the underlying motivation behind our actions, no matter how large or small? Or is it our visceral connection to nature, whether or not it is played out in specific commitments?

Aldo Leopold might reply that "saving all the pieces"—the work of the intelligent tinkerer—is key to being part of the land community and having a land ethic. Since no one person can save all the pieces, saving and restoring some pieces becomes increasingly important. But as we increase the number of pieces we are saving, we must also expand our land ethic, moving forward from saving small pieces to reassembling even lands that are not so healthy and restoring them to healthy ecosystems.

Both its scale and its isolation limit the contribution that Stone Prairie Farm can make to the health of the global ecological system. And this is true of many places where pieces of the larger conservation-worthy landscape have been lost. Biodiversity is lost, soil is depleted, waterways are running turbid, and migratory birds pass over these black holes on the landscape. We need to reassemble the pieces so we can reach critical larger-sized scales, get beyond isolated efforts, and restore ecological systems across the landscape.

Perhaps a new land ethic could be focused on fostering intelligent tinkerers who save and restore the products, services, and functions of healthy ecosystems. Such a land ethic would entail more than simply protecting a collection of disparate and disconnected pieces. It would require an individual and collective commitment to restoring global ecosystem health—an investment in ourselves, yet one on which all life depends.

Since my first reading of *A Sand County Almanac* I have succeeded in giving nature an active role in my daily life. In the years since Leopold's visionary writing, biodiversity on this planet has plummeted and ecological functions of the biosphere are on the decline. The hope offered by projects such as the restoration at Stone Prairie Farm seems overshadowed—if not thwarted—by larger-scale trends. How are we to feel?

We can still be hopeful because we appear to be entering a different time. People seek healthy lives, with safe food and ex-

ercise. Many are rejecting the status quo. Organic food production, one of the faster-growing movements right now, is one
beneficiary of changing needs, tastes, and preferences. Fortunately, it is an industry that not only depends on a healthy
ecosystem but also adds to it. The demand for conservation developments is high. Nature is rebounding on many fronts, although development, agricultural activities, and speculation still
imperil our future.

The reintroduction of the California condor and the return
of the peregrine falcon are just two of the signs that give me
hope and contribute to my gratitude for what my colleagues and
others are doing. More recently, indeed as this book was going to
press, sandhill cranes flew in, landed, and were doing courtship
displays on Stone Prairie Farm, set on taking up residency on
this land for perhaps the first time in well over a hundred years.
As individuals we can reignite life and support its needs. Working my farm has cultivated and invigorated my internal passion
for life. Now I want so badly to get my hands on the neighboring farms, sowing seeds and reversing the existing land-use patterns. But I realize the immensity of this task, and the need for
wider participation by my neighbors and the larger community.

I yearn for the day when, through a myriad of strategies
and with the right combinations of human compassion and investment, restored, healthy ecological systems will grace North
American landscapes.

For nearly thirty years I have carried out a personal exploration of Aldo Leopold's land ethic, played out on my farm and
in my life and livelihood. The joy of the recovery of a small piece
of the earth cannot be overstated. I long to see nature's second
chance supported and encouraged elsewhere. There's enough
room on every farm, in every development, and in every industrial project. It starts with finding room in our hearts to make a
commitment. The commitment to restoration and land protection can provide as fulfilling an experience in every life as it has
in my own.

Lively Seasons on the Restored
Stone Prairie Farm

Most years spring is temperamental and unpredictable in southern Wisconsin. It peeks through and teases with a few days of
unseasonably warm weather in late February. I watch with the
hope that an early spring will come, but the weather usually
transitions slowly, fading from an engulfing white blanket of
snow to a murky drizzling gray, out of which burst pelting sleet
and snow squalls. When it seems as though winter won't release
its grip, the mornings start to bring scattered clouds with gaps of
blue. A curious sun emerges, trying to cast its warmth upon the
prairie. Then I stroll out the south side of the house to catch
some rays as they burst through fast-moving clouds and dapple
the prairie floor, igniting grass stems with a golden glow and
melting the remaining drifts. The wind is still cool, but I strip to
my T-shirt nonetheless and revel in these warm pools of light.

    After a few warm days, just when it seems spring has taken
hold, gray stratus clouds smother the sky and turn mornings

into dusks. Sky and land are rendered seamless, signaling that we should brace for an ice storm or a heavy offering of wet, late-season northern snow. There is an unmistakable comfort on these gray days. My heartbeat slows and all is calm but for the whistling teakettle—and Max, curled warm and dry in his dog bed, snoring and moaning softly by the crackling woodstove.

As the melting water dribbles off prairie plants and springs gurgle behind the house, sending rivulets across the thawing ground, we know the days are heating up. Soon the snowmelt will flood the riverbanks and initiate the muddy season, and we'll hear the sounds of returning killdeer, that harbinger of spring, flying overhead. The prehistoric call of soaring flocks of sandhill cranes will resonate high in the sky, floating on the shifting breeze and sending shivers down my spine.

In spring I can't ignore the prairie wind. It is unstoppable, and may be the only vital historic piece of the prairie system not decimated by agricultural uses. Moving across western deserts and up and over the Sierras and Rockies the squeezed air masses drop their moisture as rain and snow in the mountains, becoming arid and crisp for hundreds of miles to the east of the mountains. Then the intervening grasslands and evaporating water replenish their vital moisture.

When early spring winds bluster, I listen to the groaning trees and the creaking old farmhouse. Using the right-wing rule, I point the fingers of my right hand, palm up, toward the blowing wind, so my "hitchhiker thumb" can identify the direction of the low-pressure air mass pulling the current. I want to follow that wind as it grooms the rolling landscape, whistling through farmyards, whipping the waters of the Missouri River, ruffling the backs of cows, and kicking up dust along midwestern dirt roads.

Wind is the original information highway, pulling with it dust and pollen and returning wave after wave of birds and bugs to their breeding grounds. As the punctual southerlies of early March begin to blow, Susan and I watch in envy as hawks, songbirds, and waterfowl pass by, including flocks of red-winged blackbirds flying low over the prairie to their northern breeding destinations.

⌒

Prairie life starts each spring as a silent flush of new green sprigs emerging from the charred soil left from prairie burns. Within a few months, the vegetation miraculously exceeds the height of a tall horse. Corn plantings also start small and grow to impressive heights, but they allow no room for other plants. The only other life in the cornfields is pest insects such as corn-boring moths that lay eggs directly on the developing ears or the fungus that infects developing kernels and turns them into misshapen gray forms.

When corn and soybeans dominated the landscape, I heard mainly the clank of farming equipment or maybe a bellowing cow when I went outside at dawn or at dusk. The fertilized soils produced corn that loomed higher and higher as the season progressed. At my height of five feet, four inches, I could still look out over the young corn and watch crows and other birds at a distance. But as the corn grew taller, it closed in around the back fence line. Even if I doubled in height, all I would have seen was a green wall of corn standing sentry twenty-five feet away. The wall absorbed sound and produced a raspy soundscape as the leaves and stalks rustled at the slightest breeze. This haunting memory stands in stark contrast to the symphony now playing across the prairies and wetlands, the music of wildlife and the bubbling brook carried on the meandering wind. When winter subsides, I am beside myself with anticipation as life starts anew, in a slow and steady crescendo.

In early April, there's the hum of mosquitoes; the first unlucky ones emerge from the underwater wetland world to find little sustenance from me, as I am usually still wrapped in wools, and our dog's winter coat is too thick to penetrate. At the same time, the first overwintering bird species begin their celebrations. Song sparrows, pheasants, cardinals, chickadees and others belt out their songs in the early morning, only to be temporarily silenced by random spring snowfalls.

But rain or shine, and even in quieting snow, the ambient volume is turned way up when the amphibians gather and breed. Within a few weeks of the thaw, the first lone western chorus frog sings as water temperatures in the wetlands, stream, and ponds, warm to thirty-eight degrees Fahrenheit. The best impression of the chorus frog's call is the percussive sound of an index finger stroking the teeth of a plastic comb, which is convincing enough to get the gaggle of frogs singing again if they've been startled into silence.

As the water warms further to forty-two degrees, the chorus frogs are joined by hundreds of spring peeper frogs and American toads. Eventually, a chorus of thousands of amphibians jitters in the night, and throughout the day as well. Spring peepers make loud melodious chirping calls, not unlike the sound of repetitious birds. The ever-disgruntled toads join in, barely audible against the drone of the chorus frogs. But it is the toads' harmonious and exuberant trill that captures my attention. Of all the night calls, the American toads' are the most remarkable. They feel like tones from the earth itself and carry as far as the loopy call of North Country loons but are higher-pitched, like the screech owls.'

By driving the roads and stopping to listen from varying distances, I discovered that our toad populations could be heard singing on still evenings from several miles away. They're certainly "ours," as the surrounding cornfields provided no amphibian habitat.

On still spring nights I make midnight visits to our wetlands on foot with a dim flashlight, walking quietly and getting as close as possible without disturbing these toads. When I squat down along the edge of their pond, I marvel at the sight of hundreds of bubble-throated creatures draped over floating vegetation and each other, a slow moving mass kicking across the pond surface in every direction. I sit silently, listening blissfully to the rapturous drone of the choral vibrations that resonate through their swelling throats.

If I cough or move too quickly, or if a foraging raccoon appears, pawing around the shoreline to catch some dinner, the toad ensemble instantaneously turns silent, leaving only the sound of my heartbeat and distant hooting owls. When the disturbance passes, eventually one soloist starts up again. Another joins him for a duet, and then gradually they are bobbing and vibrating again by the hundreds. As with my barrel owl calls, I have also perfected toad mimicry and enjoy adding my voice to their symphony. Depending on the pitch I choose, I have been able to create a lead that the toads will respond to with a complementary harmony. Thus in the middle of a dark night, Steven Apfelbaum and the toads celebrate together the coming of spring. I don't know that the local farmers would entirely approve of this late-night pastime.

This reawakened toad community pulses and mates with abandon. The much smaller male sits on top of his mate in an inseparable embrace and secretes his gametes on the stream of her eggs. The entwined couples dance around the wetland margins, leaving gelatinous black egg strands by the miles, shimmering slimy in the moonlight. The daily progression of this genesis reminds me of the stop-motion flipbooks we used to draw in the corners of our notebooks during grade school. By day two, the black egg develops folds, and by days three and four the nubs of the legs are discernable. By the end of the week, a body with legs, tail, and head has emerged. After they hatch, you have to watch your step, because there are tens of thousands of toadlets wandering around the wetlands and venturing into the prairie landscape. This activity continues until the mating season winds down in late June.

One evening Max found me singing with the toads at the shoreline. I tried to call him over to sit quietly with me for fear that he might leap in and go after them. Max was bred to be a herder. Sure enough, as with any good herding breed, he became entranced by the constantly moving toads, and before I could grab his scruff, he plunged into the pond in an attempt to gather the toads together. But the breeding toads were hard to corral. When they'd dive under to evade him, he'd thrust his head under the water to nudge them with his slender muzzle. But he quickly discovered that it was harder than herding cats. So Max changed tactics, gently grabbing them in his mouth to carry them to the center of the pond. He stood excitedly in the middle of the swarming mass swatting his tail, trying to figure out which one to grab next.

When most had disappeared under the surface, Max became visibly frustrated and tired from running around the shoreline. When a large coupled pair rolled over in the water not far from the shore, Max leapt over to them. But when he scooped them up, he got a load of toad juice in his mouth. Toads have a poison gland located above and behind each eye that exudes a bitter white liquid said to be vile tasting. I hadn't thought about this possibility until Max gripped a bit too firmly and I saw the white poison ooze from his mouth.

He quickly dropped the toads and started swinging his head from side to side. He salivated profusely and started hacking. He acted like he needed to dislodge something stuck in his throat, but nothing came out. When that didn't work, he started drinking the pond water, but that apparently provided no relief from the toads' chemicals. Then out of sheer helplessness, he lay down and rolled around in the shoreline vegetation for quite some time, until finally he stood up and came over to me with the same pleading look he had worn after getting sprayed in the face by a skunk a few years earlier. From then on, at the sight of a toad poor Max would lower his head and trot away, his toad-herding aspirations forever vanquished.

Not all creatures are so easily deterred. One evening my flashlight beam exposed a northern water snake consuming a toad. It was quite a sight, because the snake was small and the inflated toad was huge. It looked like someone had tried to stuff an unripe melon into a garden hose. For nearly an hour the serpent twisted his victim around with a rotating jaw movement until the helpless toad was looking headfirst down the snake's gullet. But that toad continued to sing even after it was swallowed. And as the battery in my flashlight died, I could still hear the exuberant trill emanating from inside the swollen snake.

As the water warms into the upper forties and fifties, the amphibian frenzy increases as the tree frog sopranos pipe in with their blurting, high-pitched trill. The amusing green frogs show up next, but aren't particularly melodious. Pluck an E string on a five-string banjo, and that is their sound. Initially drowned out by the toads and early frogs, those one-note banjo players build into the dominant drone on early summer evenings as they trade territorial calls.

And when the hot humid nights of midsummer smother the land in a drenching swelter, the leopard frogs and bullfrogs hop onto the scene, seeming to appear from nowhere out a magician's hat. The bullfrog, the stereotypical large green creature, is an eating machine, devouring frogs, toads, and anything else it can stuff into its mouth. All the uneaten frogs split, except the leopard frog, which somehow evades the aggressive bullfrog. From that point on, we hear the counterpoint of the leopards' wet-fingers-rubbing-a-balloon sound against the bull's classic deep throaty *ribbit.*

⌒

For me, summer really starts with the rituals of preparing the garden and the orchard. I arrange the gardening implements on the porch—shovels, rakes, and pruning shears—and inventory the boxes of bulbs and seeds, and the bags of onions and garlic that are overdue for planting. By this time I've grown flats and pots with garden seedlings—tomatoes, peppers, broccoli, eggplants, parsley, basil, and numerous herbs. They call out, demanding my immediate attention.

With my work schedule, I am never certain when I can begin my annual sojourn in the garden. I've been forced to plant as late as the end of June, but even those late-planted gardens have produced large harvests. By then there is already much to tend to in the orchards and vineyards. The bloom starts in early May, and by early summer there is an abundance of fruit. If I find time in February to prune the apple, peach, pear, and cherry trees and the grape arbors, some ninety trees and vines in all, we usually have a bumper crop. I'm actually thankful that all of the young pears and apples don't fully ripen, because it can become too much of a good thing. One year by midsummer, I harvested seven bushels from just one pear tree, and we have a total of six. The next year the cherry trees produced so much fruit that my fingers had a semipermanent red tint from the hours of picking, and my lips were stained and raw from eating too much of the acidic fruit.

Most of our vegetables, except what we eat fresh in our meals, are sliced up and dehydrated for later use. The work is arduous. But those few months tilling and mulching, seeding and planting, harvesting and preserving produce several hundred pounds of food stockpiled in airtight aluminum containers. If you think sun-dried tomatoes are great, add dried greens such as collards, chard, beets, spinach, and dried garden herbs to your winter stews and casseroles. By then I've generally forgotten the backache and the tedium of the work.

By August early-morning fog blankets the sweeping landforms. The noisy insect masses come to life with the addition of moisture. If it weren't for the bugs, I think nature could endear itself to almost anyone. The occasional chirping cricket accentuates the peaceful early-August evening, but soon afterward the sound is amplified with the onset of romantic exuberance. There is more sex and violence in the prairie than in your average B-movie, with thousands of katydids and tree crickets eating each other or being eaten. And then they breed, which also involves a lot of noise, as females lure in the males or vice versa.

The sex-starved insects continue their activities long after closing time. Come nightfall there is the Stone Prairie's headline performance, a pulsing, glowing show of lightning bugs. The males emit snappy repetitive pulses as they search for mates, while the females respond with deliberate slow beams; some illuminate on their passionate descent, others streak across the sky like pulsing shooting stars.

As dusk settles these shows become quite brilliant. Before restoration began, the lightning bugs were only occasionally seen along the spring brook, rising and falling above the few remaining patches of bank vegetation, or in overgrown areas along road margins. Now, Susan, our summer guests, and I can enjoy lawn-chair viewings of lightning bugs behind the house. This is one of my favorite summer events.

One rainy late summer evening we were delighted to witness the return of yet another wildlife species, the wild turkey. Turkeys, once prevalent but pushed to the verge of extinction, were reintroduced in our county around 1985 and had thrived. They quickly became favorite game birds for hunters, but farmers found them to be a horrible nuisance, because the massive flocks damaged countless numbers of crops.

One late summer afternoon in 1991 a van pulled to an abrupt stop in the driveway. The door swung open and a noticeably agitated person jumped out. This is not a benevolent visit by a Jehovah's Witness, I thought to myself.

As she approached, I realized it was a neighbor.

"Your damn turkeys are eating my melons! Every last one," she shouted. "They've pecked holes and devoured the whole crop! Can't you pen them up and keep them away from my melons?" She was so angry that she barely got the words out.

I raised my hand in peace to calm her and address her allegations. "If you can just calm down, I can—"

"Just tell me what you're going to do to replace my melon crop."

"Hello," I said, trying to slow everything down. "You must be Jerry, with the fruit and vegetable stand down the road? I'm Steve," I said, extending my hand. She reached and gave me a brisk handshake.

"I know you are upset," I said. "But those aren't our turkeys. They are eating our crops too. Our veggie garden is getting pillaged, and our flowers, and they are trampling and pecking apart our native plant nursery." She looked as though she thought I was speaking Chinese. "They're wild birds. They just happen to cross our farm as they come up from the creek, then they cross our fencerow into your fields."

She calmed down slightly.

"Well, what the hell can we do about them? Can we shoot 'em or trap 'em or something?"

"I called the DNR and asked the same questions. They told me that they would have to come out to determine if the birds presented a bona fide nuisance and were creating real crop damage."

"Well, aren't they?" she said, regaining a bit of her indignant fervor.

I told her that the problem was there were so many complaints from around the region about the exploding turkey population that the Department of Natural Resources was too overwhelmed to deal with it.

"They weren't particularly helpful," I said. This merely incensed her, and she started repeating herself.

"They have damaged every single ripe watermelon and muskmelon in my field, Steve. Every last one of 'em has been drilled and hollowed out by those birds. I have lost hundreds of melons, worth thousands of dollars. And the DNR won't let us cull those suckers?"

"Not yet, at least."

"I just can't believe this," she muttered, as she stepped back and looked at the ground for answers.

"What if we both called the DNR? Perhaps that would get their attention. Even better, let's start a letter-writing campaign to our legislators. That might ruffle some feathers and get more immediate results." I was quite proud of this suggestion, and my admittedly lame pun.

"But—"

"I know," I said. "Obviously not for this crop since the damage is already done, but at least for next year."

She seemed to appreciate my compassion and the encounter ended in a neighborly spirit, with her apologizing and me jokingly saying we need to encourage the turkey hunters to get busy in the autumn. "Maybe we can get everyone and their brothers and sisters to save the DNR the trouble of trying to figure out what to do," I said with a little smile.

What I didn't dare tell Jerry at first is that I had in fact tried to reintroduce a wild turkey pair on our farm one summer. I raised them well enough but was unsuccessful trying to release them. They grew to their fully feathered adult size, but they had no fear of humans. Subsequently, the female was run over one morning as it rested in the shade beneath an equipment trailer. Susan and I happened to watch the scene unfold from the house. Seeing the driver, an AES employee, start up the truck, we screamed through the window but couldn't get his attention over the clatter of the diesel engine. We watched in horror as the hen was squashed multiple times under the trailer wheels. Then the driver, finally noticing our hand waving, reversed backwards, further flattening the doomed bird.

I eventually felt compelled to mention this to Jerry but also to clarify that the wild turkeys now proliferating in the area got no direct help from me. The DNR never did help, but they kept me hanging for some months, telling me they would get back to me with a solution, but that never happened.

⌒

Like spring, fall in southern Wisconsin is complex and temperamental and can't seem to commit to the coming solstice. Early autumn mornings are cool, with a fog that eventually burns off. But what often looks like a promising day becomes a bone-chilling afternoon with pounding northerlies.

The wildlife is attentive to impending winter and begins to show urgency in early September. Goldfinches harvest thistles and sunflower seeds persistently, stockpiling for the winter. Long-billed marsh wrens sing incessantly, while killdeer, flickers, crows, song sparrows, and kingbirds form flocks in preparation for migration. Blue jays spend their mornings flying between the scattered shadowy oaks, while the grasshoppers, katydids, and tree crickets hang quietly from plant stems in suites of transparent dewdrops, hoping to avoid the hungry jays.

Sawtooth sunflowers stand brilliantly erect and golden. Grasses wave in flowing pulses as dark olive-green cherry saplings jut out against the rosy hues and drifts of gold. Visible beyond the prairie, the neighbor's cornfield is a uniform silk-tassel ocean that raises the topography into the air by ten feet. The perfect uniformity of the corn is disrupted only by a meandering drainage swale that courses through it.

By Labor Day, the fields of colorful big bluestem and Indian grass provide a jungle gym for insects. Each goldenrod plant becomes a community of eating, buzzing, and breeding insects, while butterflies prefer to sip nectar from blue lobelia, mint, and cardinal flowers.

The prairie in fall lacks uniformity. Variances in height and branch pattern create corridors of green that lace through the rich hues drifting over the land. This chaotic color scheme highlights the myriad textures of the various plant communities, which are vitally linked in a complex tango of cooperation and evolution. These rich colors, textures, and patterns contrast with the monotonous perfection of the cornfields.

During this season I'm often drawn to the windows and into the yard to watch migratory hawks or study the staging barn swallows that gather in large family groups to frolic like seals in ocean surf. They slice through the air with precision, hunting moths, flies, and other bugs. At sunrise they dart close to the contour of the land, sometimes brushing plant tips. As the day warms the heat creates updrafts that the swallows follow hundreds of feet into the sky to catch flies. In the late afternoon, they rest on power lines and make occasional swoops through the willows and across the yard, finally settling on the second-story perch of my house. Watching their acrobatics is a delight that must be savored quickly, for their visit is short and they soon depart on their annual pilgrimage southward.

Large ant mounds have developed on our fields where corn once grew. Nothing like the tiny sidewalk crack colonies I remember from childhood, these prairie colonies can be several feet wide and tower several feet above the ground, with dozens of entrances and thousands of preoccupied ants carrying drying seeds, dead insects, grass plant stems, and twigs of assorted sizes. Pushing a stick into the colony elicits hoards of swarming defenders that attack the invader. Ants are true hunters and gatherers, combing the land for seeds and insects. They burrow into hard, overworked farm ground, creating pathways for other life to follow into the soils. And they carry seeds down with them, dropping some along the way and inadvertently spreading wildflowers, nectar sources, and plants that provide food for others. They also provide much-needed overwintering and caretaking for some butterfly and other insect species. When the restoration first began I saw only an occasional butterfly, but now they are everywhere, thanks in part to ants.

I associate Thanksgiving Day with the last butterfly. In the human world I am typically assigned to the massive house-cleaning necessary to prepare for the onslaught of twenty-plus guests. I prefer passive cleaning methods. On windy days, I simply open doors on opposite sides of the house, allowing strong winds to blow most of the accumulated dust, dog hair, and crumbs into the prairie. The ants must think it is manna from heaven as they haul away the victuals.

Susan does the bulk of the cooking, and soon the deluge of relatives begins to arrive, Susan's making the long voyage from

Iowa and mine driving in from throughout Illinois. We set off for long appetite-building walks through the prairie, and people take pleasure in pointing out the annual changes. Their observations serve as another key indicator of how successfully wildness has returned to the land. Since these visitors come only once or twice a year, the changes are more noticeable to them, whereas I've witnessed the shifts in small, daily increments. It's a pleasure to hear them commenting on how the wild plum thickets are developing, the way the western ridge is now highlighted with an orange hue, or the near miraculous recovery of the compass and prairie dock plants from the previous year's weevil infestation that eliminated seed production. Each year they marvel at the increased life on the prairie and the changing aesthetics and want to know details. When the feast is ready, of course, everything shifts. The focus moves to the table, and to postdinner napping. Eventually the homeward travels begin.

More often than not Thanksgiving has fallen on sunny days, with perhaps a blush of clouds to the south or a breeze that makes the grasses bow to the north. The kids watch wildlife, frolic about, or get busy with their food harvest. One year a pheasant bolted upward from behind the house, gliding a short distance before suddenly descending into the dense prairie cover. Seconds later, a Cooper's hawk dived into the same spot in pursuit. We were all awestruck by the predatory display, which made for excellent conversation over the turkey feast. Another year the children found tracks south of the house, just above one of the tributaries of the spring. Following the tracks, they found a large oval hole beside a freshly dug mound of sand and gravel. This landscaping, coupled with the elongated toe and claw prints, confirmed that badgers had moved in and had already begun pushing up soil around the entrance of their den in anticipation of the coming winter.

The crop harvest is in full swing in fall. So as the remaining habitats decline in the wake of the combine, game from neighboring farms crowds onto Stone Prairie Farm. On Thanksgiving

weekend Wisconsin is crawling with orange-vested deer hunters, out before sunup and waiting to gun down the biggest buck
they can find. Deer move into the cover of our prairie as the corn
crops are reduced to stubble. Noah joined his first hunt as a teen,
during a year when half a dozen large bucks had sought refuge
in the prairie. We hunted together, searching for the deer, which
were difficult to see in the tall, dense, buckskin-colored prairie.
Still Noah persisted, and shot his first buck as it emerged into
a clearing. A loud shot rang out, echoing in my ears and over
the land.

Minutes later we stood over the 175-pound deer. It was wonderful to see Noah so thrilled at his success. We talked about the
noble creature, the habitats it needed at the farm, and what it
ate. Then we reflected on this life-and-death experience and on
the idea of hunting for food, not just sport. We decided to make
rawhide from the skin, which we removed carefully with a sharp
knife. The rawhide was to become a drum for Susan. Then
we decided to make several types of sausages and, together, we
carefully butchered the animal. During this experience I kept
thinking to myself about the conflicted feelings I have had in
hunting, and about making sure to honor the creature and not be
wasteful. During my younger years, at Noah's age, hunting was
exciting, but now what felt right to me was observing and pho-
tographing nature rather than shooting at it with a gun.

At the time Noah still considered me an interloper in his
parents' fractured relationship. That hunt helped bring us together, and after nearly twenty years we still share that camara-
derie. Discussing the much-anticipated annual hunting season,
we strengthen the bonds of our relationship.

⟨⁀⟩

As the cold of late autumn settles in, Susan and I begin the
chores essential to getting through the Wisconsin winter. We
stack seasoned firewood near the house and put up fresh wood
for the following year. The path around the house gets a final
mowing, and we clean up and rototill the garden beds, often

planting a cover crop. We create firebreaks in preparation for prescribed burning the following spring, as well as for fire protection should some passing driver carelessly toss a cigarette into the prairie. Depending on the wind direction, a fire could rapidly engulf our house and spread to the neighboring farms.

In late fall we start getting nostalgic for the flowering world, so the last blossoming gentians get our full attention. We hike the dry-ridge prairies each year to find the downy, cobalt blue flowers, intertwined with prairie roses that strut their scarlet hips to entice passing birds. As we hike through oak and black maple forests that border the prairie, we often find edible mushrooms, picking such favorites as chicken of the woods, hen of the woods, and sulfur mushrooms. The occasional inky caps and giant puffballs are big finds, but they must be fresh to harvest. If overripe, they are full of fly larvae or burrowing beetles. We soak them for a few hours in brine, then slice and dehydrate them. By the following morning, the mushrooms are dry and ready to infuse hearty winter stews and soups with their glorious flavor.

Once our chores are done, we retire to the sleeping porch to watch the last signs of fading autumn. We sleep there as the peaceful drizzles turn to light snow and droning crickets cease their chirp. We listen as the last of the night migratory birds pass through. And then, a few weeks later, another avian show begins on Stone Prairie Farm. Flocks of Canada geese on their southward journey emerge out of the morning fog, and Susan and I rush outside, standing in awe as the majestic V's pass through lathered cloud peaks and sail overhead. By midday they pass higher in the air, appearing as only small dots in the vast Wisconsin sky. It's as if time has reset itself.

Fall migration comes to an end with the first snow flurries, usually in early December. At this point, the weather dramatically takes center stage, throwing fast-moving sleet that slaps percussively on the windows, and sweeping curtains of snowdrifts that drape across the prairie. The silence of that first winter blanket causes both great drowsiness and a soothing sense of peacefulness.

After a fresh snowfall we are out the door in snowshoes or cross-country skis to track the local wildlife, their footprints clearly visible in the glistening powder. When least weasels detect you they burrow beneath the snow and reappear dozens of feet away, dashing quickly and quietly like fish in water. Mink follow the course of the stream, playing in the billowy snowdrifts along the banks, while raccoons wade in the water along the edge of the uplands. We find the telltale signs of a fox pursuing a rabbit, and the tracks lead us to scattered tufts of rabbit fur.

On such snowy days there are no apparent land divisions, as though our home sits in the untrammeled wilderness of the last century. From the window my 80 acres seem boundless. Black willows scattered along the spring brook lead the eye to the prairies, which seem to roll on westward indefinitely toward the Rocky Mountains.

Winter subdues nature, so we turn to indoor activities, family time, and assorted projects to amuse ourselves. No matter how hot and muggy the summer, in the dead of winter the sultry heat is only a fond memory. It was a great surprise to me initially, but it turns out the refurbished old farmhouse with radiant heating and good insulation provides a relaxing atmosphere in which one can do fulfilling things. And to think I couldn't see the logic in investing in the remodeling!

Before the big winter melt, Susan and I embark on one of our favorite wintertime traditions: maple syrup production. I first learned about syrup making when I was eight years old at the River Trail Nature Center in Northbrook, Illinois. My brothers and I learned how to tap the trees and collect buckets of the watery sap. We watched with great anticipation as it boiled down into thick sweet syrup, knowing that when it was ready we'd get to taste test it over vanilla ice cream that the ranger kept on hand for his most enthusiastic volunteers.

Since our prairie had few sugar maples, we made a sweet

deal, so to speak, with neighboring farmers; they'd let us tap their maple trees in exchange for pints of finished syrup. Some of the old-timers reminisced about tapping many of the same trees to make syrup and sugar candy when they were young, and they were happy to let us at the trees. Getting started was a bit of an ordeal, but we soon converted the old granary into a sugar shack, complete with a fifteen-foot-long maple syrup evaporator, two four-hundred-gallon bulk tanks, and a large stainless-steel sink. It occupied the entire granary and put Susan and me in the maple sugaring business.

Most of the maples grow on slopes facing north by northeast or along the terraces of drainage routes, where they escape exposure to winter winds as well as desiccating dry winds and summer heat. Fortunately, they also escaped the historic wildfires that once swept the prairie on the surrounding uplands.

To get the trees set, we pull our ash toboggan through a few feet of snow with the necessary equipment: a chainsaw with the bit-holding attachment we use to drill the tap holes, a bag of taps, coils of plastic piping, and other assorted connectors and tools. At each tree we drill a diagonal hole, then gently pound a tap upward into it. During peak production we have four hundred taps on the ridge-top maples, connected to a gravity-fed pipeline system that runs down to covered bulk tanks at the bottom of the ridge.

After a day of sap collection, we drive a pickup truck to the tanks and pump the sap into our hauling tank to take back to the sugar shack. There we put it into the stainless-steel milk coolers. On a good day, Susan and I return towing a full three-hundred-gallon tank. Every few days, after collecting about eight hundred gallons of sap, we fire up the evaporator and start making syrup. Sometimes we stand over the vats throughout the night, stirring the simmering sap and breathing the swirling, sweet vapors. Neighbors love to come over to feed the fire and dip their fingers in the goo in anticipation of a big bowl of homemade ice cream drenched with fresh syrup. It is a real community event, with everyone chattering away as the sap condenses. The real fun is pouring the cooked liquid through a strainer and bottling the syrup. In our best years we produce more than a hundred gallons of the most delicious syrup imaginable.

Soon after we started making syrup, Big Bud showed up as though he'd followed a star to the manger. Born in Vermont, Bud has syrup making in his blood, and it's something he had missed in the nearly three decades he'd lived in Wisconsin. Bud taught us how to make maple taffy, which involves carefully simmering the syrup to a thicker consistency without scorching it. At the right moment, he'll ladle it onto prepared areas of clean white snowdrifts or ice, causing it to crystallize immediately. As it cools, but before it freezes, he'll pick up the straps of semi-rigid glassy goop and start pulling it in all directions. Soon the clear, glassy substance is transformed into white taffy, which he lays out on dry strips of paper to cool further.

Every year Bud's family back in Vermont sends him a few bottles of syrup and maple syrup candy. Vermont's maple season goes on a few weeks longer than ours, so we can always count on him showing up a few weeks after our syrup making has ended with some samples of the latest vintage of Vermont's finest. We get out our Wisconsin blend and set the two side by side to debate the quality differences and "grade" the syrup. Sometimes ours will score higher, at which point Bud usually bribes us with a gift of the maple syrup candies his relatives send. So scoring be damned, that candy always wins the day for Vermont.

We certainly don't mind substituting the syrup season for an early spring. I can't object to feeding the woodstove once every few days to keep the farmhouse warm instead of twice daily in an extended winter. And once those solar panels started generating heat, it helped offset the wood burning. When the sap begins to run milky and miller moths come out, Susan and I shut down the syrup production and begin to scour the seed catalogs, mentally preparing for another lovely spring.

Acknowledgments

This book attempts to capture the richness of my experiences at Stone Prairie Farm. Although I took the initiative in developing it, my words would pale and flounder without the feelings, vision, and energy contributed by Susan Marie Lehnhardt. My contributions to this book are dedicated to her.

My formative years laid the foundation of my appreciation for all land and ecosystems, not just this farm or the prairie biome. I thank the many who have nudged and mentored me, and insisted on wide-open eyes and thoughtful inquiry. My parents, Ruth and Jerry Apfelbaum, and brothers Gary, Ronnie, and Larry all played an important part in my beginning years. So did the following naturalists at the River Trail Nature Center: Chet Ryndak, Connie Drust, Robert Clemens, Ray Schwarz, and Steve Swanson. Among the early friends who gave me room to roam were Mark Schewe, Dirk Rymer, and Robert and Pat Dunlavey.

Clients who trusted me with major projects, and their livelihoods, include David, Barbara, and Brian Hoffman of Hybernia; George and Vicky Ranney and Dorothy and Gaylord Donnelly of Prairie Crossing; and David Newman, Marc Anderson, Peter Phlaum, and Vance Operman at Wild Meadows. I also thank friends or research colleagues James P. Ludwig, Alan W. Haney, Kim Chapman, Jack White, and numerous others who have also encouraged my path. Staff members at Applied Ecological Services and Taylor Creek Restoration Nurseries have seen me come and go at odd hours over the last three decades. I thank them all for their support, including John Larson, Carl Korfmacher, Pat and Corrine Daniels, John Ochsner, Fred Faessler, Rob Baller, Tom Hunt, Mark O'Leary, Doug Mensing, Doug Eppich, and numerous others. Thanks to Ben Yalom, my tireless editor. And more than a simple thanks to Heidy Sowatzke and Lynnette Nelson, my assistants, for typing this manuscript, above and beyond their heavy daily workload. Our neighbor and fellow homesteader John Ivanko provided editorial assistance, helping bring the experiences described here to life. Brian Joiner, George and Kay Barry, Nina Bradley, Luna Leopold, and Peg Kohring are friends and colleagues who waded through earlier drafts and provided much appreciated commentary. I'm grateful for the opportunity to share my experiences in this book. Now everyone has some sense of what I've done after work for over twenty years.